Scenarios in Marketing

Scenarios in Marketing

From Vision to Decision

Edited by

Gill Ringland and Laurie Young

John Wiley & Sons, Ltd

Telephone (+44) 1243 779777

Email (for orders and customer service enquiries): cs-books@wiley.co.uk
Visit our Home Page on www.wiley.com

Other Wiley Editorial Offices

John Wiley & Sons Inc., 111 River Street, Hoboken, NJ 07030, USA

Jossey-Bass, 989 Market Street, San Francisco, CA 94103-1741, USA

Wiley-VCH Verlag GmbH, Boschstr. 12, D-69469 Weinheim, Germany

John Wiley & Sons Australia Ltd, 42 McDougall Street, Milton, Queensland 4064, Australia

John Wiley & Sons (Asia) Pte Ltd, 2 Clementi Loop #02-01, Jin Xing Distripark, Singapore 129809

John Wiley & Sons Canada Ltd, 6045 Freemont Blvd, Mississauga, ONT, L5R 4J3, Canada

Wiley also publishes its books in a variety of electronic formats. Some content that appears in print may not be available in electronic books.

Library of Congress Cataloging-in-Publication Data:

Scenarios in marketing : from vision to decision / edited by Gill Ringland and Laurie Young.
p. cm.
ISBN-13: 978-0-470-03272-5
ISBN-10: 0-470-03272-3
1. Marketing—Management. 2. Strategic planning. I. Ringland, Gill. II. Young, Laurie, 1955– .
HF5415.13.S276 2006
658.8′02—dc22 2006020354

British Library Cataloguing in Publication Data

A catalogue record for this book is available from the British Library

ISBN-13: 978-0-470-03272-5 (HB)
ISBN-10: 0-470-03272-3 (HB)

Typeset in 10/12 Garamond by Laserwords Private Limited, Chennai, India
Printed and bound in Great Britain by TJ International, Padstow, Cornwall, UK
This book is printed on acid-free paper responsibly manufactured from sustainable forestry in which at least two trees are planted for each one used for paper production.

Contents

List of Figures

List of Tables

Contributors

In alphabetical order

Lloyd Burdett joined Henley Centre Headlight Vision in 2003 having previously held a number of long-term strategy and delivery roles in the public sector. His work at HCHLV has focused on a wide range of futures, scenario planning and long-term strategy projects with clients in both the private and public sectors. Along with Andrew Curry, Lloyd now leads HCHLV's futures work, focusing particularly on the development of new approaches to action-oriented futures work, including scenario planning, and adapting them for use in fast-moving sectors. He is also currently responsible for HCHLV's scenarios work in international markets, particularly the USA, and is due to move to HCHLV's New York office late in 2006.

His e-mail address is Lloyd.Burdett@hchlv.com.

Andrew Curry joined Henley Centre in 1999 from Cable and Wireless Communications. Andrew combines an expertise in futures work, particularly scenarios, with an in-depth knowledge of media and new media. Andrew leads Henley Centre's public sector team, and has developed many of our facilitation and workshop techniques. He has directed projects for a wide range of clients, including Vodafone, DEFRA, the Army and *Sport England*. Andrew previously worked as a financial journalist, as a television producer, and in the new media sector. He launched Britain's first interactive TV channel in 1993 and was part of Cable and Wireless's digital TV project team.

His e-mail address is Andrew.Curry@hchlv.com.

Paul Fifield has run his own consultancy business for over 20 years. Paul's clients are loyal and enjoy the 'life-long learning' that comes with working with him. He has worked with clients in a wide range of industries. He specialises in strategy and is preparing the third edition of his book *Marketing Strategy*. His mother tongue is English, he is fluent in French and has a working knowledge of Dutch.

He holds a degree in Business Studies as well as an MBA and a PhD in Marketing Strategy, from Cranfield University. He was elected a Fellow of the Chartered Institute of Marketing (CIM) in 1988, an elected member of CIM Council 1999–2001 and the CIM International Board of Trustees 2002–2004. Paul is currently President of the CIM Southern Region, a member of the Marketing Society and a Fellow of the Royal Society for the encouragement of Arts, Manufacturers and Commerce (FRSA).

His e-mail address is paulfifield@fifield.co.uk.

David Haigh, BA, ACA, FCIM, MIPR, read English at Bristol University before qualifying as a Chartered Accountant with what was then Price Waterhouse in 1980. He then became the European Financial Controller of an international group of companies, Financial Director of a marketing consultancy, then of WCRS and Partners. In 1988 he became Managing Director of Publicis Dialogue. David joined the board of directors in the global brand valuation practice of Interbrand, before setting up his own company, Brand Finance Limited, in 1995, which focuses on marketing accountability.

David lectures on the importance of brand promotion and valuation. He is the author of several books including *Strategic Control of Marketing Finance* and *The Future of Brand Valuation*. For over 10 years David has been a regular columnist for journals such as: *Accountancy Age, Marketing Business* and *Brand Management*.

His e-mail address is d.haigh@branfinance.com.

Crawford Hollingworth is Executive Chairman of Headlight Vision, part of the WPP Group. Following degree and post-grad work in applied social psychology he was tempted away from academia into the advertising world as a strategic planner. He worked for BMP DDB Needham, AMV BBDO and then joined Chiat Day as Vice President Strategic Planning. He finished his planning career as the executive planning director of Bates Dorland. During this time he had worked for Sony, Landrover, American Express, Qantas, RSPCA, Bass and Yellow Pages among others. He started Headlight Vision in 1995.

From an early age he has always been fascinated in why people behave in the ways they do and in how one could influence that behaviour. His overall personal expertise lies in consumer trends, strategic brand planning and qualitative research. His ability is to create more holistic solution-based research from this perspective.

His e-mail address is Crawford.hollingworth@hchlv.com.

Gill Ringland's career has spanned academic and industrial worlds, taking a leading edge role in physics, software and information technology, strategy and scenarios in turn. She has been active in five start-ups, and was responsible for building a £3-billion new business over five years for ICL.

She started to use scenarios when responsible for strategy at ICL, and as a result wrote the amazon.com bestseller *Scenario Planning*. She is a Liveryman of the City of London through the Information Technologists. She has a BSc, MSc, FBCS, MIEE, and is a graduate of Stanford University's Senior Executive Program. She is a past Member of SRC's Computing Science Committee and of Council of the Economic and Social Research Council

She writes and consults widely as a Fellow of St Andrews Management Institute. Her books are "why, what, when, how" guides to the use of scenarios: *Scenario Planning—Managing for the Future, Scenarios in Business*, and *Scenarios in Public Policy*—all published by John Wiley & Sons, Ltd.

You can contact Gill at: gill.ringland@samiconsulting.co.uk

Don E. Schultz is Professor (Emeritus-in-Service) of Integrated Marketing Communication, Northwestern University, Evanston, IL. He is also President of the global marketing consultancy Agora, Inc. also located in Evanston. He was founding editor, *Journal of Direct Marketing*; 1989 DMEF Direct Marketing Educator of the Year; 1992 AAF Advertising Educator of the Year; member, National Advertising Review Board; co-author, *Strategic Advertising Campaigns and Integrated Marketing Communications*; former senior vice president, management supervisor, Tracy-Locke Advertising and Public Relations, Dallas/New York/Columbus; BBA, Oklahoma. He has an MA and PhD from Michigan State.

His e-mail address is dschultz@northwestern.edu.

Merlin Stone is the author of many articles and 30 books on transforming marketing and customer service capabilities. He is a Founder Fellow of the Institute of Direct Marketing and a Fellow of the Chartered Institute of Marketing. He is on the editorial advisory boards of the *Journal of Financial Services Marketing*, the *Journal of Database Marketing and Customer Management Strategy*, the *Journal of Targeting, Measurement and Analysis for Marketing* and the *Journal of Direct, Data and Digital Marketing Practice.* He writes monthly columns for *Database Marketing and Direct Marketing International* and for the website *What's New in Marketing*.

He is a Director of WCL, specialists in change management in the public and private sectors and of Nowell Stone Ltd. He has a first-class honours degree and doctorate in Economics from Sussex University. He has held posts at University of Manchester Institute of Science and Technology, The Jerusalem Institute of Management, Henley Management College, Kingston University, Surrey University and Bristol Business School. At Kingston he was Dean of the Faculty of Human Sciences. He is now a Visiting Professor at Bristol Business

School—University of the West of England, and Brunel, Luton, Portsmouth and Southampton Solent Universities.

He can be contacted at Merlin.Stone@w-c-l.com.

Tim Westall is a Director of April Strategy, a management consultancy with a specialism in marketing. Tim has spent 12 years in consulting, working on strategy and innovation projects with a wide range of blue-chip clients. Prior to that, he spent seven years in a number of international marketing roles within Unilever.

His e-mail address is tim.westall@aprilstrategy.com.

Laurie Young is a specialist in the marketing of services and customer care. His career includes senior positions with PriceWaterhouseCoopers, BT and Unisys. In the 1990s he founded, built and sold his own professional service firm, focusing on service marketing. Over the years he has advised firms ranging from small single partner practices to large multinational organisations on the contribution of services marketing to shareholder value. He has published three books: *Competitive Customer Care* with Merlin Stone, *Making Profits from New Service Development,* and *Marketing the Professional Services Firm.*

He can be contacted at Lauriedyoung@aol.com.

Acknowledgments

This book owes its genesis to Clare Plimmer of John Wiley & Sons, Ltd, who was convinced that a book should be written on scenarios in marketing. She discussed this with Laura Mazur of Writers 4 Management, who suggested that Laurie Young (author of *Marketing the Professional Services Firm*) and Gill Ringland (author of books on scenarios) might pair up. This book is the result, and the editors would like to thank John Wiley & Sons, Ltd for their support and patience during its gestation.

We attracted an excellent set of contributors to provide chapters within the overall theme of "how scenario thinking can be used to improve the creativity and discipline of marketing". Their contact details and a short biography are included in the section on contributors: we thank them for their time and contributions, which—of course—were in addition to "a day job". We would also like to thank Dr Wendy Schultz of Infinite Futures and Paul de Ruijter of De Ruijter Management who contributed additional case studies.

Gill Ringland would like to thank a number of her colleagues at SAMI Consulting for helpful critiques as the work progressed, and to Adrian Davies's thoughts on the conclusions we reached.

Both of the co-editors would like to thank Laura Mazur for her work on the case studies and the chapters as they came in from the contributors: if we are still sane it is down to Laura!

ONE

Introduction to Scenario Planning

Gill Ringland

SUMMARY

This chapter answers three questions:

- ***How can this book help you?***
- ***What is a scenario?***
- ***How can scenarios be used?***

It defines scenarios and gives the theoretical and experimental underlying basis for their application. It also contains a discussion of when not to use scenarios.

The chapter is contributed by Gill Ringland, the author of several books on scenario planning and the chief executive of SAMI Consulting, which aims to help its customers to make robust decisions in uncertain times.

HOW CAN THIS BOOK HELP YOU?

You have opened this book because you are a marketer, who has heard about scenarios and want to know what they can do for you. Can they bring both creativity and discipline both into marketing? Can the use of scenarios make your organisation more successful?

Scenarios in Marketing. Edited by G. Ringland and L. Young.

It's well known that scenarios have made headlines by helping to anticipate events, improving the ability of an organisation to get ahead of the curve. For example, scenario planning has helped:

- Pacific Gas and Electric to prepare for the earthquake in California;
- Shell to anticipate the fall of communism in Russia and its effect on natural gas prices;
- countries such as Guatemala and South Africa to defuse tensions and map a way forward.

These examples suggest that scenarios work over a long timescale in large geographies. Is scenario thinking then relevant to the types of problems tackled by marketers? The answer is "Yes". Scenarios allow you to explore alternatives to "the official future", which is the set of shared assumptions about the future in the organisation. This official future is usually more comfortable, and hence more potentially misleading, than other possible futures or scenarios.

In Scenario Planning, Gill Ringland (2006) has described a number of marketing case studies where scenarios were developed that effectively challenged "the official future":

- Erste Allgemeine Versicherung, the Austrian insurance company, anticipated the fall of the Berlin Wall and entered new markets in central Europe.
- KRONE, the wiring and cable supplier, developed 200 new product ideas.
- Unilever decided on marketing strategies for Russia and Poland.
- United Distillers (now Diageo) set market strategies for India, South Africa and Turkey.
- Electrolux spotted new consumer markets.

The purpose of this book is to provide a straightforward account of the use of scenarios, oriented towards the concerns and disciplines of people facing marketing decisions. It is intended for marketing practitioners who want to get a view and experience of how to use scenario techniques. It will also appeal to corporate planners and MBA students, as it shows how scenarios fit as part of the marketing tool kit, spanning the space between the signals from the outside world and decision making (see Figure 1.1).

Figure 1.1

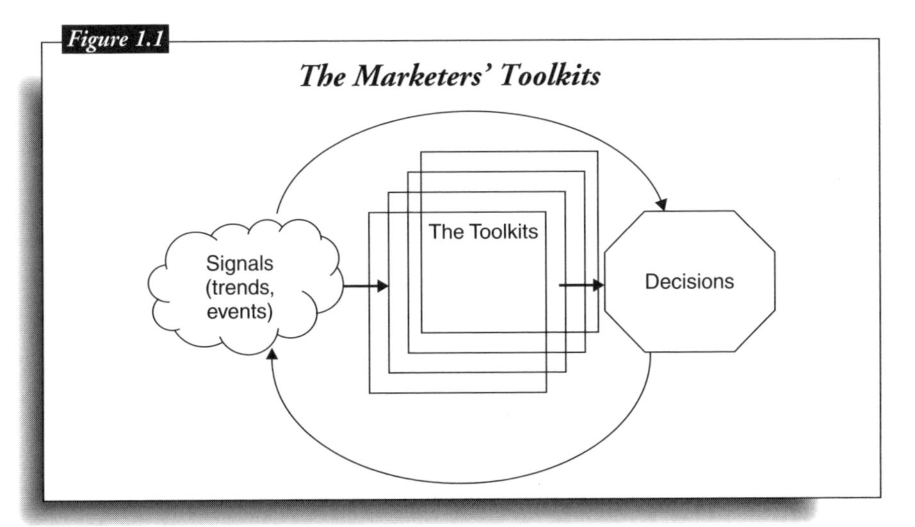

MODELS OF THE WORLD

Scenarios are just one example of using models of the world to explore or anticipate "real life". For instance:

- Wind tunnels are used to test car shapes for aerodynamic features. Does the car become unstable at high speeds, and does it have higher or lower drag factors than other shapes?

- In fatigue tests for airframes, either a life-size airframe or a scaled-down airframe is subjected to stresses and strains in a test rig, where early signs of cracks, fractures or breakages can hopefully be encountered before they are seen in the airframes that fly passengers.

- Mathematical or computer models are used to schedule and allocate resources, within sets of constraints. Linear programming techniques are used to solve problems such as forest management, agricultural production, production planning in factories, and even the selection of hospital menus.

It is clear from these examples that whether physical or computer modelling is used, the predictions for real life are only as good as the ability of the model to contain enough of the rules and constraints of real life. Thus, for instance, a model based on fixed proportions of income being available for discretionary spend, as a way of calculating the market for luxury goods, would cease to be applicable if changes in lifestyle meant that increasing proportions were in fact being spent on food, through eating in restaurants or snacking on the move (Moore and Hodges, 1970).

Two aspects of a successful model are suggested by these examples:

- The ability to anticipate real world behaviour—which may be unexpected—through exploring the constraints or changes in the external environment, or the relationships between forces.

- The creation of a mental model which allows the user to look for early confirming or disconfirming evidence.

In the case of the airframes that are used to fly passengers, the model could identify the weaker section of the frame and indicate when (after how many flying hours) to look for signs of stress.

In the case of the market for luxury goods, the model might cause the distributor to investigate the cultures in which this change might occur.

How Can Marketers Get Better Models of the World?

This is a difficult question. If we compare good marketers with the Israeli Intelligence Service, for instance, we can look at what happened in the run up to the Yom Kippur War. This example of the difficulties in maintaining a view of alternative possible forms of threat, and hence the ability to react to signals, is given by Cohen and Gooch (1990). It describes how the Israelis, in spite of a superb intelligence operation, were essentially taken by surprise by the Arab attack during the war.

So, how can we avoid being taken by surprise?

Consider the approach taken by the Prussian military thinker Carl von Clausewitz—a major strategic theorist. He became interested in the effect of chance and uncertainty on war because the *"juggernaut of war, based on the strength of its entire people"* defined a new era. War had become one of the largest and most complex of endeavours, and in this context he dismissed the simplistic use of mathematical techniques, which he suggested illuminated tactics but not strategy. On the topic of how to act boldly despite the inherent uncertainties of war, he suggested making *"an educated guess and then gamble that the guess was correct"*. For a more detailed analysis, see Herbig's article in Handel (1989).

In this context, then, it could be said that scenarios improve the quality of the educated guesses and also provide a framework for deciding what the implications are, and when to gamble.

In Chapter Four and Chapter Eight, and in Appendix One, we discuss some of the methods that have been developed to try to improve the quality of these educated guesses in a marketing environment.

WHAT IS A SCENARIO?

Think of a scenario as a fairy tale or story. Michael Porter (2004) defined scenarios as:

> *"An internally consistent view of what the future might turn out to be—not a forecast, but one possible future outcome."*

A good set of scenarios are plausible in that they can be "imagined" in terms of current, visible, events or trends that might cause them to happen; the set should not only include a visionary (or normative) scenario, but also some scenarios that challenge the organisation. Scenario planning is the art of using scenarios for decision-making.

The Experimental and Theoretical Basis for Scenario Thinking

Scenario thinking explores the future in a way that provides not only plausible and consistent but also qualitatively different views of the future. Scenarios allow default assumptions to be surfaced and discussed. As an example, see the discussion over business plans at D2D (see Case Study 1.1).

CASE STUDY 1.1 SCENARIOS TO EXPLORE ASSUMPTIONS AT D2D

D2D was ICL's manufacturing division. The management team of D2D had produced a five-year strategic plan, and headquarters reviewed it with them as a basis for a prospectus for spinning D2D out as an independent company or as part of a contract manufacturing company.

ICL had developed two scenarios for the future of the information industries, shown in Figure 1.2. ***Coral Reef*** was a colourful IT world, with many small companies, a hectic pace of development, and consumer and business customers interested in the latest products. ***Deep Sea*** was a world in which a few large suppliers dominated their own territory for both consumer electronics and business computing, and customers preferred dealing with these established suppliers because they were big enough to sue.

When the management team was introduced to the scenarios, they recognised that their strategic plan had assumed that the world was a ***Coral Reef*** world, but that their competitive advantages—for instance European quality awards and staff policies—were aligned to the ***Deep Sea*** scenario. This meant that

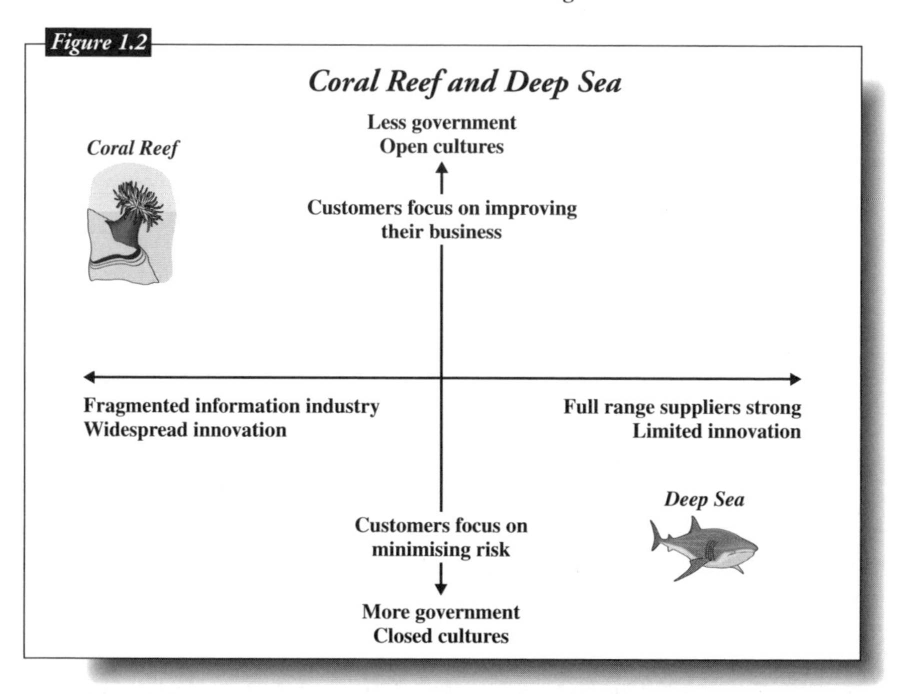

the part of their assumed future growth relating to consumer electronics was too optimistic. The team rethought their strategy and plan, focusing on their competitive strengths.

The business was successfully sold to Celestica, to provide the European contract manufacturing facility to add to those in China and Canada.

What Works and What Doesn't

Over the years practitioners have built up a number of rules of thumb on what works and what doesn't.

- Scenario thinking needs to take in a wide range of potential inputs to provide a useful basis for decisions. This may mean extensive desk research, horizon scanning, or interviews, or a mixture of all three, and the presence at the scenario building sessions of "external" or "remarkable" people. Scenarios that are built by only insiders tend to become introverted and pessimistic, with a focus on problems rather than opportunities.

- Scenario building is most useful when it is done in the context of an understanding of why it is being built. Is it to provide a context for decisions;

or as part of building management skills? In the first case it is important that the supporting desk research on the trends is in place; in the second it may be more important to discover what is in the participants' heads.

- Scenarios should be describable in an "elevator speech"[1] with a clear theme, and a set of names. They should relate to a key issue facing the organisation.

- It is often said that there should not be an odd number of scenarios because, in many cultures, it will be assumed that there is a middle or "right" scenario.

The process of scenario building is described in Appendix 1.

The Theoretical Basis Behind Scenario Thinking

Interestingly, a decade or more after the processes were first used, neurobiologists (e.g. Ingvar, 1985) discovered that the brain is actively rehearsing futures even when asleep. This means that by using scenarios to provide additional futures for exploration, the brain can be preparing for potential actions.

As Arie de Geus (1999) says

Every moment of our lives, we instinctually create action plans and programs for the future—anticipating the moment at hand, the next minutes, the emerging hours, the following days, the ongoing weeks, and the anticipated years to come—in one part of our mind.

These plans are sequentially organised, as a series of potential actions: "If this happens, I will do that." These are not predictions. They do not pretend to tell what will happen. They are time paths into an anticipated future. . . .

Not only does the brain make those time paths in the prefrontal lobes, it stores them. We visit these futures and remember our visits. We have, in other words, a "memory of the future", continually being formed and optimised in our imaginations and revisited time and time again." This process "apparently helps us to sort through the plethora of images and sensations coming into the brain, by assigning relevance to them. We perceive something as meaningful if it fits meaningfully with a memory that we have made of an anticipated future."

The stored time paths serve as templates against which the incoming signals are measured. If the incoming information fits one of the alternative time paths, the input is understood.

We will not perceive a signal from the outside world unless it is relevant to an option for the future that we have already worked out in our imaginations. The

[1] A description taking less than the time it takes to go from the ground floor to the top of the building in an elevator.

more "memories of the future" we develop, the more open and receptive we will be to signals from the outside world".

When Not to Use Scenarios

There are times when it is not useful to have a filter for sorting through external signals. This is when one, overwhelming, tidal wave is about to engulf an industry or organisation.

A good example is given in Ringland (2006). A scenario exercise in the computer industry looked at a number of factors, but missed the total sea change in the industry which was about to be caused by the collapse in industry margins from 40% to less than 10% as the industry growth shifted to semiconductors and PCs from proprietary mainframes.

CREATIVITY AND DISCIPLINE

Scenarios bring creativity into marketing by posing the question—what if· · ·?—in a number of articulated and qualitatively different worlds. One scenario can be "the official future"—the future that most people expect, but the development of which may also pose the question about different futures. The Electrolux case study is a good example (see Case Study 1.2).

Discipline is also an integral part of the scenario process, as described in Appendix 1. It is an auditable process in which futures are created from a combination of external signals, some of them weak, others posing questions, other signals being trends. These are combined to give alternative time paths which then can be analysed by the subconscious as well as the conscious brain.

CASE STUDY 1.2 DEVELOPING NEW BUSINESS STREAMS AT ELECTROLUX

Environmental issues are key concerns for the Electrolux Group—a major supplier of white goods—and working with environmental issues is all about dealing with short-term uncertainties and understanding long-term trends. In the mid-1990s the management team wanted the group staff in Environmental Affairs to develop an awareness of those trends and strategies for dealing with environmental issues integrated with the business process throughout the company.

Environmental issues needed to form part of the thinking process of the businesses. The scenario process was key in developing a picture of what was happening in the broader market and business environment that affected the product groups.

The Framework

Electrolux surveyed the literature available on scenario planning, internal experience from change programmes, and received advice from Graham Galer, former strategic planning manager at Shell, about Shell's experience of using scenario planning.

A scenario methodology, called the Environmental Change Programme (ECP), was developed using internal expertise, the services of the academic partner Gothenburg Research Institute and a management consultancy.

Two pilot projects were run, one with a group from the consumer side and one with a group from the commercial side—commercial cleaning appliances. On the consumer side, the group had already experienced pressure from environmental issues.

The first step of the ECP was to undertake a strategic investigation of the business environment with a special focus on environmental issues and demands. The second step was to look at the impact on the current strategy of the current and possible future conditions. The process and results were used as a way of broadening management thinking. However, the key was to integrate the concern and awareness of the environmental issues with the business strategy and to set up action plans.

The scenario process worked as an eye opener. The group started with the product line managers and then rolled it out to other management teams on lower levels.

The Scenarios

The process of building the fact base for the scenarios took around three months. During this period there was an extensive data collection process. Interviews were undertaken with suppliers, customers and environmental organizations. The scenarios were developed by a core team of four to five people from Environmental Affairs. The process was finalised by a brainstorming session based on a presentation of the fact base. The resulting skeleton scenarios were then formulated by obtaining additional information from experts and desk research.

Three scenarios were developed:

- ***Summer Time:*** (focusing on global warming): Global warming had caused strict legislation to be put in place to restrict the use of fossil fuels; energy prices were rising.

- ***Cocktails:*** Focusing around the use and abuse of toxins, both real and perceived.
- ***Evergreen:*** Focusing on material use, reuse and recycling.

The Use of the Scenarios

The process of introducing the scenarios with the businesses was started with a slide presentation of the driving forces behind environmental problems and demands. During the first pilots, this was followed by a set of slides highlighting the most important aspects of each scenario. This was presented to the full product line management team and other key managers—about 15 people. The managers were then formed into three separate groups to look at the different scenarios. Each group was asked to consider what they would do if they were working in Electrolux in 10 year's time and their scenario turned out to be a reality. For their assistance, they were provided with five pages explaining each scenario in detail.

After presenting their ideas to the other groups, each group was asked to consider what strategies could or should be put in place in any case—whatever scenario happened. The management teams recognised that it would be good to implement many of the strategies even if the scenarios did not occur. The actions they had identified made sense in terms of current environmental and business pressures.

The Results

There were several impacts of the change in thinking. One was a major strategic change in the commercial cleaning business. As a result triggered by one of the scenarios, the division became more service oriented. Electrolux became more aware that there was value in its products even beyond the economic use for the customers. As a supplier, the materials or parts of the product could be reused. The idea was then to sell the customer a service and not a product. This can be compared with a successful scheme developed by Rank Xerox of renting copiers with full service, guaranteed function, and charging based on the number of copies made, instead of only selling a copier machine.

The scenario process at Electrolux is ongoing. Less effort is now put into data collection and more effort is put into rolling the scenarios out to the businesses. The objective is to pass it on to all the product lines. Two years later, around 25% of product lines had used the techniques.

This case study was contributed by Jan Agri of Electrolux.

NEW USES OF SCENARIOS

While the popularity and application of scenarios has varied since the emergence of the technique after the Second World War (see Appendix 3 for a detailed history), in the last few years there has been a resurgence in interest for a number of reasons

- Since the mid-1990s there has been a renewed emphasis on sources of value and growth in corporations after the downsizing and retrenchment of the 1980s. See, for instance, Case Study 1.4: Pfizer's use of scenarios for organisational learning and change.
- Many senior managers now have MBAs and "know about" scenarios—perhaps, however, with a jaundiced view (O'Brien, 2004) through hurried exposure.
- The public sector in Europe has proactively developed the use of scenarios in policy discussion (e.g. European Commission, 2005).
- The non-governmental organisation (NGO) sector has realised the effectiveness of scenarios for harnessing the energies of members and the public. (See Case Study 1.3: Scenarios in Arts Marketing.)

CASE STUDY 1.3 SCENARIOS IN ARTS MARKETING

The Arts Marketing Association (AMA) has about 2000 members, consisting of people who persuade the public to experience the arts. The Symposium for its 150 senior members in 2005 was based around some key questions: What is the utopia for the future of the arts? What could and should the arts look and feel like in 2025? How could the AMA bring this about?

The Symposium had three parts. In the first part, "Visioning Utopia", a panel discussed "What could the UK arts sector look like for audiences in 2025?"; the second part, "Informing the Road Map", considered the opportunities and challenges in the world at large that might help or hinder this vision, and, the last part, "Building the Road Map", used the knowledge from the first two sessions to start the journey.

- ***Visioning Utopia.*** This was a panel discussion involving a range of senior figures in the arts and media. Each panelist was given time to outline his/her arts utopia and the discussion was then opened up for panel and delegates to debate these ideas together. These ranged from creating a new vocabulary and contract between the funding system, arts providers and the public ("both the National Theatre and the army are paid for by tax but only the arts are described as 'the subsidised sector'...") to a 10-year moratorium on revivals in order to display and promote new art.

- ***Informing the Road Map.*** The next session introduced four speakers to forecast developments in the key areas of technology, society, economics and politics between now and 2025. This session explored certainties, sources of surprise and new trends.

- ***Creating the Road Map.*** The task of the final session was to harness the plethora of ideas and information in order to agree on a utopia, and a road map for its implementation. The large number of people involved made this unusually challenging, and required detailed planning, organization and execution. With help from SAMI Consulting, the AMA designed and facilitated a process around some well-used scenarios—the Foresight 2001 scenarios—to provide a context for the discussion.

A short briefing in a plenary session covered an introduction to scenario thinking, an outline of the scenarios and a description of how the arts world might look under each scenario. So, for instance, a ***World Markets*** scenario could see increased private sector funding but the arts remaining a minority interest (as in the USA); compared with a scenario with wide participation in the arts but little public funding, or another where arts were seen as a social good and public funding was secure.

The delegates were divided into 16 syndicates to answer two sets of questions for each scenario:

- First, what are the desirable and undesirable factors of each?

- Second, ideas for reaching utopia under each—divided into "blue sky" ideas and "green" ideas—the latter obvious, "why don't we just go ahead?".

The syndicates were allowed an hour for each set of questions. The facilitators collected the output from the syndicates and synthesised it into headlines for the final, plenary, discussion and decision session.

Successful Outcome

Many aspects of the vision of the arts in 2025 could be summarised under the umbrella heading "Arts as an integral part of everyday life". Priority lists for ideas were also created, some eminently achievable in the short-term and some requiring a longer-term view, to deliver this vision. It was an incredibly creative and stimulating session that brought forth numerous good ideas, not just those identified as priorities. These ideas are being followed through in a series of regional think-tank meetings across the country involving arts organisations and arts funders.

CASE STUDY 1.4 USING SCENARIOS FOR MARKETING STRATEGY AT PFIZER

Organisational Context

The UK marketing division of a global pharmaceutical company decided to create scenarios to refine their strategies. Scenario use was already accepted within the corporate culture, as the global headquarters had previously built a set of strategic scenarios looking 10 years ahead. The UK marketing division faced the twin tasks of identifying potential new revenue streams, and clarifying their perception of external threats and opportunities.

The marketing division's strategic development team embarked on its scenario process within the usual constraints of corporate planning: a tendency to use straight-line forecasting, and the necessity of any output feeding directly into strategic imperatives already established by the global headquarters. Within those strategic imperatives, however, the developers had relative freedom of approach in managing uncertainty.

The Scenario Process

In 2004, the strategic development team began its change management process with a broad scan of current trends and emerging issues of change. This information collection and analysis sparked deep discussion within the team, and some interest outside it, but the team members found that people were not using the trends data in decision-making.

Upon consideration, the development team concluded that lack of familiarity with the foresight process dictated adoption of a new definition of strategic planning, based more on organizational learning. Furthermore, both global headquarters and UK headquarters were generating a growing number of strategic initiatives that needed to be checked for their robustness against the changing external environment.

Having attended an external training session in participatory scenario building, the development team decided to explore that approach. They contracted Fast Future to create and facilitate a scenario-planning process that would involve not only the strategic development team, but also senior managers, team leads and division heads.

The process had three primary phases:

1. ***Analysing the change data***—Review of the change data; identify and priorities driving forces; articulate the key questions that scenarios should address.

2. ***Creating scenarios***—Identify the driving forces with the greatest influence on key questions; rank them on importance and uncertainty; identify four potential end states for each critical uncertain driver; compose four scenario frames by layering related end states of each driver; use the scenarios to answer the key strategic questions; determine the impact of each scenario on customers, competitors, and other stakeholders.

3. ***Discerning opportunities***—Identify opportunities created by each scenario; agree evaluative criteria for opportunities, and priorities; map to existing high-priority strategic initiatives; evaluate non-priority strategic initiatives in the context of emerging opportunities to determine need for re-evaluation; establish next steps.

The results were transcribed, and a professional media team produced them as four "special issues" of a newspaper: "He@lth e-Nation", "Can Pay, Will Pay", "Bleak Health" and "Bureaucracy Rules". Each "special issue" consisted of a number of articles, side-bars, and commentaries written from the perspective of the future each scenario depicted, with vivid, often witty, details.

Lessons Learned

The process benefited organisational learning from the beginning: the raw materials—the brainstormed trends and emerging issues of change—proved just as useful as the scenarios themselves. Exposing a wide range of senior managers to such a wide range of change issues created a common language of change among top management.

Concrete change resulted: a new service provision division emerged as a result of the workshop. Senior management has also used the scenarios to support the role-out of "customer-focused" competence as a priority. This support takes the form of "customer workshops" in which teams role-play a specific customer within the context of each scenario, exploring the issues customers face and their resulting needs.

The UK marketing division as a whole continues to use the scenarios to support conversations on what the company can do given the uncertainties of a dynamic environment. As a result of these activities, more people on staff now see the link between the present and potential futures arising from emerging trends of change.

One characteristic of this work that could, in purely theoretical terms, be seen as a weakness, is instead the strongest lesson: neither the trends chosen, nor the resulting scenarios, strayed very far from the immediate operating environment of the company, or very far into the future. But the use of trends closely related to the current operating environment of the company has made this new, and relatively unfamiliar, process within the company's culture legitimate.

People hear the issues they identified and built into these scenarios mentioned in the daily news; they see the impacts they discussed evolving towards one or another of the scenario stories. This maintains interest in, and familiarity with, the issues, and reinforces acceptance of the technique. The strategic development team is currently considering approaches to involve not only management but also external stakeholders in building the next round of scenarios, which will explore further into the future.

This case study was contributed by Dr Wendy Schultz of Infinite Futures: wendy@infinitefutures.com

These factors have meant that new uses of scenarios have become prominent:

- Scenario creation as a management development tool. This uses workshops—typically two days—to develop young high flyers, to create a common language in a management team (for instance after a merger), or to brainstorm ideas as a framework for research.

- Using scenarios already developed, perhaps with some implications for the organisation drawn out, as a basis for decisions on research and development, country risk, mergers and acquisitions, corporate social responsibility, portfolio management or the location and capacity of manufacturing plants.

- Using scenarios already developed to "wind tunnel" test a business plan or strategy, by asking the question: "What if this scenario happens?"

- Using scenarios already developed as a basis for action planning. An example was the use of existing Foresight 2020 scenarios (Berkhout and Hertin, 2002) to provide a framework for action planning for the Arts Marketing Association.

- As part of the communication during change management in an organisation or public consultation in local or national government, as in Arnhem (see Case Study 1.5).

CASE STUDY 1.5 USING REAL ENVIRONMENTS TO MODEL THE FUTURE

These case studies are based on conversations with Jaap Leemhuis of Global Business Network (GBN) Europe, and on work with a UK supermarket group.

The Example of Rotterdam

Rotterdam City Council wanted to mount a "50 year" celebration of the rebuilding of Rotterdam in 1945. But instead of looking back, it wanted to look forward. It thus asked GBN Europe to design a process that would engage the public in thinking about the future of Rotterdam in 50 years, time.

The celebration began with six "town meetings" held in the evening in the large fifteenth-century church in the centre of the city, the Lagenskirk. Each was organised around a different dimension of the future (e.g. economic, social), and introduced by 30-minute contributions from experts before discussion from the floor. The meetings were videoed and taped, and used as the inputs to a scenario group of professors. This group worked with GBN Europe to develop two scenarios.

- One was for Rotterdam to maintain its industrial quality and role as the largest port in the world, with all the impact that has on quality of life—the environment, traffic, etc.

- The other saw the port activity move "out to sea" and the city redevelop to focus on services and amenities.

The scenarios were formulated by 30 senior civil servants, and written up by professional writers and editors into a booklet widely distributed throughout Rotterdam. The scenarios were given to six architects who were asked to produce projects for city renewal that would be robust in both scenarios. The projects were discussed by the architects and the public in six open evenings at the Architectural Institute. They were then the basis of an exhibition that was open for three months, with visitors able to walk through the scenarios and projects.

Applying the Lessons Learned to Arnhem

The example of Rotterdam was in the mind of the city planners for Arnhem, when they asked GBN Europe to help with their planning process. Arnhem sits on the main route from the industrial Ruhr in Germany, and Rotterdam. It is also a very beautiful part of the Netherlands, attracting many retirees. The question for Arnhem was: how to manage development?

Using a similar process to that developed for Rotterdam, the project began with town meetings, this time in the Musee Sacrum Concert Hall. One of the evenings was devoted to the logistics hub dimension of Arnhem's future, that is very dominant.

The scenario group was made up of City administrators, who developed four very different scenarios for Arnhem in 2015. Each scenario was presented in a brochure via the impressions of a sympathetic visitor to the future: for instance, a young technician visited the ***Logistics Hub*** world; and a 75-year-old gave his impressions of the ***Retirement Haven*** future.

The City created a "Villa 2015", with each of four large rooms representing one of the scenarios. All the inhabitants were sent a postcard of the Villa, inviting them to visit, and visitors were asked to fill in a questionnaire on their preferences.

The scenarios have since been used extensively by the planners of Arnhem. Even the chief of police is an advocate.

Customer Scenarios for a Supermarket

A leading UK supermarket group was exploring new retail formats, and developed three customer lifestyle scenarios as a basis for designing the stores at which they would be trialled.

- One customer type was "cash rich—time poor": here parking access for short stops was near the doors, and fast access food and convenience items were provided with self-scan payment.

- A second type was "cash poor—time rich" where facilities included food stations with chefs to discuss meals from scratch and seats near "how to" and "best buy" articles.

- The third type was the hardest of all—cash poor–time poor—for instance, single mothers. Here trial formats included crèches, and it was found that these needed to be on a veranda floor to be visible from all over the store.

CONCLUSION

Scenario planning can thus be an effective way for marketers to try to deal with the ever more complex challenges they face in a fast-moving environment. The following chapters will discuss how this can work for different aspects of marketing in more detail.

REFERENCES

Berkhout, F. and Hertin, J. (2002) "Foresight Futures scenarios—developing and applying a participative strategic planning tool", *Greener Management Journal*, **37**, 37–52

Cohen, E. A, and Gooch, J. (1990) *Military Misfortunes: The Anatomy of Failure in War.* The Free Press.

De Geus, A. (1999) *The Living Company.* Harvard Business School Press.

European Commission (2005) *Converging Technologies: Shaping the Future of European Societies.* Luxemburg.

Handel, M. I. (ed.) (1989) *Clausewitz and Modern Strategy*. Frank Cass & Company.

Ingvar, D. H. (1985) "Memory of the future", *Human Neurobiology* **4**, 127–136.

Moore, P. G. and Hodges, S. D. (1970) *Programming for Optimal Decisions.* Penguin.

O'Brien, F. A. (2004) "Scenario Planning: Lessons for practice from teaching and learning" *European Journal of Operational Research*, **152**, 709–722.

Porter, M. (2004) *Competitive Advantage*. The: Free Press.

Ringland, G. (2006) *Scenario Planning*, 2nd edn. John Wiley, Sons Ltd.

TWO

Securing Future Revenue

Laurie Young

SUMMARY

This chapter provides an overview of how marketing operates in different settings. It then summarises how scenario planning can be integrated with the wide range of marketing functions to improve future revenues. Later chapters look in more detail at these individual functions and the use of scenario planning.

The chapter has been written by Laurie Young, who is a marketing specialist with a successful career both in business and as an author.

INTRODUCTION

"*Marketing*" is the term used to describe the means by which companies raise their revenue. As all companies have to draw in revenue, all undertake aspects of marketing. In fact, even charities or organisations with no revenue, like government bodies or lobby organisations, can undertake aspects of marketing in order to communicate effectively with groups of people. Presenting credentials to potential buyers, managing press relations, hosting seminars, creating new products and giving presentations at public conferences are all part of the marketing mix. So, whether they call it marketing or not; have specialist marketing managers or not; firms undertake a range of marketing activities to develop their business.

In publicly—owned companies these are likely to be the responsibility of a relatively small specialist unit comprising people who are qualified and experienced

Scenarios in Marketing. Edited by G. Ringland and L. Young.

in marketing. They will be responsible to the management team for creating strategy, plans, budgets and programmes to grow the business. They will also be expected to balance the skills, resources and processes of the marketing department to optimum effect and for the benefit of the business in its market. Responsibility will have been delegated to manage the function effectively and they will need to ensure that their group has good knowledge of relevant concepts, develops appropriate competencies, uses reliable techniques and installs robust processes or systems. On top of this, they will need to engage with the whole firm to ensure that the customers' experiences are appropriate to meet the firm's objectives. In short, the marketing function needs to keep up-to-date and act as a catalyst for the business in its approach to market.

Yet, not all marketing is undertaken in the carefully organised departments of large publicly owned companies. In small firms, professional partnerships and charities, the situation tends to be more fluid and less clearly defined. Different people will initiate different marketing activities, which are frequently handled by people who have no specialist marketing knowledge and may not be aware of other marketing initiatives in different parts of the company. Even if a marketing manager or marketing department exists, they may not have exclusive responsibility for all revenue generation tasks.

This chapter introduces the range of responsibilities, organisational structures, managerial processes and marketing activities in different settings. It then discusses how scenario planning can be integrated with these different marketing approaches to improve future revenues.

ONE MORE TIME: WHAT IS MARKETING?

Marketing has been variously called an art (because it is creative, requiring judgement and experience), a science (because market-oriented companies use data and analysis to inform decision-making), a management discipline (one of the functions of many firms), an academic field of study (most universities have dedicated faculty) and a profession (because it requires deep knowledge of techniques with the experience to know how and when to apply them). In reality it has all the elements of these but, above all else, it focuses on how a business can generate future revenue.

Opinion formers have defined marketing as follows:

- *Marketing is the process of planning and executing the conception, pricing, promotion and distribution of ideas, goods and services to create exchanges that satisfy individual and organisational goals.*

  (American Marketing Association—AMA)

- *Marketing is the management process that identifies, anticipates and satisfies customer requirements profitably.*

  (UK Chartered Institute of Marketing—CIM)

- *Marketing is the social process by which individuals and groups obtain what they need and want through creating and exchanging products and value with others.*

  (Philip Kotler, 2003)

Marketing is therefore a management process by which leaders of a firm draw in revenue and increase the business. It is not limited to the specialist function within a firm or to highly trained marketing managers. When business managers of any kind are engaging in activities or plans that affect the revenue line, they are marketing. As in all aspects of business life, these activities can be undertaken using common sense by anyone in the firm. However, they are likely to be more effective, and generate more income in a more cost-effective way, if the right techniques are used and if experienced specialists are engaged using management processes and systems that enable them to contribute appropriately to the health of the firm.

The activities of marketing, in no particular order, are:

- *Competitive intelligence*—understanding what competitors are doing and adjusting the firm's direction in the light of that.

- *Opportunity analysis*—agreeing which opportunities in the market are likely to create more revenue for the firm and how they might be addressed.

- *Managing relationships and interfacing with buyers*—the approach by which the firm gains new customers or relates to existing buyers.

- *Internal communications*—creating and managing messages between the employees and the leadership of a firm.

- *Pitch or bid processes*—the process by which the firm presents its credentials or specific proposals about an offer to potential buyers.

- *Press management*—the way the firm handles its public appearance in the media.

- *Sponsorship*—any paid involvement in sporting/entertainment/arts events to improve the reputation of the firm.

- *Corporate and social responsibility*—engaging in the support of community projects to encourage a positive reputation for the company.

- *Customer events*—hosting social or issue-based events in order to attract new business.

- *Direct communication*—electronic or physical mailings and presentations at public conferences.

- *Thought leadership*—producing reports, books or other projects to demonstrate the skills of the firm and draw in new business.

- *Collateral design*—the production of leaflets, brochures and case studies to illustrate issues.

- *Advertising*—using paid advertisements in TV, radio and print to spread awareness of the offer.

- *Customer database management*—using technology to ensure that buyer details are assets of the whole firm.

- *Networking*—managing relationships with a wide range of individuals in order to generate business.

- *Pricing*—setting charges for the firm's products and services.

- *Creating new products or services*—designing and launching new concepts or offerings.

- *Point of sale*—displays on premises.

- *Premises selection and design*—layout of shops to create the optimum traffic flow and sales.

- *Sales promotion*—campaigns designed to make certain products or services attractive in order to increase sales.

Most organisations, of all sizes and ownership types, will undertake some aspect of many of these activities. All are aimed at gaining revenue in the future and are based on a combination of judgement, research and analysis. But, because they are future-oriented, all involve risk. The issue for the marketer is whether the rich pictures painted by scenarios can reduce the risk of failure.

DIFFERENT MANIFESTATIONS OF MARKETING

The Intuitive Business Leader

Rivals in the market had been conducting a competitive and high-profile marketing campaign for 10 years. The product had been recut, repackaged, repriced and renamed. There had been advertising on railways stations, in newspapers and eye-catching outdoor sites. At one point, billboards appeared on streets, the length and breadth of Britain, which were filled with a message that could be read from 10 metres away: "Why does a woman look old sooner than a man?" Messages had been projected onto leading monuments, like Nelson's column, and one overenthusiastic foreign competitor had even daubed a message on the white cliffs of Dover; prompting the *Times* newspaper to criticise "gratuitous exhibitions of dissolving views".

Salespeople were employed to call on retailers and to visit homes across the country. An elaborate range of competitions had captured the imagination of the population and a scientific sounding instruction booklet had been widely distributed. There had even been a long running dispute with an aggressive British tabloid, the *Daily Mail*, about a questionable price change.

A typical modern marketing campaign, using all aspects of the marketing mix, you might think. But this was conducted in the 1880s by the young soap entrepreneur William Lever (MacQueen, 2004; Turner, 1965). Lever was an ambitious, driven and eccentric (for much of his life he slept in a bedroom specifically designed to be open to the elements) business leader. When he took over his father's grocery business, he built it into a major, international concern that still dominates its market today. Yet this highly effective and well-rounded marketing campaign was designed by him before the advent of radio or TV and 80 years before Philip Kotler wrote his seminal work on marketing management. Moreover, his rival, Pears soap, had been launched by Thomas Barret one hundred years before Lever (the 1770s) using catchphrases and celebrities (Lillie Langtry, an actress and the king's mistress) to be "the face of Pears".

These creative entrepreneurs were using the principles of marketing, based on their business experience and intuition, long before they were codified. Similar individuals (from Richard Branson and Philip Green to Donald Trump) have become billionaires today through similar attitudes; and many thousands of less famous business leaders do the same. They are the pre-eminent practitioners of marketing, creating enormous wealth for themselves, their investors, their employees and society as a whole. They frequently succeed by breaking rules

(Harvard would not have advised young pop entrepreneur Branson to go into the airline business) and shake up or create markets. Their emphasis is on customers and markets, so they push all elements of their business to focus on external opportunities rather than internal activities. They also tolerate both risk and failure.

As their businesses grow, the most successful learn to use specialists to round out or refine their vision and instinct. They routinely employ accountants, lawyers and merchant bankers; and most use marketing specialists (either as employees or through agencies) to great effect. The culture of their highly successful, market-oriented businesses is focused on understanding and executing the leader's will. Much time is taken to tease out, develop and communicate their vision and implement it throughout the firm. Scenarios can be powerful tools in this context, crystallising futures envisaged by the leader so that different business functions, including marketing, can develop them in their part of the business.

The Bureaucratic Company

While the bureaucratic organisation has been heavily criticised by academics and business thinkers, it is seen in most large, modern businesses representing, as it does, the need to specialise. These businesses are owned either by the public through shares, or by venture capitalists or families. Authority is delegated down a professional management hierarchy by the leadership team, giving them authority to run the business on behalf of the owners. It is unfortunate that "bureaucratic" has become a pejorative term. Specialisation of work and skill has been one of the main contributors to the evolution and success of the human race. There are, therefore, real benefits to the specialisation, clarity of reporting, accountability and decision-making emphasis of this type of structure.

The prime marketing activities in a bureaucracy are the responsibility of a specific specialised unit, the marketing department, depicted in Figure 2.1. It reports to a chief marketing officer (CMO) and has the delegated authority to generate revenue and create all marketing programmes. The diagram depicts typical functions within the unit but these can vary enormously. For instance, brand management might exist within market management (because it focuses on categories) or in marketing communications. Sales and sales support might be combined with marketing under one "sales and marketing" director or vice president. Also, there may be elements of the marketing mix in other parts of the organisation. For example, some firms place new product development and pricing under a separate director. Others have separate directors for corporate relations; responsible for reputation, brand, corporate social responsibility (CSR) and public relations (PR).

The CMO, as leader of the function, has several roles. The first is to provide marketing experience, judgement and advice to the firm's leaders about policies; to round out and inform decision-making and strategy development. The second

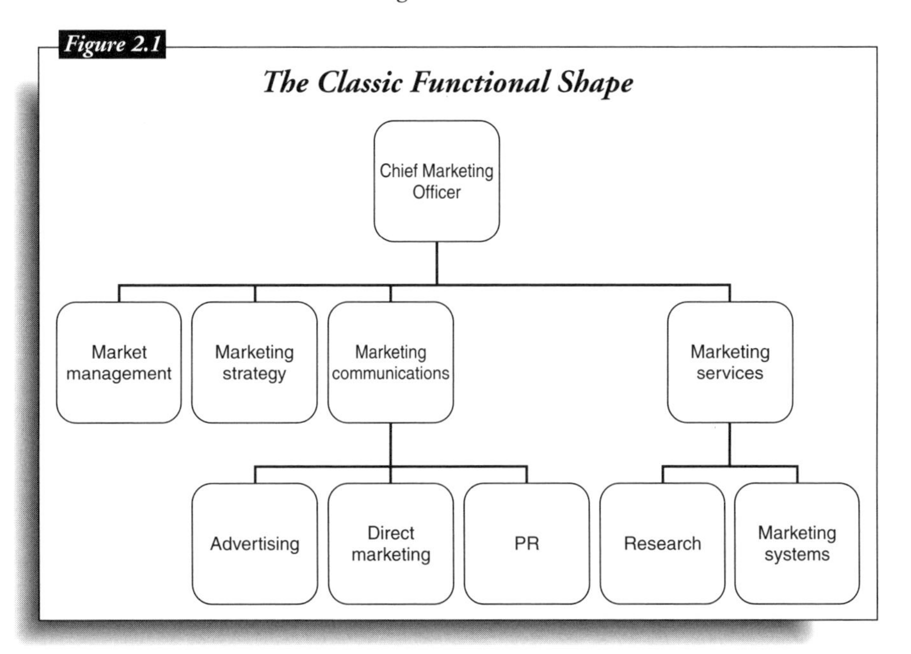

is to lead the function, ensuring that it is properly resourced and contributes appropriately. The third is to be the voice of the market within the firm, challenging it to embrace opportunities and understand customer needs.

The ability of the marketing function to contribute effectively to income generation and the health of the business depends on the status and recognition it has in the organisation. In many long-standing consumer goods businesses (Procter & Gamble, Unilever) or confectioners (Mars), it is a lead function of the business. The firm recruits the cream of the graduate crop into a professional apprenticeship scheme which provides some of the best marketing training in the world. Alumni of the programme progress through the firm from junior brand managers to marketing directors. Their role is to generate income from branded value propositions using the full arsenal of marketing techniques.

In other industries, however, the contribution of specialist marketing people is limited to minor functional roles like sales support or brochure creation. The income of the business is generated by other means such as a strong and healthy natural demand for an innovative product or systematic account management.

In this type of firm scenario planning has been most often used to create corporate strategy, most famously at Shell. Marketing specialists are frequently engaged in the creation of the corporate scenarios, contributing market insight, but

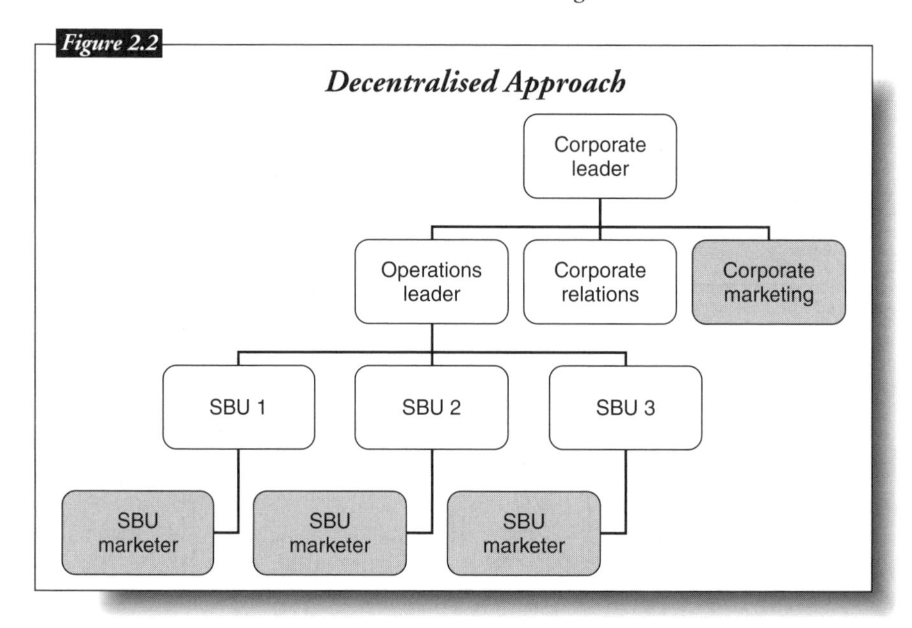

it is led by corporate planners or their equivalent. Once agreed, though, corporate scenarios give context and direction to the work of the marketing function.

The Conglomerate or Decentralised Business

Figure 2.2 depicts a decentralised organisation with devolved business units. These might be businesses specialising in different disciplines or in different geographic countries. The effectiveness of the approach and the behaviour of the marketers depend on the degree of autonomy of the different units. For example, this structure is often adopted by large technology companies. In these, a "strategic business unit" (SBU) will be expected to work within tight corporate guidelines. The marketer is likely to have a clear job description with defined competences and objectives. They are also likely to report regularly to the corporate function and participate in clear, firm wide processes. At the other extreme, there are large conglomerates which own separate firms with different profit pools (like ABB, Hanson and WPP). The marketers in these firms are likely to have greater autonomy within very broad corporate guidelines. Scenario work in both these, though, is likely to be at corporate rather than business unit level, if at all.

The Smaller Firm

By far the majority of firms range from medium sized enterprises to tiny start ups. In these, specialist marketing units are limited by resource constraints; often to

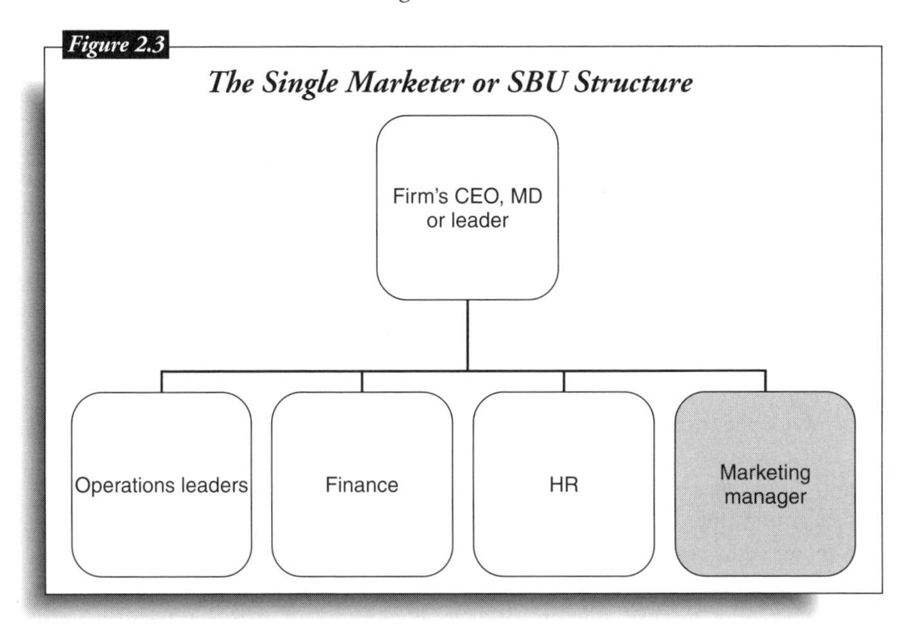

a single, or isolated, marketer, depicted in Figure 2.3. This person might report to the firm's leader, gaining authority to create programmes, strategy and change from the closeness of that relationship. Constrained by lack of resources, the single marketer needs influence to get the wider organisation to take on work and the budget to rely on external contractors.

Single marketers need the capability to handle a wide variety of tasks and the humility to do much of the work themselves. In some firms they report to a functional leader who manages all specialists (HR, finance, IT, etc.). This, however, tends to be less effective because it weakens the assumed authority behind the speciality, reducing the influence of marketing. For these, scenario approaches will help to facilitate debate with the firm's leaders about strategic direction, prioritising revenues and activities.

Professional Partnerships

In many ways partnerships are the embodiment of the decentralised, flat and flexible organisations recommended by recent management theorists, and have been so for many decades. They comprise cells of "practices" each led by an owner of the firm, a "partner". They include some of the world's biggest, influential and most international businesses with revenues in excess of $16 billion at the time of writing.

In a large partnership, employees work their way through their firm, conducting client projects, until they "make partner". For many, this is a defining moment of their career. They are included in meetings and discussions of which they were unaware and they become part of an inner circle of colleagues. Reward is different but so too is responsibility. For instance, one of the main characteristics of a partner is the ability to build a book of business and to win work, through an external profile that grows with experience.

As a result, as years go by, they gain an external reputation for a specialist skill. At this point, the client weighs both the firm's reputation and the specialist skill of the partner when buying. In fact, part of the strength of the company becomes the leading partners in its offer. The brand of the firm and the reputation of key partners become inextricably linked. Both are the major marketing tools, the key revenue earners of leading partnerships, and any other activity is seen as supportive to them.

While the strength of partnerships lies in their autonomy and closeness to the market, a drawback is the tendency towards confusion in the skill, deployment and competence of "support" functions. "Support" is an ill-defined term for non-fee earning employees and normally includes any specialist marketing functions. Support people can be directly employed or subcontracted but the role and nature of the resource depends on the vision and aims of the partners in the various practices. For instance, sole practitioners might employ a secretary as demand increases. This frees them from basic administrative tasks in order to carry out more client work and they may take on marketing activities, such as arranging client hospitality events.

Some practices might use client service staff to execute marketing work, others will use administrators and yet others will use marketing specialists. Some surprisingly large professional networks have no central marketing department, or a very small one comprising inexperienced people. As a result, they miss out on the input of high quality specialist insight into their firm's direction and, from the perspective of the network, this results in diseconomies of scale and a less than optimum impact on the market.

The organisational shape depicted in Figure 2.4 reflects the thinking among several leading firms to overcome these drawbacks. First, there is a specialist function handling corporate reputation, media relations and chief executive communications. Secondly, there is a separation, at both corporate and local level, of "practice marketers" (who directly interface with partners in each practice) and, thirdly, a number of "marketing services" specialists. The latter are grouped into a firm-wide shared service to optimise effectiveness, budgets and supplier management.

In some firms, all practice marketers report directly to the CMO but work with the practices as consultants. All are linked in a professional community that sets standards and direction. In these organisations, though, the main income generation is through the client service teams. The marketing task is as much

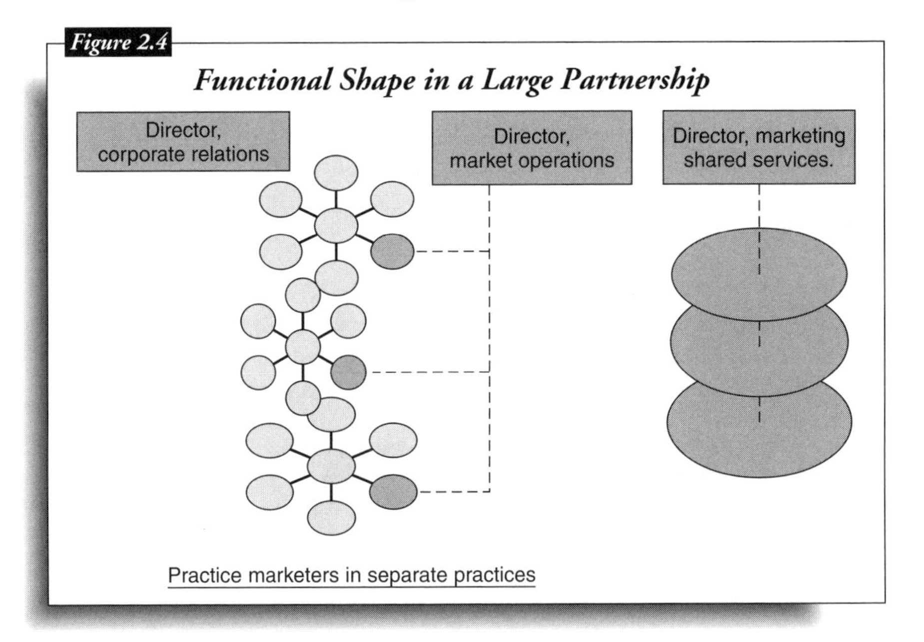

about facilitating a cross-organisational market-oriented culture as it is about managing a relatively small unit of specialists.

A number of the larger partnerships have people at partner level leading marketing in much the same role as the "chief marketing officer" in publicly quoted companies. These are frequently partners of the firm, qualified in its prime discipline rather than marketing, who are undertaking a management role for reasons of personal development. If the role is occupied by a marketing specialist, they have often come to it through a consultancy route within the firm. Few are recruited externally, as in other business sectors. Whatever their skill or background, the CMO is as likely to be concerned with improving the account handling skills of colleagues or the proposal management capability of business units as the creation of a communications campaign or new service.

Scenario planning has been used at corporate level by partnerships. It is an excellent device to achieve the consensus needed among all the firm's partners regarding any strategic direction. For instance, one of the "big four" accountancy firms used it to create a new direction after the upheavals created by the regulatory response to the Enron débâcle.

The Voluntary Sector and Non-Governmental Organisations (NGOs)

Charities and their like have a variety of marketing roles. Most, though, put emphasis on their "fundraising" specialists who, like salespeople in profit-oriented businesses, generate the organisation's revenue. There are also likely to be a range of specialist marking communication people dealing with press and PR. The development and management of key messages through concerted campaigns is a key skill and a critical success factor. In many ways, groups like Amnesty and Greenpeace are consummate marketers, even if they may not like to be called such.

The Marketing Supply Industry

Much marketing occurs on behalf of clients within various specialist agencies. This is a hugely diverse range of businesses. It includes advertising, direct marketing and new product development agencies, as well as a variety of consultancies. They range from the huge conglomerates like WPP to single person businesses. Yet they frequently create revenue and profit for their clients (Case Study 2.1).

CASE STUDY 2.1 HATHAWAY SHIRTS

In his 1960s best seller, *Confessions of an Advertising Man*, David Ogilvy (Ogilvy, 2004) describes the campaign he created for Ellerton Jetté who owned Hathaway shirts.

It was Hathaway's debut as a national American advertiser but, at the time, it could only spend $30,000 against its competitor's spend of $2,000,000. Ogilvy's use of clear copy and "the magic ingredient" of an eye patch on a male model put Hathaway on the map after 116 years of relative obscurity. It launched the brand and also made Ogilvy internationally famous. Moreover, after eight years, the company was successfully sold at many millions of dollars profit. It is a classic example of the genius and creativity that the marketing supply industry can provide for their clients. Despite the fact that much writing and theory is developed from and for marketing specialists in large companies, much of the real added value comes from agencies.

THE EVOLUTION OF MARKETING IN AN ORGANISATION

Much of the academic study of marketing focuses on issues of theory, concept or practice. By and large it makes assumptions about the way the function works in a firm. It is assumed that there is a well-developed organisation led by a marketing director or CMO, able to call on financial and human resources to undertake research, manage advertising or adjust product features in the light of rational, justified arguments. There is little talk of the need to convince organisations of the need for marketing, of competing for resources or of organisational politics.

The situation is rarely so clear cut. The marketing function is often undeveloped. It has to argue for its role in the organisation and has to invest in processes, as well as running projects to generate revenue. Some companies do not understand their own need for certain marketing skills and restrict the contribution that the function makes, limiting it to, say, a minor promotional role. Professor Nigel Piercy's research (Piercy, 2001) showed that there was rarely consistency about the functions for which marketing leaders are responsible. Nor was there consistency in the shape of organisations. He observed four types of marketing departments:

- *Integrated/full service*—closest to the theoretical models and with a wide range of responsibilities and power in the organisation.
- *Strategic/services*—smaller units with less power and integration. Their influence is in the area of marketing support services or specific policies/strategies.
- *Selling overhead*—often large numbers and dispersed but primarily engaged in sales support activities.
- *Limited staff role*—small numbers with few responsibilities and engaged in specific staff support such as market research or media relations.

Also, it appears that marketing departments evolve (from a limited staff role to fully integrated) as firms grow and marketing grows in importance within them. When a company is initially formed much of the marketing role is undertaken by the founders or specialist subcontractors (such as PR agencies or merchant bankers). Some time after that a marketing specialist will be hired to manage activities such as brochure production, new product launch and perhaps some advertising.

As the firm grows, marketing specialists are recruited into different places in the organisation, such as public relations and sales support. Later, this develops into the fully integrated marketing function seen in many corporate firms. A large corporate entity might have up to 500 marketing specialists running campaigns, integrated by both a hierarchical senior management team (culminating in a CMO) and by the use of common processes and technology.

THE "MARKETING CONCEPT"

The marketing concept suggests that the buyers and the market, not exclusively the operations of the firm, should be at the centre of management's attention; and that, by putting attention on the market, long-term profits can be achieved. It has been called "market oriented" or "customer led" but is the antithesis of the internal orientation of many firms. Some are sales led, some are fascinated with technology or product enhancement, while others are monopolies, preoccupied with internal rivalry. These approaches can be successful for a time, generating funds for owners, until market conditions change. If new regulation is passed or an aggressive competitor changes market dynamics, firms without a market orientation can fail.

This simple concept is in all marketing textbooks and can sound like wishful thinking by marketing theorists, keen to press for greater influence for their discipline. The experience of many marketing specialists is the opposite; that the function is not appreciated or allowed to shine. They become absorbed with changing daily priorities, tactical rather than strategic work and the need to engage in internal politics to protect the contribution of their function. But the marketing concept is more than an academic wish or theoretical fantasy.

Numerous research papers from "What the hell is market oriented" (Shapiro, 1988) to "Marketing is everything" (McKenna, 1991) and long-term tracking surveys (like the PIMS database—Buzzell and Gale, 1987) have shown that market oriented companies produce long-term shareholder return. Perhaps the clearest example, however is America's GE. Under Jack Welch this huge conglomerate exceeded expectations in terms of shareholder return and, for over a decade, came top in survey after survey as the most admired company. But this success was built over the long term (see Vaghefi and Huellmantel, 1988).

As far back as 1957, Ralph Curdier, the then CEO, announced that "marketing would be both the corporate philosophy and the functional discipline to implement the philosophy". Until then all planning had been internally oriented, focused on solving internal problems. This set the foundation for an externally oriented culture. Evidence suggests that, since then, each CEO has chosen his successor as a means to continuing this philosophy and the consequent enduring legacy has been the foundation of GE's outstanding success.

A marketing oriented company understands its market and anticipates future trends, exploiting emerging opportunities. It is forward looking and intimately engaged in understanding the minds and responses of its buyers. Scenario planning, as a future-oriented tool, is a powerful mechanism to aid the development of different marketing strategies and programmes in this context.

SCENARIO PLANNING AND DIFFERENT MARKETING FUNCTIONS

Marketing is focused on exploiting future opportunities to gain future revenues. It is risky because past events or previous buyer behaviours are not reliable indicators of future action. For instance, despite popular belief, satisfied buyers, whether they are consumers or business groups, do not always buy again. They will willingly change if another supplier offers a better value proposition no matter how good the service has been on previous occasions. Successful marketing is therefore based as much on good judgement and risk assessment as on research and statistical analysis of past trends. But it remains risky.

How does scenario planning, as a future-oriented technique, relate to various marketing activities or functions? How can it round out perspectives on markets and improve the execution of activities designed to draw in revenue? How might it reduce uncertainty and risk?

First, if the firm has developed corporate scenarios, it gives direction to its people. Leaders of all functions will build their activities around the corporate direction the scenarios paint. Whatever organisational structure or culture exists, consensus will be achieved through communication of a clear direction. As with other functions, this clear corporate direction will influence the components of marketing from market research and new product development to brand and communication programmes. The mere fact that all the firm's resources are committed to one or two clear directions is likely to increase impact and reduce risk.

However, how does scenario planning relate to the individual functions of marketing itself? Specialists in various aspects of the function are likely to find scenario planning relevant to their job, but how can they deploy the technique if there is no corporate backing for the approach and no developed, firm-wide, scenarios? Is it a tool, like market research or portfolio analysis, that can be used easily within the function itself? This is explored in depth by expert writers in this book but a brief overview follows.

Scenario Planning and Customer Research

Field research is familiar to most business people. They may have seen the results of research presented at internal meetings or read public research reports on various subjects. Unfortunately, familiarity can breed contempt, making the processes, the techniques and the outcomes seem deceptively simple. As a result, there are many unconvincing or poor research reports resulting from poor specification or poor use of the research industry.

Yet, undertaken properly, field research yields insights into buyer needs, their views (which can be different to needs), competitor performance and market trends. It can reveal the different elements of an offer which people value and how they combine with different price points to form packages that they will buy. Moreover it can indicate how these differ between buyer groups, creating opportunities to vary an offer for different market segments. It can also save money by stopping new ideas, marketing programmes or advertising initiatives that the market will reject.

However, to do all this it has to be properly specified and managed. It needs a clear requirements brief and a robust managerial process if it is going to produce results. This needs to ensure that the sample frame, the approach, the technique and the questionnaires are appropriate. However, even if properly specified, research can reveal conflicting and confusing buyer views and needs.

People are not straightforward. Frequently they do not know what they want until stimulated. Moreover, they make decisions as much by emotion and intuition as by rational need. In fact, recent thinking suggests that people are assailed by so many stimuli during any day that their conscious mind selects what to receive and respond to but their unconscious mind receives and assimilates much more. This, in turn, drives much "intuitive" decision making. Recent pioneering approaches at Harvard University (see Zaltman, 2003) are beginning to delve into these hidden attitudes. The different interpretations of these research results can be captured in scenarios, creating representations of confused, emotional and intuitive human responses which can be used by practical business people in development projects.

Scenario Planning and Market Analysis

Many marketing academics and theorists have an economic background. As a result they have given an impression that market analysis is a straightforward, objective process that tries to make sense of rational or efficient markets. Techniques such as the "market audit" and competitor positioning maps create an impression that there is one view of a market. These are reinforced by industry research analysts who tend to adopt a herd mentality and reinforce entrenched views. There are, for example, several established agencies tracking trends in the IT industry which drive the views of most suppliers.

Yet market analysis is not straightforward at all. At its most basic, the interaction between buyers and suppliers over the development of a product or service can affect the rate of purchase and the speed of adoption. It took, for instance, the development of feature film length video cassettes for VHS to become the video recorder standard and for the world-wide market to really take off. Similarly, various attempts were made to offer public information databases (Prestel in the UK in the 1970s and Mintel in France in the 1980s) but it took the anarchic nature of the internet for this to really fly.

The rate at which a market matures is as much dependent on a complex mix of supplier and buyer interaction as it is on impersonal economic forces. In fact, some suppliers take a behavioural view of a market. While economic drivers are not irrelevant to them, they think that demand is more strongly influenced by the depth of relationship between suppliers and buyers. Their policies of revenue generation are reliant on stimulating and deepening this relationship.

There are, then, different ways of understanding supplier competences and competitor actions, giving different market perspectives. These can be distilled into different scenarios that will give direction to strategy and programmes.

Scenario Planning and Marketing Strategy

Ideally it should be difficult to separate marketing strategy from corporate strategy. The strategic intent of the whole firm should be based on a perspective of the market or markets in which it operates. In the development of corporate strategy there should be iteration with marketing strategy to ensure focus on achievable opportunity and market objectives. If a company is adopting a scenario planning approach in its corporate strategy, it will create possible futures based on perspectives of potential market developments which should developed from marketing skills and techniques.

Within the marketing strategy itself, however, the planner is dealing with alternative futures. The famous Ansoff matrix, for example, is a tool to focus thinking around market penetration, product development, market development and diversification. Each is an alternative future that can be dramatised and explored through scenario techniques. In the various approaches to opportunity analysis and investment prioritisation, similar alternatives are explored. The "directional policy matrix", for example, identifies markets and businesses that the leadership team regard as the most attractive and have the greatest potential. Investment is prioritised around their criteria of what makes a market attractive and what makes a business strong. The potential development of these alternative investment strategies can be explored in scenarios.

Scenario Planning and New Product or Service Development

Innovation of new offers and their successful adaptation in the light of market reception are both very important and very difficult. There is evidence that large established firms find it particularly difficult to innovate due to their lumbering cultures; whereas a number of suppliers find it difficult to turn ideas into replicable, viable offers to customers. Scenarios can be used to stimulate creativity and ideas. They can also be used to test alternative development routes with the market. Portfolio strategy is particularly open to scenario interventions. The alternative stories of different products can be used to model potential returns and growth volumes.

Scenario Planning in Brand Valuation

To arrive at the expected future earnings of a "brand", it is necessary to decide, either explicitly or implicitly, which growth scenario is most likely to occur (and then determine valuation assumptions that are appropriate to that scenario). This means it is inevitable that the consideration of alternative scenarios, and their probability of happening, is central to the "brand" valuation process. The use of scenarios to explore brand valuation and develop a "Fair Market Value" is central to most modern brand valuation techniques.

Scenario Planning in Communication Programmes

However good a new product is, the reception by the market is unpredictable. Much relies on how it is communicated to groups of human beings. The ability to communicate with markets and customer groups is therefore an important competence for all firms. The relevance of message and ability to persuade can be crucial to revenue growth. Scenarios can be used to test and design communication programmes, modelling the most effective media and communication strategies. They should be particularly helpful in the development of integrated communications strategies and response mechanisms that are crucial to most modern marketing.

Scenario Planning in Action

The following case study for mobile commerce illustrates many of the above aspects.

CASE STUDY 2.2 STRATEGIES FOR MOBILE COMMERCE

Following the UMTS (3G) licences auction in Holland in 2000, one of the telecoms companies involved embarked on an exploration of the future of mobile commerce. It concluded that mobile telephony alone was not enough to allow it to survive as a telecoms organisation. Consumers needed to be persuaded to use their mobile phones for more applications and services than just phoning. But there were a number of questions that needed to be looked at. For example:

- How could this be done?
- Would consumer behaviour really develop in that direction?
- What if it went the other way?
- And which players actually determined what happened in this market?

The Process

The research and development (R&D) department initiated the project. External consultants, an internal project team and 20 employees got involved. The overall goal was to increase insight into what mobile commerce meant for the organisation.

Four Dilemmas

During the interview period, it became clear that mobile commerce requires a totally different mindset than mobile phoning. Mobile telephony is one service with a simple price structure. Mobile commerce, on the other hand, demands cooperation with other providers, and the means of payment were still totally unclear.

Four dilemmas surfaced which proved to be crucial to the development of mobile commerce strategy:

- Should the company exploit its position in the Dutch market to become a market leader? Or should it take advantage of the worldwide scope of its parent company?

- Should the organisation open its infrastructure to all possible commercial providers and allow them to reach their target groups that way? That would mean the profit would come from the increase in data traffic. Or should it choose a selected number of parties, who would be allowed to use the infrastructure (at a charge) to offer commercial services to subscribers?

- Should the company be a "Lone Ranger", and use its dominant international position to dictate the standard for m-commerce? Or should it work together with the other telecoms providers as a sort of "United Nations" to offer consumers and providers one European standard?

- Should it stimulate supply of services or create demand by users instead?

Through systematic study and discussion of external developments, the model shown in Figure 2.5 was constructed based on the most important factors and their interdependence.

If mobile commerce were to become successful, it would obviously be necessary to have customers for the services provided. On the other hand, customers will only show up when interesting services are offered. Also, these services will only be offered when there is enough demand.

On the customer side this problem was increased by the absence of applications (on mobile phones, PDAs, laptops) necessary to run mobile services. Unclear standards were a major obstacle on the supply side. With GSM, the success story of the nineties, standards had been enforced by the European Union. That was straightforward, because most operators were publicly owned. The economic boom of the nineties also helped things along. Providers could give away free mobile phones and hence drive the market. But by 2000 it was illegal for providers to cooperate; in a liberalised market they were supposed to compete. It was also uncertain whether the economic boom would last, or whether a dip would follow.

The Three Scenarios

Deadlock (see Figure 2.6)

Efficiency-driven consumers are focused on low prices, and they use their cell phone just to make phone calls. There is hardly any interest in m-commerce. Moreover, severe competition for clients has meant lowered tariffs and shrinking profits for operators. The capacity that the provider has for data transport (UMTS) does not provide income. Possibilities for m-commerce activities are found exclusively in the business-to-employee market and in telecoms solutions for the automobile industry. The only way a business can survive is by using reserves, operating as efficiently as possible and looking for alternative sources of income.

Digital Hub (see Figure 2.7)

Although consumers use their cell phones mainly for making telephone calls, they slowly but surely discover new applications. The cell phone is viewed as a portable version of the Internet, so comparable content is therefore expected. Dot.com companies, which have survived the crisis, jump into this new niche, partly to support their e-commerce activities. But they quickly discover that earnings are restricted. If users have to pay too much for content on their cell phones, that will lead them to move to other, cheaper technology like wireless LAN. For telecom operators a focus on telephony is still essential. They can only distinguish themselves from competitors by operational efficiency.

New Wave (see Figure 2.8)

Cell phones are no longer used primarily for phone calls. Because of broadband and very consumer-friendly mobile services, the cell phone has become the nerve centre of personal activity. Providers of m-commerce make good money. These providers are telecoms operators or specialised m-commerce businesses. Their growth comes from the possibilities inherent in integration of mobile services and the cell phone. The competition is very tough, because the fastest, most accessible and smartest provider with the most desirable hardware will dominate the (world) market.

Wishful Thinking or 'What If'

When these scenarios were developed in 2001, everyone in telecoms land fervently hoped that the ***New Wave*** scenario would become the future. It wasn't for nothing that hundreds of millions of euros, money earned from good old-fashioned telephony, were spent on UMTS licences. After such a major purchase people were loathe to think that the future might be different. But this company was not afraid to consider the possibility that m-commerce might not take off. Hence the scenario project. The scenarios created space to formulate clear options for the company, a number of which were acted upon.

Looking Back

Despite all wishful thinking, reality today looks more like a combination of "Digital Hub" and "Deadlock". Making telephone calls is still the most important application for cell phones. Except for commercial text messaging, which is incredibly profitable, phones in Europe are hardly used as mobile information and entertainment units. This is in contrast with the Far East, where people using public transport every day immerse themselves with their cell phones as their only source of entertainment.

Nevertheless, the industry still hopes that the ***New Wave*** scenario will come true sooner or later. The roll-out of UMTS is in full progress and expectations are still optimistic. In 2004 several telecom providers introduced a fast UMTS internet connection for laptops. Later that year UMTS was applied to fast internet connections via cell phones. With this connection it is possible to send and play small films, television excerpts and video clips. Image telephony, with which callers can see each other, is also now possible.

With hindsight, it is safe to conclude that over the last five years UMTS has turned out to be a bottomless pit in terms of expenditure, although some providers have prevailed over others in the battle. It is still possible that the next five years might bring the "mountains of gold", which have been awaited for so long. But then the industry will have to acknowledge that it will be essential to collaborate in order to win over a larger number of potential purchasers. This will not come easily to companies that have been fierce rivals.

Successes and Failures

The main success of the project was the fact that scenario planning offered a method of looking at an important problem in a particular way. The topic we had chosen was very complex there were many different opinions on how to solve the issue. The process enabled us to simplify the complexity and the issue became "graspable". What to do slowly became evident during the process.

Apart from that, we learned a lot from the interviews we conducted to prepare the workshops. The many different opinions in the company were made explicit and registered and offered a very clear view on what was happening internally. A rare and most interesting opportunity!

Lessons Learned

Although the scenario process in itself was a success, the impact of the results turned out to be disappointing. Afterwards, it became evident that this was due to the fact that we did not appoint one specific owner of the project who was to make something out of the findings. Shortly after the process the whole company changed and the suggestions from the project were not taken forward. So I would advise others to determine a topic carefully and select the right person to take the deliverables forward into the organisation.

As I said before, the major conclusion that resulted is that you never really realise how people within the organisations look at the same topic in so many different ways and from different angles. Also, the level of creativity of the ideas we suggested was very high. We could not have achieved that level if we had looked at the issue internally. That was a huge benefit for me; bringing more players together stimulated the creativity.

This case study was contributed by Paul de Ruijter of De Ruijter Management, paul@deruijter.net.

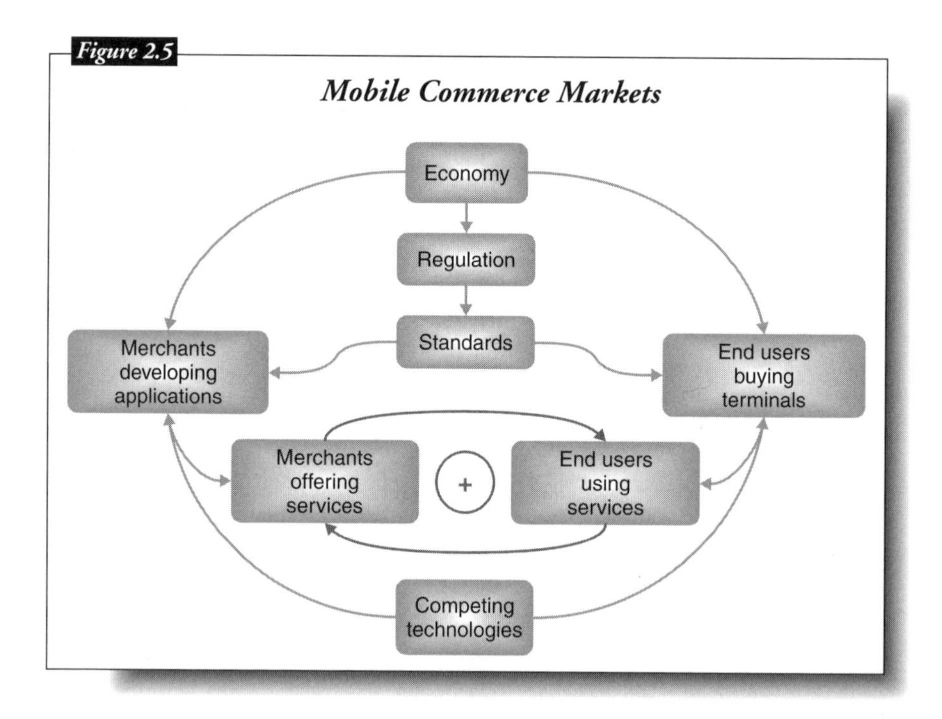

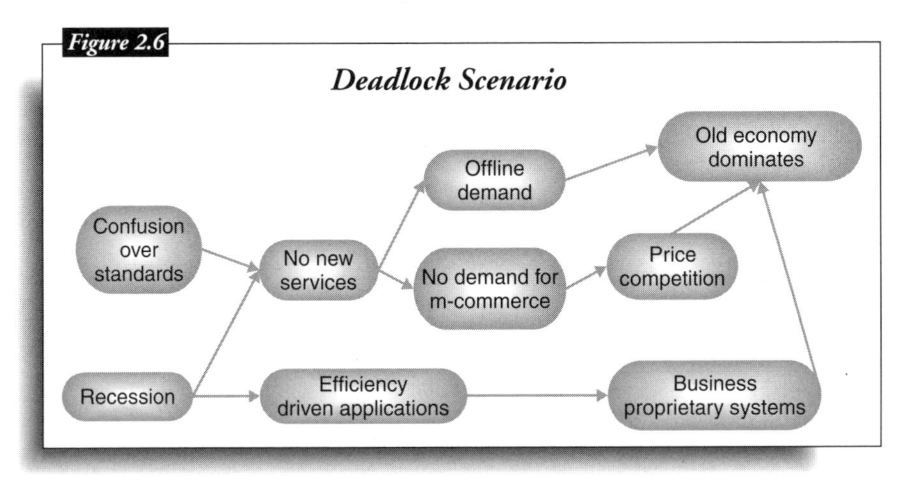

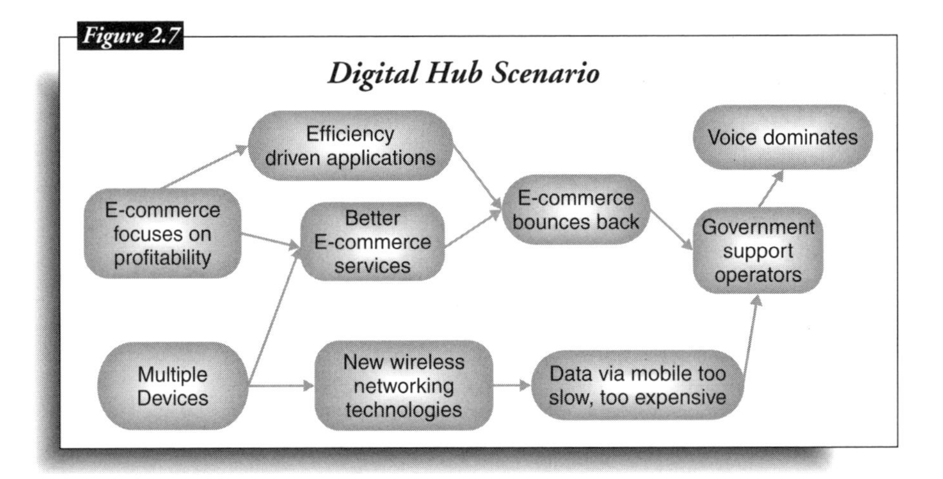

CONCLUSION

Whether conducted by line managers, leaders, specialists or agencies, marketing comprises activities and management processes that generate an organisation's revenue. Over the long term it is most effective if the firm is focused around the market and future oriented. Marketing evolves in firms over time. When

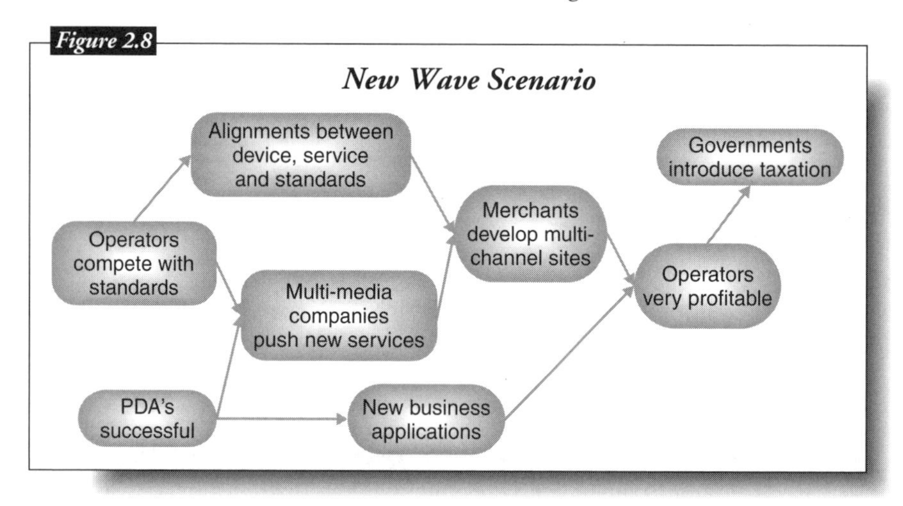

a firm is small, it is often undertaken by the founders or is subcontracted to specialists. As firms grow, however, the way they approach marketing should become more sophisticated, to the point where marketing is developed into a fully integrated function with well-defined roles and responsibilities, processes and proper measurement techniques.

Various aspects of marketing (strategy, research, NPD and communication), in all these environments, work well with scenario planning. The futures created by scenarios allow marketing strategies and plans to be better developed and more effective. The technique should allow marketers to work with perspectives that are less bound by past behaviours or entrenched views; as a result, they should increase success and mitigate risk. Case study 2.2 for mobile commerce illustrates many of these aspects.

REFERENCES

Buzzell R. D. and Gale B. T. (1987) *The PIMS Principle*. Free Press.

Kotler P. and Armstrong, G. (2003) *Principles of Marketing*. Prentice Hall.

MacQueen, A. (2004) *The King of Sunlight*. Bantam Press.

McKenna, R. (1991) "Marketing is everything", *Harvard Business Review*, January.

Ogilvy, D. (2004) *Confessions of an Advertising Man*. Southbank Press.

Piercy, N. (2001) *Market-led Strategic Change: Transforming the Process of Going to Market.* Butterworth–Heinemann.

Shapiro, B. (1998) "What the hell is market oriented?", *Harvard Business Review*, November.

Turner, E. S. (1965) *The Shocking History of Advertising*. Penguin.
Vaghefi, M. R. and Huellmantel, A. B. (1998) "Strategic leadership at General Electric", *Long Range Planning*, **31**(2), 280–294.
Zaltman, G. (2003) *How Customers Think*. Harvard Business School Press.

THREE

Marketing Strategy and Scenarios

Paul Fifield

SUMMARY

This chapter answers three questions:

- ***What is marketing strategy?***
- ***How marketing strategy can build market-based scenarios of the future.***
- ***How marketing strategy can help turn scenarios into reality.***

It provides a quick overview of the key elements of marketing strategy, focusing on the two elements that are essential to building scenarios that are rooted in customer need. It also shows how strategic marketing scenarios can be used profitably in the medium term.

The author, Paul Fifield, is an independent consultant and author in marketing strategy. He is also Visiting Professor of marketing strategy at the University of Southampton, School of Management.

WHAT IS MARKETING STRATEGY?

Although the term is familiar, marketing strategy tends to be the "Cinderella" of marketing theory and practice. Books on corporate strategy are to be found in every boardroom and the words of academic strategists, such as Harvard economist Michael Porter (1983, 1990), are regarded almost as law. Likewise, books on

Scenarios in Marketing. Edited by G. Ringland and L. Young.

Figure 3.1

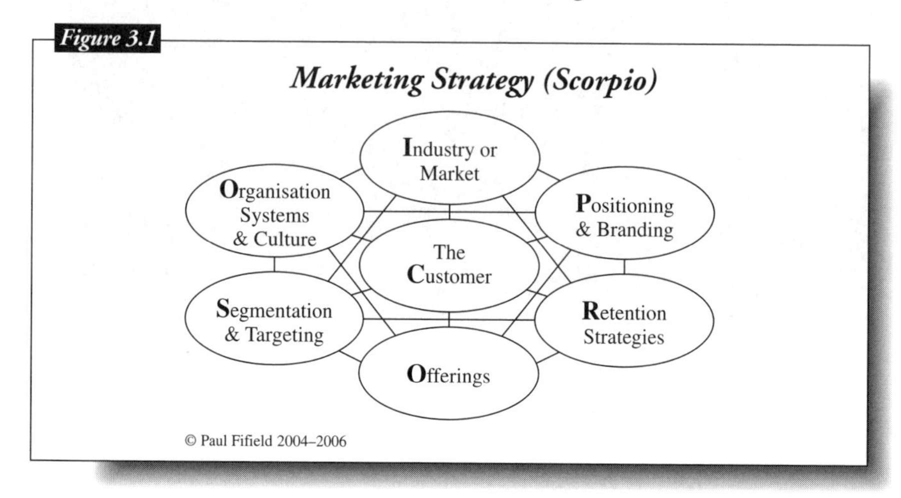

marketing tactics, where the models explained by Philip Kotler are applied with both enthusiasm and reverence, prop doors open in marketing departments the world over.

Marketing strategy, on the other hand, fits neatly into neither stronghold. Each side assumes that the other has dealt with it, so nobody does. As this is both wrong and dangerous to corporate health, it is important to start by considering a definition for "marketing strategy".

Using the Scorpio Model of Marketing Strategy

The newly developed ***Scorpio*** model in Figure 3.1 shows the key elements of marketing strategy. They include:

- **S** *Segmentation and targeting*—What are the segments in the marketplace and which ones should we own?
- **C** *The customer*—Who are our customers and what do they want from us?
- **O** *Offerings*—What is our unique offer to the customer?
- **R** *Retention*—What are we doing to ensure that our customers come back to us?
- **P** *Positioning and branding*—How are we "unique" and what brand values do we support?

- **I** *Industry or market thinking*—Do we describe our business in industry terms or in customer terms?

- **O** *Organisation*—What do we do to ensure we have the organisational structure and processes that will support a customer approach?

The model is arranged so that all the elements are linked together since they *all* need to be assessed. Marketing strategy is emphatically not a "mix'n match" business.

Although there should be nothing "new" here for the marketer, the ***Scorpio*** model can be seen as an *aide-mémoire* for those who sometimes find that some of the elements get "lost" in the excitement of developing new strategies for future growth. But what is essential is that everything is centred around the customer, who should inform whatever aspect is being considered. The ***Scorpio*** set thus contains groups of elements that need to underpin different objectives, such as:

- Understanding the future—industry/market and segmentation/targeting

- Driving for growth—positioning/brand and offerings.

- Taking off the brakes—retention and organisation.

In this chapter we will focus our attention on the two elements that help to understand the future and build scenarios: industry/market and segmentation/targeting.

HOW MARKETING STRATEGY CAN BUILD MARKET-BASED SCENARIOS OF THE FUTURE

Marketing strategy is not just a section that fits into the business plan, somewhere between corporate objectives and advertising slogans. The "lost space" between business strategy and marketing planning/tactics is critical for organisations that need to survive in a competitive environment (see Figure 3.2). This lost space is marketing strategy.

The marketing strategy scenario has a serious role in the business. It can be a guide to the future of the business while reducing some of the unknowns to manageable risks and choices. However, always remember that there is a world of difference between "scenarios" and "vague hopes". Even more importantly, a scenario that is not firmly rooted in an understanding of customer needs and want can never be more than a vague hope.

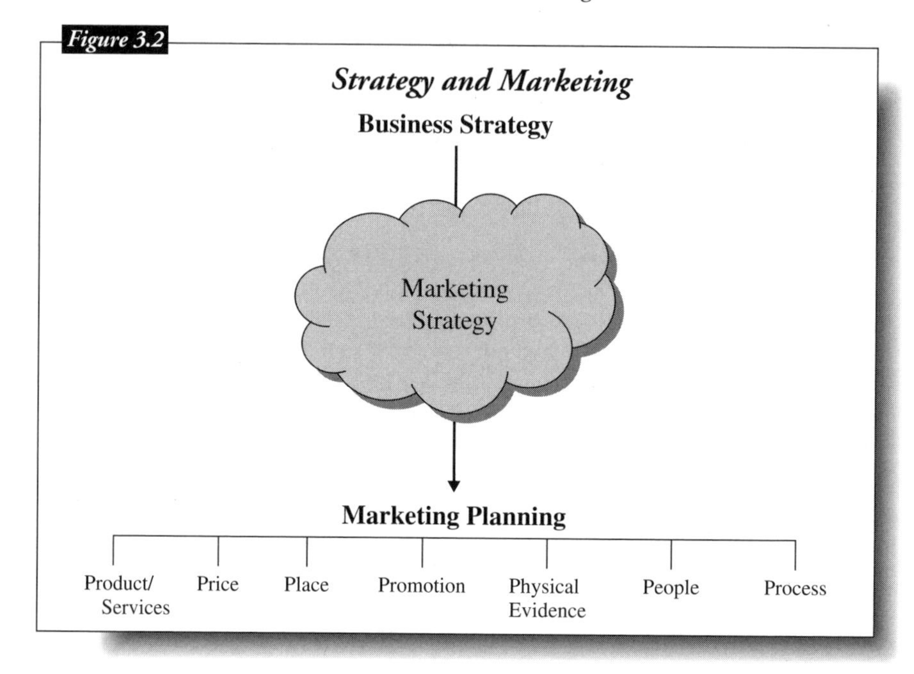

The Customer

In business the customer has to underpin all activity. Certainly, modern business would find it difficult to do without ingredients such as employees, operations, finance, cash flow and logistics. However, in these days of scientific management, many people tend to forget the obvious. More fundamental than anything else, the organisation needs revenues and profits if it is to survive (and many don't) and grow. And where do revenues, and therefore profits, come from? Customers.

Customers produce all the organisation's revenues and profits and are the only reason for any organisation's continued existence. At the very least, the organisation intent on survival will need to know who its customers are and what they want. The organisation intent on achieving success rather than simple survival, however, will need to know much more than that if it is to compete successfully in ever more competitive markets. Although it is a fact of commercial life that "knowing" may itself be a tall order: often customers don't really "know" what they want. They just want—and need.

The problem with many scenario exercises is that they simply don't take the customer into account. But it is critical to have some idea about what the customer is going to want in the future. Because no "want" means no revenues—which means no business.

Industry or Market Thinking?

This is the first step in understanding the marketplace and developing a marketing scenario. Traditionally there are two ways in which "the business" might be described and defined by the organisation:

- *The industry the organisation is in or the technology that it will use to produce products and services.* This is the usual approach but not good.

- *The customer needs that the organisation will satisfy.* This is rarer but much better.

For example, Louis Vuitton looks like a very different business as soon as it declares itself to operate in the "art of travel" rather than just "luggage". The key point to remember is: What is the market in which you are trying to build the scenario? For example, there is an advantage for Kelloggs of not being obsessed with "cereals" because it would lose business to non-cereal competition. But where should it see its future? Business definitions such as "breakfast cereals", "breakfast", "morning goods", "first meal of the day", "snacks", "nutrition", "children's health" will all offer very different competitors, opportunities and threats to the organisation. Strategic marketing scenarios should thus be driven by precisely these issues. However, they are often selected without making any conscious decision at all.

Experience shows that when wrestling with this difficult question, defining the business based on customer needs (even though it can appear rather esoteric in its definition) will have a much stronger effect on the organisation and is more easily communicated to the marketplace than definitions based on industry or technology (see Case Study 3.1). Some well-known definitions are shown in Table 3.1.

For a strategic marketing scenario, the market-led business definition is essential because:

1. It is based on the *customers' needs*, so is securely linked to revenues and profits.

2. It focuses the scenario on *which customers* to serve (segmentation).

3. Helps focus the scenario on the (real) *competition*, which might not just be other players in the same industry.

4. The scenario can focus on the critical *strategic threats and opportunities.*

5. Only customer needs identify the *potential to differentiate*, a key source of additional profit so central to the scenario assessment.

TABLE 3.1 INDUSTRY VERSUS MARKET LED BUSINESS DEFINITIONS

Industry-led	Company	Market-led
Motor cycles	Harley Davidson	Big boys' toys
Watches	Swatch	Fashion accessories
Electronics	Sony	Entertainment
Cars	Jaguar	Status
Watches	Rolex	Jewellery
Cosmetics	Revlon	"Hope"

6. Establishes *directions for growth*, because it uses customers' existing and future needs as guides.

7. Establishes *boundaries for effort*, which means it helps the scenario builder establish which future "effort" will be rewarded by customers—and which will not.

CASE STUDY 3.1 TELEPHONE DIRECTORIES

This company was responsible for publishing specialised directories with business telephone numbers supported by paid advertising to help people to buy products and services over the telephone. They produced directories by the million and distributed them free to all homes and business. Pre-internet, this was an important route to market for many small and local businesses.

When we started working with the company, it was convinced that it was in the directory publishing business and this was clearly what its operations did. It thus followed logically that the primary competition was other directory publishers and local press which also took paid advertising.

Looking forward and trying to build scenarios for the longer term development of the market, the organisation and the brand was very difficult since scenarios for 'directories' were limited.

We spent some time with customers and users of the directories and soon were able to suggest an alternative definition: The company was in the business of *providing information prior to a purchase*.

It took the organisation a year to get used to the new definition, but when we then began to develop strategic marketing scenarios for the newly defined market, the richness in the outputs was evident:

- The previously dominant competition (other directories and local press) became almost insignificant.

- Substitute competition such as word of mouth, magazines and personal data lists became much more important.

- We discovered the size of the problem when we found that the company's publications were the preferred directory source, but that directories in general were the information source of last resort.

- We succeeded in segmenting the "information prior to a purchase" market quite successfully and produced a number of real alternative scenarios for senior management to develop into new market offerings.

Segmentation and Targeting

So far we have considered the need to drive scenario development by:

- A focus on customers and their needs and wants

- A focus on a market rather than an industry-driven business definition.

Both activities are essential to developing scenarios that offer real, profitable and practical insight to a business problem. From a marketing strategy perspective, these two activities are not optional, they are essential. Without them, any scenarios produced run the risk of being elegant, but unusable mind games, which is not good for the company or the reputation of scenarios for long-term planning in general. With these two elements added to the traditional scenario approach, there is a good chance of making a substantial return on the scenario investment.

Market segmentation, on the other hand, is not strictly an "essential" component for a strategic marketing scenario, but it is strongly recommended that this technique be added to the two described above. Market segmentation is a "refinement" to the previous work, but today an ever more important one.

From a purely marketing perspective, market segmentation (sometimes called customer profiling) is one of the basics of good marketing strategy. This is especially the case given that the "mass market" is long dead, and where, today, one size no longer fits all. For most organisations that want to compete effectively, segmentation is not a "like-to-have" tool, it is a "must-have" tool. Ted Levitt said many years ago that if the organisation isn't talking segments, it isn't talking markets (Levitt, 1960). Without an understanding of the different groupings of needs and wants in the marketplace, no organisation can hope to have the clarity and depth of customer focus required to stay relevant.

From the perspective of building a strategic marketing scenario, segmentation is helpful in key areas:

- First, market segmentation helps to focus on those parts of the market that are interested (or will become interested) in the offer and who are going to be part of the organisation's future market. Trying to deal with the whole market in a scenario is complicated, costly, time consuming and pointless. After all, why build painstaking views of the future for prospects who are never going to be customers?

- Secondly, market segmentation helps the organisation to understand the whole market for which the scenario is being developed. As Table 3.1 showed, we have already moved from the impractical but recognisable industry-defined labels such motor cycles, watches, electronics, cars, watches and cosmetics to big boys' toys, fashion accessories, entertainment, status, jewellery and hope. These are more practical, powerful and recognisable definitions—at least from the customers' perspective—but they do tend to present traditional managers with more problems. Simply measuring these markets with suppliers from different industries is different/more difficult than traditional methods. Knowing the constituent parts (segments) of the total market is the only way to bring the market to life and make measurement possible.

So what do we mean by *market segmentation*? It was first developed as a concept in the late 1950s but started to enter regular marketing parlance in the 1980s. Although it slowly rose in importance during the 1980s and 1990s, it is really only recently that market segmentation is (finally) starting to be recognised as a foundation for the development of any form of customer-driven marketing strategy. The reason for this growth of interest in market segmentation is directly related to the evolution of most marketplaces. This is certainly the case with consumer markets and, over the past few years, increasingly it is used in industrial/business-to-business markets.

The whole segmentation issue has been driven by customer needs. While the 1960s were typified by mass production and volume sales, the 1990s started to break this obsession and the new millennium will be typified by people's search for a greater sense of individualism and identity. People nowadays, whether buying for themselves or for their organisation, are much less ready to settle for a mass-produced standard product or service. The search today is for something special, something different, something that reinforces their own sense of identity as a person, as an individual, as a professional buyer—certainly as someone separate from the "herd".

The modern day array of product choice—all you need to do is find out how many different Sony Walkmans or iPods you can buy, how many different forms of coffee/beverage you can buy in Starbucks, the bewildering array of mobile phone tariffs or the range of options open for the buyer of back hoe diggers for construction sites—stands witness to this growth in choice which seems to be demanded in many advanced marketplaces in the world.

It has been regularly argued, certainly by some of the more purist marketers, that, given the evolution of society and its needs, individualism and so on, the ultimate market segment is a segment of one; that every individual is moving to create his or her own position, own identity and own space in the world, and as everybody has different needs we have segments of one person. Unfortunately, for most producers, this is unlikely to be commercially viable. A compromise position must be found, and segmentation is just that—it is the most economic way of managing a diverse market without forcing the identical offer onto different people or trying to create unique offerings for everyone.

When talking about segmentation it probably makes some sense to start with the definition. A simple one would be:

> *Market segmentation is the sub-dividing of a market into homogeneous sub-sets of customers, where any sub-set may conceivably be selected as a market target to be reached with a distinct marketing mix. (Kotler, 2003)*

From this quite precise definition it can be seen that the key to market segmentation is all about the identification of *"homogeneous sub-sets of customers"*; that is, customers who are alike in some way or other. All the problems centre on how to determine the best way of segmenting a market. Simplistically, the choice is between:

1. *descriptors and demographics*—which describe the size, location, industry, family size, etc. of the target market; or

2. *motivations and attitudes*—which identify the needs and wants that drive the perception of the offer and the needs behind the purchase

Descriptors and demographics are the easy way of identifying groups because the data is readily available. Motivations and attitudes give more powerful segments because understanding different needs or problems allows the organisation to produce products and services that customers really want. Case Study 3.2, about an IT hardware company, shows how this can work.

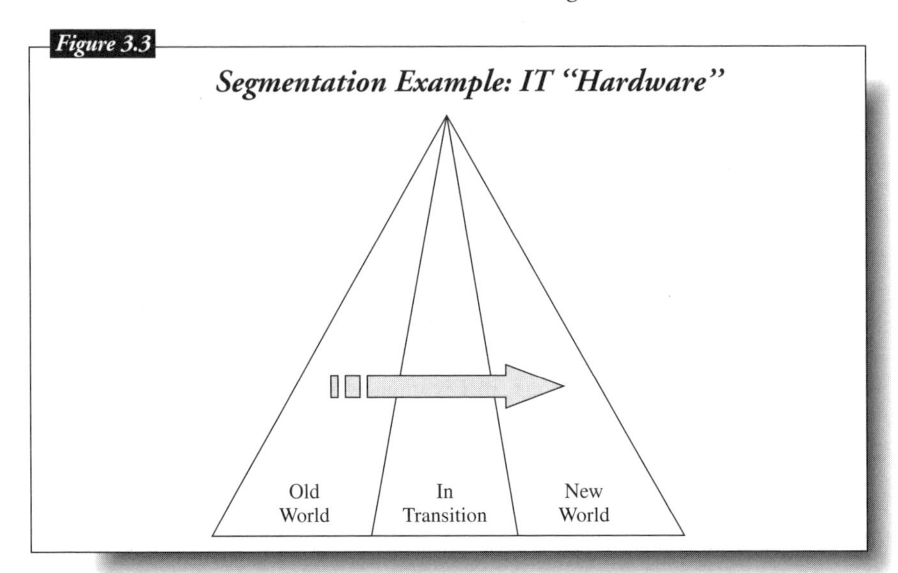

CASE STUDY 3.2 IT "HARDWARE"

Working with a large IT company, we were concerned about the long-term development of the marketplace and the effect that market changes would have on sales and the sales organisation.

We looked at market segmentation to shed some light on what was going on and later to form the basis of the strategic marketing scenarios. Through a process of internal and external analysis (qualitative and quantitative) we started to see that the market naturally broke into three (very) different types of client organisation, as depicted in Figure 3.3.

1. ***"Old World" Organisations.*** These were dealing quite badly with the structural change of the late 1990s and finding it difficult to compete in a world of rapid communications, pervasive technology and international competition. Rather than deal with reality, their history and size had convinced them that this uncomfortable period was merely a "blip" and they were firmly convinced that "normal service would be resumed"

2. ***"In Transition" Organisations.*** These had worked out that the change was structural, not temporary, and knew they had to change the way that their business operated. At the moment, however, they were not sure exactly

of the direction in which they should go. They were waiting to see what they should become.

1. ***"New World" Organisations.*** They had already changed in response to the market demands and were rapidly working out how to apply new business models. Broadly, this group had discovered that they had to change from a "product" to a "customer" focus.

In addition, when we cross-analysed organisational and purchasing behaviour against each segment, we made even more discoveries:

1. ***"Old World" Organisations.*** They were still buying IT from old style organisations (including the client) and wanted to be approached by sales forces in the traditional manner. They were constantly seeking reassurance from all their business contacts that the world had *not* really changed. In addition, they were focused on buying IT hardware solutions that constantly increased the *efficiency* of their organisation so allowing them to do what they had always done, but quicker, easier and cheaper

2. ***"In Transition" Organisations.*** They were not buying additional IT hardware because they were uncertain what the future was going to look like. As they still had the day-to-day issues about replacement and growth, they would only lease new equipment that was absolutely needed. At that point the client organisation did not offer leasing or flexible payment methods because they had not been required.

3. ***"New World" Organisations.*** They were still buying IT solutions, but were buying from all sorts of different suppliers. They were focused on acquiring IT solutions that increased the effectiveness of their organisation, so allowing them to do what their customers wanted from them, which meant systems that allowed the offerings to be innovative, flexible, simple and fast to market. Much more interesting was the discovery that these organisations had mostly removed the IT director (chief technology officer) from the board. Purchases were made by different line managers on the basis of what the system would do for them rather than what the system was. Few of these organisations were currently buying from the client organisation, not least because the salesforce only dealt with IT directors and did not approach other line managers.

The implications of these results will be obvious to anyone interested in developing scenarios.

The scenarios were then developed based on the information we had discovered from the segmentation analysis. We plotted the expected development and growth of each of the three segments and were able to choose between different strategic responses. Later, the model was scaled to a global level and played its part in the eventual reposition of the entire business—which was out of IT hardware.

HOW MARKETING STRATEGY CAN HELP YOU TO TURN SCENARIOS INTO REALITY

So far this chapter has looked at creating strategic marketing scenarios by specifically using three key techniques: customer focus, market business definitions and market segmentation. These are the three elements of the ***Scorpio*** model discussed earlier (and shown in Figure 3.1) that are most relevant to scenario development.

The other four elements really come into their own after the scenarios have been developed in two ways: analysing scenarios to identify probabilities and turning scenarios into plans and market action. More specifically, the other four elements of ***Scorpio*** are used as follows:

1. ***Positioning and branding.*** This is about understanding the unique market position (the word or concept that the organisation should "own" in the customers' mind) that should be developed. Success is about being different—not the same. How should the organisation be different? What should it make, sell, do to be noticeably different? How can we achieve this unique position? What are the roles of the product, service, staff, communications and behaviours in achieving and maintaining the position? Who is competing for the position? Scenarios can help to see market positions outside typical industry classifications. Positioning and branding can help to put "real" flesh onto the scenario skeleton.

2. ***Offerings.*** This is about the complete offer (product or service plus support plus partners plus channels to market plus after sales care plus image, etc.). Often we need to look more closely at what we do, but from the customers' perspective rather than the producer's, to see where we are succeeding in adding value—and where we are inconveniencing our customers for little or no good purpose. Scenarios can help us to take another perspective. Offerings can help us to bring the scenario to life.

3. ***Retention.*** Customers who come back again are the most profitable. But retaining customers is not something that happens without care, attention and planning. Working with different scenarios to identify how the organisation could retain different customers can give great insight to the differences between scenarios.

4. ***Organisation.*** This is about deciding the type of organisation needed to deliver what the customer demands. Not every organisational design or structure is capable of delivering customer needs: systems, processes and culture determine behaviours within an organisation. Customer needs change over time (this is the root cause of the whole problem) and either the organisation is able to change to keep pace with its customers, or its customers leave to find better/more appropriate service elsewhere.

Since strategic marketing scenarios are always based on future assessments of customer needs, it doesn't take much analysis to work out exactly the nature and shape of the organisation needed to deliver the future customer benefits. It might take longer to agree whether such organisational change is possible. Remember, it is absolutely not a question of "how close" the organisation can get to the customers' needs. It is only a question of either being able to deliver on the future customer needs, or not. In the latter case, there is never a shortage of competitors willing to step in.

A WORD ON TIMING AND OTHER PRACTICAL ISSUES

Experience with many clients has proved that building strategic marketing scenarios is a methodology that will provide an organisation with real competitive advantage. However, there are a small number of annoying but important barriers to this obvious and simple process.

1. ***Understanding the preoccupations of managers.*** Any project such as developing plans, strategy or scenarios needs to be much more than a plan. It needs to be *implemented* if it is going to show a return on the investment in the time and money that it cost to develop the plan. Implementation ultimately depends on the manager in the organisation wanting to apply it. Whether the manager wants to apply the strategy and implement the plans arising from the scenarios depends on what's in it for him or her. This is not intended as a criticism of the state of management in the early twenty-first century, but rather a lesson in pragmatic leadership. Getting anything done is a case of understanding certain facts:

- Most managers who are driven by the future, are not typically responsible for doing things (implementation).
- Most day-to-day managers (who do things) are not worried about the future.
- Those responsible for using/implementing the scenarios are (mostly) motivated and measured according to what happens in the short term.
- Managers today are doing more work than in the past.
- They are working with less administration support.
- They tend to be less loyal to their employer than previously (there are many reasons for this) and more loyal to themselves and their networks.
- They are just as ambitious.
- They do not tend to stay in the same job (or sometimes company) for very long.
- They have a "day job" which, for most, involves achieving business outputs that can be measured in the current financial year.
- If they are to implement longer-term actions, they need to be sure that they will achieve some credit for the risk that they take.

2. ***A question of time.*** This can make anything that is focused on the future problematic. There are some key time issues:

    - Scenarios are, by definition, a view (or several views) of the future.
    - Most managers are driven by and focus on the short term, the next 12 months.
    - Good managers can be motivated by the medium term, if it covers the period they expect to remain in the job or the organisation.
    - This medium period normally stretches to about three years.
    - Managers generally believe that their (and any) market becomes unpredictable beyond five years, so it is pointless (academic) looking out any further.
    - Customers (depending on the nature of the purchase) live in the present but can vision themselves into the future, using products and services that exist and of which they are aware.
    - Customers cannot envision themselves using a "new" product or service.

- Customers generally "learn" about new products and services more slowly than organisations would like.
- There is absolutely no point launching a product or service offer:
  (a) before it is wanted, because the customers will not understand its benefits and will not buy;
  (b) after it is wanted and they have purchased; "me-too" offerings tend to be far less profitable.

3. ***The (inevitable) issue of marketing.*** Many organisations (in many industries it is the majority) are determinedly fighting against becoming customer-focused. The reasons for the continuing tension between the product-focused and the customer-focused organisational/business culture are many and varied—and will not be covered here. What we can say is that this chapter on strategic marketing scenarios has been directed at the customer-focused organisation.

Organisations that are still focused on products and processes are fighting a competitive battle they can never win. They only know how to "push" products at markets, and, if they could take a moment to stand back from what they are doing, they would see that there is another way. Figure 3.4 shows the dimensions of "the great debate" and the "armoury" employed by each camp

Figure 3.4

Products and/or Markets

The Great Debate:

"PRODUCT" Focus	**"MARKET" Focus**
Product features	Customer needs/wants
Product sales	Customer satisfactions
Technical excellence	Customer expectations
Product service	Customer service
Rational solutions	Emotional solutions
Product profitability	Customer/segment profitability
'PUSH' Strategy	**'PULL' Strategy**

CONCLUSION

What, then, can we say about strategic marketing scenarios? I use them constantly with my clients, and have done so for over 20 years of consulting in marketing strategy. But note, I never mention the word "scenario".

My background and training is such that I am qualified to be an "academic". However, I work mainly with practising managers rather than with students. In the UK, to the practising manager, the word "academic" means the same as "theoretical, impractical, useless". I really have no idea why this should be, but it is strongly felt and the gulf between practitioner and academic seems as wide now as it did 20 years ago. One thing the successful consultant learns early is not to use words that create a barrier between himself and the client.

Why do I use scenarios in this way? Because they are a useful and practical technique to get to the future. I work almost exclusively in the future and it is my job to get my clients to understand what the (their) future looks like and what they will have to do today to be successful tomorrow.

The future is always uncertain, but the future is not totally uncontrolled and can be influenced to a greater or lesser degree by an organisation's actions. Thus, to some extent, the organisation is (partially) in control of its own destiny. To have an idea of today's actions, and of the influences the organisation might have, we need to have a sense of the possible futures facing us.

This way I obtain the greatest return on scenario investment. I use medium term (3–5 years) scenarios (called strategic visions or plans or insights—but not "scenarios") to inform what the organisation should be doing *today*.

And today is what counts for the practitioner.

REFERENCES

Kotler, P. and Armstrong, G. (2003) *Principles of Marketing*. Prentice Hall.
Porter, M. (1983) *Competitive Strategy*. New York, Free Press.
Porter, M. (1990) *Competitive Advantage*. New York, Free Press.
Levitt, T. (1960) "Marketing myopia", *Harvard Business Review*, July–August.

FOUR

Scenario Planning and Innovation

Tim Westall

SUMMARY

This chapter describes how scenario planning has been used to drive creativity in a number of consumer marketing applications, and contains an agenda for a sample workshop. It has been contributed by Tim Westall who is a director of April Strategy (www.aprilstrategy.com). April is a new kind of strategy consultancy, founded in 2004 and working with leading global organisations on their toughest challenges to deliver powerful, customer-driven strategies that improve business performance.

INTRODUCTION

Innovation is one of the top three priorities for most chief executives. But many companies are not as successful at innovating as they would like to be. A lot of what passes for innovation is stuck in "today", and is often little more than incremental rearrangement of the familiar. When looking ahead, people tend to extrapolate individual trends, missing connections and overall patterns.

Scenario planning can be used as an overall innovation framework or as a discrete creative catalyst. It builds a radically different set of environments, which, if brought to life in a vivid and engaging way, will inspire big strategic ideas and smaller product/service improvement ideas, many of which will actually be relevant to today.

At April Strategy we have evolved the central tenets of scenario planning into a powerful, practical innovation approach. This chapter gives some details of this

Scenarios in Marketing. Edited by G. Ringland and L. Young.

approach, together with examples from European and global projects in food and beverage, personal care, financial services, healthcare, travel and leisure.

The benefits of using scenario planning for innovation are:

- A greater quantity of bigger, better new ideas.

- A means of prioritising and managing a complex innovation portfolio.

- A management forum for "thinking the unthinkable" in a constructive, non-judgemental environment.

WHAT IS "INNOVATION"?

'Innovation' is defined as *the act of introducing something new*, and most chief executives will tell you that it is their number one priority. So it's important to do it well.

Across different categories and levels of maturity of business, innovation means different things. It is useful to distinguish between two broad types:

- **Type 1—*PUSH innovation*.** Borne of a new technology and/or a charismatic inventor, push innovations often begin life in garages or labs. Some become huge multinationals (think of Microsoft or Dyson), while the majority meet no market needs and fail (think of videophones or Segways). Push innovations succeed through luck and perseverance. By their very nature, they cannot be researched in order to demonstrate market potential (famously, the Sony Walkman failed in market research many times). Many of the past decade's IT and telecoms firms began life as push innovations, but are now migrating towards the "pull" model.

- **Type 2—*PULL innovation*.** Pull innovation starts from the point of view that people's needs are fairly well satisfied, so any new product or service must be better than, or different to, the items available today. Consequently, the innovation process tends to be rooted in research and customer insight rather than technology. What marketers are looking for first is unmet needs, unsatisfied needs, be they rational or emotional. This is the approach pioneered by mainstream marketing-led companies like Procter & Gamble (P&G), Unilever and Diageo, and is now becoming the dominant model across many categories.

For these reasons, this chapter focuses on "pull" innovation, applied in the context of large, successful organisations attempting to do things better or differently.

Having been through years of cost-cutting and rationalising, innovation is now seen as the key to growth. Yet most innovations fail—supposedly 18 out of 20 new products are withdrawn within 12 months of launch, and hundreds more never see the light of day. It's clearly not a perfect process, so how can scenario planning help?

INNOVATION'S LIMITATIONS

Real innovation in a large corporation is very difficult to achieve. It's about changing how you do things, which can be disruptive and uncomfortable. It's often about promoting ideas and strategies that will cannibalise your existing business if successful—the classic "innovator's dilemma", according to Clayton Christensen (Christensen, 1997).

The most successful innovators tend to take the innovation process very seriously, designing and running complex "innovation pipelines", with perhaps only one in 500 initial ideas eventually making it through to market. There are detailed process designs, including idea generation, development and refinement phases, with complex criteria and action standards to be hit at each stage. Millions are spent on trends research, opinion leader surveys and creative workshops.

Other "follower" businesses deal with innovation by calling it 'new product development (NPD)' and producing either 'flavour' variants of core products and services or rapid copies of what others have already done (such as *The Guardian* moving to smaller page format over nine months after *The Times* led the way).

Whether leading or following, a lot of innovation has some common limiting characteristics that you might recognise:

- 'Re-shuffling the pack', where new ideas are generated by taking what already exists and rearranging them in new ways. In fact, author Arthur Koestler defined the creative act as something that "selects, combines, reshuffles, synthesises already existing facts, ideas, faculties, skills". He went on to say "the more familiar the parts, the more striking the new wholes".

- A "static" marketplace benchmark, where innovation is referenced against current customer needs and competitor activities, rather than potential future needs and future competitor strategies. For example, "our new call centre is so clever that the average wait-time is down from 10 minutes to 8 minutes. That's 2 minutes less than our nearest rival"—even though, from a customer point of view, 5 minutes is the longest wait that 80% are prepared to tolerate before hanging up.

- "Uni-trend extrapolation", where trends are considered in isolation and taken as only moving in one direction, therefore leading to a predictable outcome.

For example, "there will be 15% more over-50s in 2020, therefore the market for carpet slippers will grow in proportion"—ignoring the fact that over-50s are becoming so much more active that it's more likely that the market for carpet slippers will decline, and the real opportunity will be in orthopaedic climbing boots.

- A presumption of a zero-sum game, where a new solution needs to displace an old one, e.g. "recorded home-movies will wipe out the cinema"—whereas home DVDs grow at double digit rates at the same time as cinema box-office takings hit a 20-year high.

The compound effect is a strategic innovation process that is driven reactively (look at what our competitor has done, how can we respond to that?) and consequently too many timid innovations that are no more than rearrangements of the familiar. A lot of the time that's fine, but in today's competitive marketplace, market leaders are always looking for a real innovation edge, and that's where scenario planning can help.

THE BENEFITS OF SCENARIO PLANNING

When it's done well, a scenario-based approach to innovation can provide:

- A radically different shared context from which to operate that will guarantee fresh new ideas—from big new thoughts around a business model down to neat twists on today's products and services.

- A process that gives managers permission to think "unthinkable" ideas in a constructive and non-judgemental environment.

- A way to "unlearn" all the subconscious assumptions and connections that normally enable us to make sense of the world around us, but inhibit really new thinking.

- A series of robust challenges to a new idea to "pressure test" in a way not achievable by conventional market research.

- A means of "connecting the dots", making sense of disparate and contradictory trends.

- A means of ratcheting back to today, in order to come up with innovations/quick wins that are relevant to today's context.

Applications

Apart from a platform for new idea generation, scenarios built in the manner described in this chapter have also been used for:

- Challenging and shaping business purpose and direction
- Informing M&A strategy
- Brand portfolio positioning
- Issues/crisis management early warning.

HOW TO USE SCENARIO PLANNING TO IMPROVE INNOVATION

Whether as a complete strategic innovation framework or as a more *ad-hoc* creative catalyst, we follow the central logic of scenario planning (see Figure 4.1). In other words, we identify, cluster and synthesise trends to create a number of vivid, plausible pictures of the future. We then explore what the business/brand should do in order to thrive within each world.

The methodology outlined here was inspired by classic scenario planning and developed at New Solutions with Paul Tidmarsh and Richard Woods. Subsequently, at April Strategy, we have gone on to develop the technique further, using it recently with clients such as Procter & Gamble (P&G) and Wrigley.

Overall Approach

The overall approach to scenario use has the following steps:

1. Define the question—for example:
   - *What is the future of x and how should we exploit it?*
   - *What are the biggest opportunities and threats to our current business model over the next 5–10 years?*
   - *How should I reinvent my customer service over the next five years?*
2. Identify relevant trends.
3. Analyse trends and group into:
   - certainties (things that are definitely going to happen)
   - uncertainties (where things could go one way or the other).

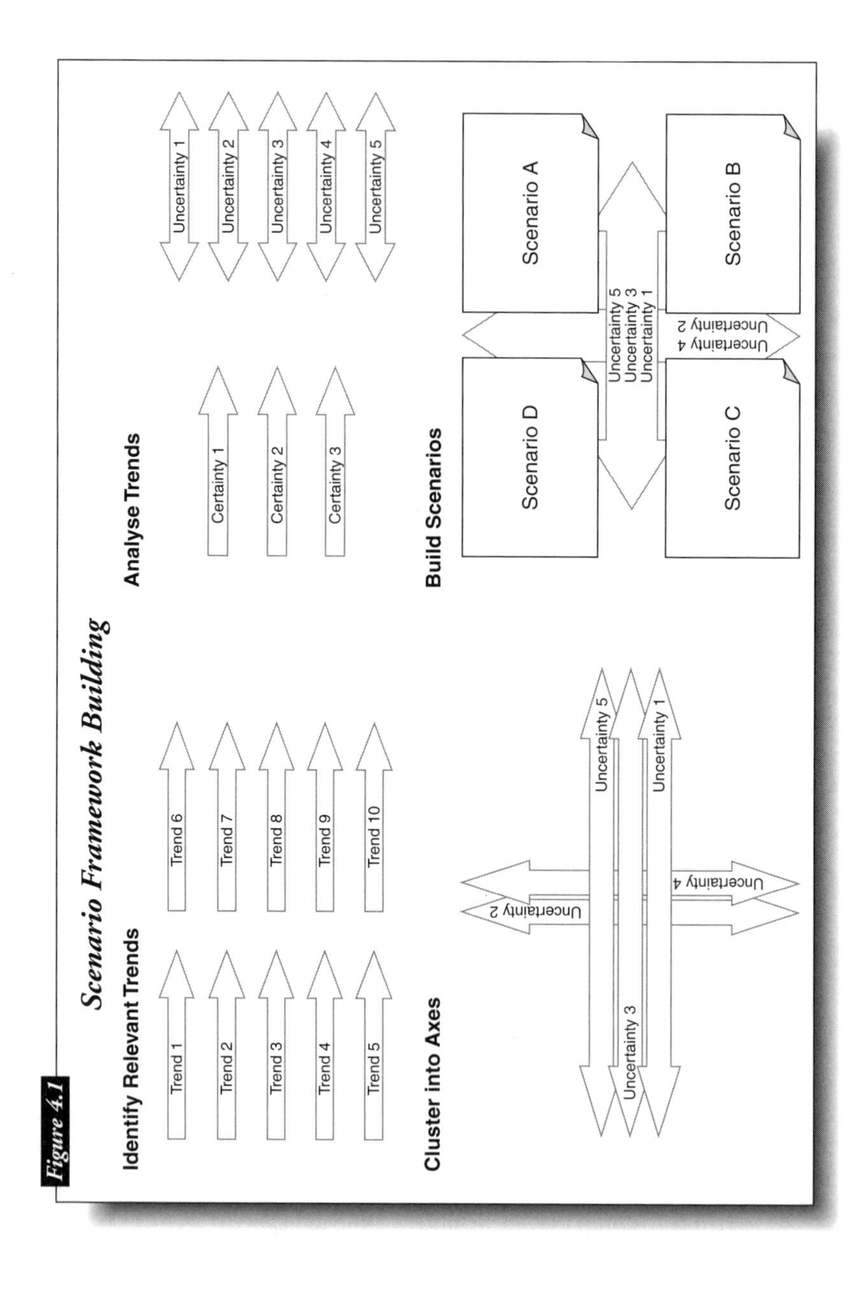

Figure 4.1 *Scenario Framework Building*

4. Cluster uncertainties according to those that are alike or will lead to similar outcomes (to create axes against which worlds are differentiated).

5. Decide on the number of scenarios to be developed (two to six, usually four).

6. By factoring "certainties" into all scenarios, create a vivid picture for each scenario, imagining what the broad picture would be like and the narrative from here to there.

7. Conduct idea generation against each scenario. With the aid of creative prompts, we explore what the business/brand would need to do in order to thrive within each potential future world. Those innovative ideas are then clustered and sorted into three groups:
   - ***Action***—Ideas that would be new and different today would meet an obvious market need and can be readily done, so are worth doing immediately.
   - ***Plan***—Ideas that are new and different, would meet an emerging market opportunity but would be challenging to deliver, so are worth more serious thought and planning.
   - ***Prepare***—Ideas that you would only actively develop in response to an undesirable turn of events, i.e. contingency preparation.

GETTING INTO THE DETAIL

Over the course of 20–30 scenario-based innovation projects, we have honed the process and learned which specific techniques seem to work most effectively. For the sake of clarity, these are detailed across the three typical stages of a project with a client manager, i.e.

- Scenario preparation—gathering key inputs
- Scenario creation—building the scenarios
- Scenario interpretation—idea generation and implications of scenarios

Scenario Preparation

Engaging the Client

As most managers do not spend much time contemplating radical future alternatives for their business, we need to warm them up to the idea of the future. How can we do that?

- Persuade business leaders to relax "on the couch" and get a feel for their personal point of view of how things might play out. They are paradoxically the best informed but most constrained. They know all the trends but prefer to twist them in support of whatever the current business plan might be. Taking them "off-line" and using some of the questioning techniques from psychotherapy (exploring dreams, nightmares, hopes, fears) always produces insightful connections and powerfully intuitive proto-scenarios. Central to this technique is to write down and playback *exactly what they said* (not the usual paraphrasing practised by most consultants) and then use their words to frame the exercise for others.

- A great way to get the broader team engaged is the "postcards from the future" exercise. We give each person a handful of (pre-prepared) newspaper cuttings mounted on postcards. We ask them to read out each headline and map the card onto a continuum of probability on the wall (see Box 4.1)

- The group thinks that Story 1 might happen, Story 2 is unlikely to happen and Story 3 also might happen.

- These and other stories (usually about 20 "postcards from the future") are then stuck on the wall chart as indicated in Table 4.1.

- This creates a distribution pattern that is nearly always weighted towards the left—revealing a healthy scepticism about the likelihood of many of these "postcards from the future" ever happening. Of course the opposite is true. The stories have been prepared in such a way that at least half have already happened. With our three samples in Box 4.1 the VeriChip in Story 1 is already under test in the USA, childhood obesity levels in Greece do now exceed the UK, and Story 3 is a November 2005 report from the BBC. So the message for the team is simple: the future is closer than you think.

Acquiring Trend Information

- These days there is so much available on the internet that a lot of effective secondary research can be done very quickly.

- There are also a lot of trend bureaux and research agencies with continuously updated trend reports. They have 'trend-watchers' installed around the globe, so if you want to know about leading edge trends in cocktail drinking, their people lurking in style bars in the metropolitan centres can always give an up-to-date view.

BOX 4.1 EXAMPLES OF NEWSPAPER STORIES

Story 1

Is the VeriChip the "Mark of the Beast?"

Within a few years a service will be available that will allow consumers to pay for merchandise using a microchip embedded beneath their skin. The VeriChip, which is about the size of a grain of rice, is Applied Digital's new subdermal chip that could someday replace the use of all credit and debit cards. Instead of standing in long checkout lines customers could make purchases by scanning themselves with special readers.

Story 2

Greek kids fatter than Brit kids

Levels of childhood obesity in Greece overtook those in the UK this year, so rather than being a lithe, tanned Adonis, your average Greek teenager is even more of a burger-munching blob than over here!

Story 3

Learning the lessons from America

Growing genetically modified crops in the USA and Canada has been an economic and environmental disaster. That's the verdict of a new report assessing the impact of growing GM soya, maize and oil seed rape published by the Soil Association.
It puts the bill to the US economy at $12 billion in lost exports, lower prices, increased farm subsidies and environmental damage. The report raises important questions about the promise held out for biotechnology.

TABLE 4.1 PROBABILITY WALL CHART

	Will never happen	Unlikely to happen	Might happen	Will happen	Has already happened
Event	Story 4	Story 8	Story 1	Story 7	Story 5
	Story 6	Story 9	Story 3	Story 15	Story 12
	Story 11	Story 2	Story 10	Story 16	
	Story 18	Story 14	Story 13		
		Story 17	Story 20		
		Story 19			

- We find that there is no substitute for original customer research. Typically, we will identify avant-garde/leading edge customers of a particular brand and find out what else is going on in their world. We deploy a range of insight-seeking tools such as introspective writing, provocation, paired-depths, accompanied shopping and so on.

- More provocative and better informed points of view will often come from opinionated experts; people with an intimate understanding of the factors determining the survival of the business under scrutiny, who may be loudly partisan in favour of or against the type of business in question. For example, when looking at the future of food we spoke to an organic farmer in Devon and a food-processing technologist in London. They disagreed on almost every point.

Making Sense of Trends

- An important step is to make a judgement between "certainties" and "critical uncertainties". Some are obvious, such as the availability of new technologies or demographic changes. What is less certain is, for example, how quickly 3G mobile phone technology will be adopted, and by whom. After all, text messaging was around for years before it was accepted.

- To understand critical uncertainties, take a look at our "favourites" in Table 4.2. These are recurring contradictory trends that we see in our work and are worth considering as a bank to start from. While they are rarely dominant, they tend to colour things sometimes significantly.

- For the purposes of differentiated scenario creation, it is better to focus on the trends that are more attitudinal, behavioural and cultural (rather than political, economic and technological)—i.e. those factors relating to mainstream consumer sentiment and values. This then enables the creation of a broad cultural context—a 'zeitgeist' or spirit of the times. The interesting thing about the 'zeitgeist' is that it is only usually apparent in hindsight. We all remember the swinging 'sixties, but that's not what many people experienced. Likewise the 'eighties only became defined by power-dressing and "greed is good" towards the very end of the decade.

Bringing Trends Alive

- One of the challenges with introducing the rich contextual information that aggregates into trends is how it is presented to a client. PowerPoint is a bit of

TABLE 4.2 TEN COMMON UNCERTAINTIES

Trend	Polarity 1	Polarity 2
Cultural outlook	Inward, defensive	Outward, exploring
Attitude to technology	Resistant and suspicious	Welcoming and enthusiastic
Attitude to brands	Prefer local, 'no-logo' brands	Prefer global, well-established
Attitude to choice	Simplicity seeking and unwilling to make effort	Willing to navigate the world of 'superchoice'
Work/life balance	Family and community come first	Work comes first, 'stress = success'
Attitude to gender relations	Post-feminist convergence	Vive la difference
Optimism/pessimism	The glass is sadly now half-empty	The glass is happily still half-full
Social cohesion	Community focused	Individual focused
Attitude to environment	Not my problem	Must take individual responsibility
Attitude to institutions	Trusting, accepting	Sceptical, seeking other opinions
Attitude to politics	Passive, disengaged	Active, engaged

a killer and big fat documents or books just won't get read ("thank-you for sticking with us so far"). One way is to create huge trend collages, bringing together quotes, excerpts and images onto a single piece of board. We then mount up to 30 of these trend collages around a room to create a "gallery", and give people the time to study and contemplate what it all means.

- Another useful technique is to video or record some of the expert interviews from earlier and play excerpts to the team.

Scenario Creation

The best scenarios are built when the client team is fully engaged in the process of discussion and construction of the future map. We allow them to be immersed in the complexity of the variables. This sometimes leads to impasses, heated arguments and head-scratching: all grist-to-the-mill for a good set of scenarios, but it does mean that having an experienced facilitator is important. (The steps in scenario creation is discussed in Appendix 1.)

When projecting what a scenario will look like, it's helpful to give everyone a pen and ask then to draw. Apart from being a great hierarchical leveller (managers are not usually promoted on the strength of their cartooning skills), it encourages more lateral thinking than the "list" approach that mere words tend to encourage.

It also helps to engage professional artists/illustrators to tidy work between iterations, and to help in creating the name and core identity for each scenario. This is essential if a scenario is to be understood and remembered by people who were not part of its original creation.

Be rigorous and ensure that all key prompts are covered (see Table 4.3 for a picture prompt sheet).

- Don't just create the picture of the future; ask people to write narratives, describing how we got here—how did things play out?
- Use storytelling techniques to describe the implications for a particular industry or business.
- Spend at least two days immersed in the scenario, to get it to feel as real as possible. To ensure the concentration and focus required, it's helpful to choose a 'minimalist' venue—an isolated monastery is ideal.

Scenario Interpretation (Idea Generation)

Having created a rich, high-level set of scenarios, the challenge is then to generate ideas about what the business would do to thrive under these conditions. We have found that four techniques provide an effective combination, each used as a 60–90-minute breakout session. To illustrate each technique, we've taken examples from (unrelated) projects in retail banking, healthcare and snacks.

1 Improving the Customer Experience

In this example you should imagine how a customer would ideally like to experience your brand in the new world, defining the steps, the customer touch points, the quality standards and expectations, and the "moments of truth", i.e. the customer touch points that really matter.

Example (from a retail banking project)

The business under question is a high street bank. The scenario is one where the creeping feminisation of the workplace (cooperation rather than competition,

TABLE 4.3 PICTURE PROMPT SHEET
Questions
• What is the broad environment like? ◦ What do the newspaper headlines say? ◦ Who's famous and why? ◦ Which companies are admire? ◦ What new businesses have been created? ◦ What's on the shelves in the supermarkets?
• What do people do all day? ◦ What type of work are they doing? ◦ What do they do with their spare time? ◦ What do they think about?
• What is work life like? ◦ How do people get to work? ◦ What is their work environment like?
• What is home life like? ◦ What's on TV? ◦ What's the routine in the evenings/weekends?
• What's going on the fringes of the world (outside the mainstream)? ◦ What are the signs of the future/where are things heading?
• Which brands have disappeared/what else is in the graveyard?

empathetic listening rather than strident declamation) has led to a world where feminine values are dominant in society. What would banks be like, from the point of view of the customer experience?

When contacting remotely:

— *"For a start, there wouldn't be muzak'n' menus call centres in Mumbai. You'd always want to speak to a real local person, and there might be special numbers or codes that you could use as shortcuts next time round."*

— *"They would recognise you as an individual, they might ask about other things going on in your life."*

When going into a branch:

— *"It wouldn't be all dominant male colours like blue, black and red. There would be softer colours—whites and pastels, maybe a touch of pink and lilac."*
— *"It's not about comfy chairs like a salon or a living room—it's a bank after all—just smart and purposeful."*
— *"There would be (probably decorative) safes on the wall, to remind you that the place was about money and that yours is safe."*
— *"The front of house staff would be more like a low-cost airline crew: young smart, friendly and efficient, mainly women."*

When seeking a loan:

— *"Definitely not open plan, nor authoritarian offices. It would be 'snugs' like in a bar, where you could have confidential conversations. Maybe like karaoke bars in Tokyo."*
— *"You wouldn't need to fill in loads of forms if you already have an account, and the person you were speaking to would be able to make a decision there and then."*

When drawing cash:

— *"There would be ATM points within the 'snugs'. That way you'd never risk anyone looking over your shoulder."*
— *"The ATM machine would be designed by Alessi—swooping curves and angles. It would be an objet d'art, not a rectangular industrial lump."*

When there's a problem:

— *"The people on the front desk would be empowered to sort things out. Rather than you having to go and meet the manager or escalate things, they would do that for you."*
— *"Even if something was your fault, they wouldn't make you feel bad about it—they'd be firm and fair, on your level. Not condescending and scolding like they are today."*

2 Top-Down "Raison d'Être"

The idea here is to challenge and revise the core purpose of the organisation in the new world, and then trickle-down to specific product ideas. It is essentially the same sort of thinking that underpins brand strategy: the search for a single unifying concept that defines and aligns the business

Example (from a healthcare project)

Our client is a healthcare organisation. Its stated purpose is to "provide cost-effective healthcare for all". We have created a scenario where an older population means a higher demand for healthcare, where GPs have disappeared, to be replaced by larger, more specialist providers and the main role of the NHS is in "traffic management"—directing people towards the right specialist.

The emphasis on "care" and "cure" has gone. Today it's all about "maintaining well-being" and "prevention". Our client's core purpose transforms to "improve self-sufficiency in wellbeing across the population". Following this through, there are then huge implications for the organisation, with, for example, education, communication and political lobbying (of government and food companies) becoming new strategic priorities.

3 Bottom-Up Deconstruction

More tactical improvement ideas, whereby each element of today's value proposition is deconstructed and we ask: "Is it fit for purpose?"; "How can we improve it?", "What new benefits do we need to be able to deliver?"; "How would we do things differently?"

Example (from a snack project)

Our client makes breakfast snack products. People are going to be more health-aware and discerning in our future scenario, then what should we do about:

Product formulation:

— *"It's not enough for us to do lite or low versions. Why don't we kick-off a program to radically reinvent our core products, and let's change the benchmark so we're working against how we think people's palates will have changed by 2009, rather than setting ourselves up to fail against the (moving target) of today."*

Packaging and labelling:

— *"It doesn't make sense for us to keep pushing our own label protocol if the government is going to prescribe it. Why don't we work with them a bit more proactively on this one?"*

Distribution:

— *"Well, there won't be vending machines around in schools for much longer, maybe we should think about taking convenience stores a bit more seriously? And what about NAAFI (grocery distribution channel for the military) stores?"*

Pricing:

— *"Wouldn't it be great to do a super-premium ultra natural version of our flagship product?"*

Brand positioning:

— *"I suppose it's not going to be very differentiating to be 'healthy'—everyone will have that. Why don't we aim to be the fruitiest, so we can claim one of our bars is the equivalent of one of your recommended five daily portions of fresh fruit? That would be an ace positioning"*

TABLE 4.4 EXAMPLE AGENDA: SCENARIO-BASED INNOVATION WORKSHOP

Day 1: Scenario Creation

- Warming up to the future
    - My dream and nightmare scenarios for my business
    - "Postcards from the future" exercise
- Gallery tour
    - Half-hour guided tour of the range of key driving forces (expressed as collage boards)
    - Half-hour individual tour and reflection against key questions:
        - What further evidence can we think of to exemplify each driving force?
        - Which driving forces matter the most?
        - Which seem pretty certain, and which seem uncertain or contradictory?
- Scenario framework
    - Clustering and mapping the driving forces to give scenario framework
- Scenario building
- Creating "rich pictures" of the future, setting out the broad environment with lots of "micro" examples of what life will be like

Day 2: Innovation

- Scenario sense-check
    - Are they plausible, directional and discrete?
- Idea generation—round 1—customer experience
- Idea generation—round 2—top-down "core purpose"
- Idea generation—round 3—bottom-up "deconstruction"
- Idea generation—round 4—10-point plan
- Feedback and synthesise
    - Each team feeds back to the full group their strategic and tactical innovation plan
        - Favourite ideas are captured and grouped into three buckets:

          A. Action / B. Plan / C. Prepare
- Wrap-up
    - Ideas we love (projects/ideas to get moving on soon)
    - Stuff we need to think more about (questions, gaps)
    - "Aha!" moments (what we have learned that we didn't know before)

4 Ten-Point Action Plan

Often when looking at 10-year future scenarios, action-oriented executives can get a bit impatient with what they see as abstract doodling. Now is their chance to bring things back to reality. Give then the "innovate or die" brief. Tell the team that this isn't a scenario, this is a certainty and it's just around the corner. Go away for an hour to work out a turnaround plan. This is about survival. Come back with a 10-point plan on the actions that have to be taken tomorrow to get the business in shape—not ethereal strategic headlines or objectives, but tangible actions.

Table 4.4 outlines an example of an agenda for a scenario-based innovation workshop.

CASE STUDIES

Detailed below are four case studies in which scenario planning was used as a tool to catalyse innovation.

CASE STUDY 4.1 GLOBAL PERSONAL PRODUCTS RANGE EXTENSION (2005)

Within the fast-growing male grooming market, P&G wanted to leverage the Hugo Boss brand in the prestige skincare area.

The company could see that the market for male grooming products was growing at an exponential rate, albeit from a low base. One of the characteristics of many of the early entrants was that they were all line-extensions from feminine-provenance brands. Was this the future of the market? Would female authority dominate, and would men become a little more feminised as they took yet another step down the road of gender convergence? Or was the whole "new man/metrosexual" phenomenon just a media contrivance that marketers would be best advised to ignore, given the innate and enduring differences between men and women? It was a difficult question that sounded like a job for insight-led scenario planning.

We spoke to many men across Europe, who were at different stages of engagement, with the object of finding out where they thought things were heading. In a spirit of open-minded enquiry, we visited spas and men-only salons. We hung out in Selfridges, Samaritaine and Douglas to observe the product purchase process. We studied the evolution of media portrayal of masculine and feminine archetypes.

We soon had the fodder we needed to build a series of rich, varied and plausible scenarios. One thing that became clear was that the supposed "certainty" that men would follow the lead of women in personal care was actually highly uncertain. We built one scenario where today's claustrophobic political correctness and studied androgyny was replaced by play and flirtation between men and women, but this time on very much equal terms. Another scenario took things a stage further, where men competed with other men to look their best, employing ever more extreme measures to look the part.

Once we had sketched the initial scenarios, we used them "behind the mirror" with consumer focus groups, listening out for indications of movement towards different scenarios, giving the evidence and inspiration to start to innovate straightaway for these emerging needs. The more we looked, the more it became apparent that the whole territory of "unapologetic masculinity" appeared to be a big un-met need. We were able to foresee a world where men were much more confident and comfortable with the category, leading to a new strategic innovation programme to cover this "blind spot", developing new language, new brand architecture principles, new product types and product formulations specifically for men.

CASE STUDY 4.2 GLOBAL SOFT-DRINKS INNOVATION AND MERGERS AND ACQUISITION (M&A) (2002)

Our client was a growth-oriented global soft drinks manufacturer, based in North America with a significant European presence. The question was "How do we believe the soft drinks market will evolve over the coming five years, and therefore where should we direct our innovation and M&A effort?" Part of the subtext was the relationship between national and retailer brands, and whether national brands would continue to lead. For example, would the recent tilt from national brand-led carbonated soft drinks (colas and the like) towards retailer brand-led "new age" drinks and water turn into a stampede?

After meeting and speaking with a wide range of industry luminaries and observers, eight certainties and seven critical uncertainties were identified that gave the basis for scenario creation. The two most interesting scenarios were:

It's a Wonderful Life

"Well, life hasn't doled out what we thought it would. Our 401k is only worth half what it was a few years ago and good jobs are a little thinner on the ground. But having said that, things are good, we've pulled together in a way that you typically only see in the movies. Even the kids seem happier, more centred and other-oriented. As far as eating and drinking is concerned, we go out a bit less, but we love going

to our local Sam's Club and stocking up on great value healthy new age drinks and sometimes mineral water."

Implications

- Retailer brands experience strongest growth.
- Growth of new age brands is checked and they struggle to hold a price premium.
- "Healthy balance" trend has moved decisively against high-sugar carbonated soft drinks (CSDs).
- Therefore, stay close to Wal*Mart and get into bottled water.

Wall St Revisited

"I jut knew things would get back to normal. Everyone was screaming like Chicken Little—"the sky is falling"—but I just knew that, typical to the American way, things would recover. Now I can get back to my to-do list, which is on my Palm pilot in my wife's Fendi bag in her SUV in our three-car garage. But first we must party! Champagne anyone? And if I overdo it, I know this little tea bar in Soho which can cure any hangover."

Implications

- Retailer brands suffer and are relegated to "cheapest on display" niche.
- Big shift towards out-of-home consumption.
- National brands, especially exotic imports, are "must-have" items.
- Category explodes with growth in most directions (water, new age less so).
- Therefore, explore foodservice channels and retain CSD focus.

Once the scenarios had been fleshed out, it became apparent that the most probable outcomes all indicated that CSD consumption would decline, and in an industry plagued by over-capacity, defensive consolidating deals should be sought in preference to offensive, diversifying deals. From the point of view of innovation, the health trend clearly identified water as the place to be, and preferably in partnership with retailers to capture economies of scale.

CASE STUDY 4.3 EUROPEAN FROZEN FOOD STRATEGIC INNOVATION (2000)

Our client made frozen food and ready meals. The company was frustrated by the fact that each new product it launched seemed to take share from something else in the range, while the big new trends (like vegetarianism, organic food and slow food) seemed to be passing it by. It was particularly worried that many of the trends in the industry were heading in an unfavourable direction: there had been numerous food scares about meat. Any food perceived as "processed" was being questioned, particularly in relation to kids' diets. The proportion of semi- and full-on vegetarians continued to rise, and chilled food and take-home meals were grabbing more share from in-home cooking. Of course there was some good news. In an age of time-poor culinary incompetence and fussy eaters, everybody wants convenience.

The question was simple: "What is the future of frozen food, and what should we do about it?" A sub-question was that the brand and product range needed repurposing and rationalising.

To understand trends and uncertainties, we spoke to farmers, retailers, dieticians, politicians, food scientists and consumers. Looking back on a piece of work done in 2000, it is interesting that much of today's "healthy eating" climate was foreseen at that time. All the scenarios assumed the new orthodoxy of "less fat, less sugar, less salt", "no additives, no preservatives" and new legislation to govern food labelling (emerging now). One of our scenarios had the education secretary banning junk food and vending machines in schools (which happened mid-2005) and food companies all converging around the same strategy of wellness/health/vitality (which has also happened).

CASE STUDY 4.4 EUROPEAN HOLIDAY OPERATOR—STRATEGIC INNOVATION (2001)

With the fast growth of low-cost airlines and online flight/holiday purchase, there was a worry that our client's existing packaged holiday business model couldn't survive. The basic question was: "What is the future of packaged holidays?" Should the company vertically integrate and offer the whole service, or should it completely disaggregate the business and leverage the brand as more service-based portal?

The real insight that emerged from trend research was that the public's attitude to the sun was actually the main determinant of the company's future success. Would the sun continue to be seen as synonymous with health, vitality, relaxation and well-being, or would it come to be regarded as a cancerous villain? We built extreme scenarios around these polarities of "solar attitude".

One scenario was about unreconstructed "Holidays in the Sun", with people basting themselves on the Spanish beaches. The opposing "Brighton Rocks" scenario was based on a world where everybody took their holidays in the UK or somewhere similarly shady, and there had been a renaissance of the classic British seaside resorts. This inspired dozens of new ideas on how to address both "lap up the sun" and "avoid the sun" attitudes. Beach resorts were reinvented for shade-seekers, with free parasols, sun cream and sun advice from the newly sun care-trained reps. And UK-based holidays moved a long way up the corporate agenda.

Another outcome of the work was the impact on the "corporate radar". The company had previously just tracked the travel press and mainstream media. It soon opened a subscription to the *Lancet* in order to keep an eye on what key influencers were saying about sun and skin. It was now aware and prepared for outcomes it had not considered before the scenario planning exercise.

CONCLUSION: TOP TIPS

From the practical point of view, if using scenario planning for innovation, there are some tips to bear in mind:

DON'T...

- Confuse scenario planning with forecasting.
- Look on scenario planning as a panacea for innovation: it's just another tool to catalyse fresh insights and ideas.
- Rely on caffeine and sugar to create the ideas and insights.
- Try and do it on-site in half a day with mobile communication devices switched on.
- "Black box" the process—the broader-based the team involved, the better.
- Leave useful ideas for today concealed within some notional future world.

DO...

- Be very careful to choose the right question for framing the scenarios.
- Choose the timescale with care—from six months to five years.

- Be rigorous in exploring eclectic sources and creating discrete scenarios.
- Create a reflective environment and allow time and space for the "complexity hump" to be overcome by all participants.
- Package and market the scenarios in a catchy, memorable way so that people "get" them fast.
- Bring ideas back to today's frame of reference.
- Recognise that we don't know what we don't know.

REFERENCE

Christensen, C. (1997) *The Innovator's Dilemma*. Harvard Business School Press.
Kaestler, A. (1964) *The Art of Creation*. Penguin Books.

FIVE

Scenarios in Customer Management

Merlin Stone and Neil Woodcock

SUMMARY

This chapter discusses the use of scenarios in customer management. The scenarios—models of the world—are those relevant in the new marketing paradigm, where customer relationship management (CRM) takes its place alongside the "traditional" models of customer management. It is contributed by Professor Merlin Stone and Neil Woodcock, who are Directors of WCL, a company focused on customer experience management and change management.

INTRODUCTION

This chapter discusses the use of scenarios in distribution, channel management and customer management strategies. All companies need to ensure that their products and services are accessible to their customers—managing the best and most cost-effective method by which customers can access their offers. In recent years, however, distribution strategy has been complicated by new technologies. First, the internet has disrupted many long-established distribution chains in many different industries. It has allowed manufacturers to reach around established distributors and sell to customers directly—a process called "disintermediation"—and it has also allowed new suppliers (such as Amazon) to establish new methods of access through online services. In many industries, there is now a mix of established and online providers offering a new balance of distribution channels.

Scenarios in Marketing. Edited by G. Ringland and L. Young.

A second, major advance in technology has also had profound impact on the customer interface: the ability of computers to store data on customers and their purchase habits. This, in turn, has allowed suppliers to respond to customers with improved offers and more tailored communications. From this innovation has arisen the concept of "customer relationship management" (CRM) and a phase of major investment by firms in CRM systems. Many are now able to engage in a two-way, responsive dialogue with their buyers which has to be managed through distribution channels. In some industries there is now a struggle between producers and distributors to determine which of them will relate to the customers.

Both of these changes have had a dramatic impact on distribution strategy in consumer and business-to-business markets. Marketing directors are now faced with complex dilemmas because of the disruption of established distribution methods and are having to test new means of customers access requiring large investment at a very fast pace. It is no exaggeration to say that, for many, this is a new model of marketing in their industry. Scenarios, models of the world, can build rich pictures that explore the issues relevant in these new marketing paradigms. The impact of CRM strategies, and how they take the place of "traditional" models of distribution, can be examined in depth by their use. They are a major contribution to risk/return analysis in modern channel strategy.

CUSTOMER MANAGEMENT AND DISTRIBUTION STRATEGY

Until relatively recently companies, and the marketing profession in general, thought exclusively in terms of channel and distribution strategy. They produced products and services which were taken to market through the most cost effective means. However, a change in social expectations (with modern consumers expecting suppliers to be more responsive to their needs) and new computer technologies have confronted suppliers with the need to interact with their customers; to listen to them and respond with adapted offers. Customer relationship management strategies and technologies have therefore profoundly changed the approach of most sectors to product management and distribution. In fact *distribution*, as a one-way process, is almost a defunct term. A two-way, responsive dialogue enabled by CRM must be a prime consideration in all channel and distribution strategies.

Actually, companies have managed relationships with customers (and vice versa) long before CRM became a popular term. They were managed in many ways; from explicit management of named customers (as in direct marketing) or implicit management of customers (as in consumer goods brand management). In the latter, customers were managed by a combination of product, packaging, advertising, sales promotion, merchandise display and, although they might have be managed directly (e.g. if they respond to a sales promotion), they have normally been treated in groups, or market segments.

Nor is the idea of customers managing relationships with suppliers new. Customers have done this for years—whether in deciding which stores to visit, which advertisements to watch, listen to or read, which products to buy, or which direct marketing contacts to respond to.

Generally, in each market, a "model of customer management" emerges, in which suppliers and customers manage each other in a particular way. Each competitive player makes similar assumptions about the relative effectiveness of different elements of the marketing mix for this model. A market is therefore a sector of an economy in which a distribution pattern has become established. For example, "brand management", "mail order", "key account management", "territory selling", "mass market retailing" might be the normal method by which suppliers and customers interact.

Models of customer management often vary by industry or sector. Particular tools and techniques are used by suppliers, while customers respond or take the initiative in particular ways. Of course, at any one time, some suppliers and customers might be more proactive in how they manage each other, and others much less so. It is one of the marketer's main functions to appraise the situation and decide which marketing mix elements will work best and most cost-effectively, given the norms of customer management for the product and market.

There is no single model of customer management that works well in every market, or even a single model that is best in a particular market. The model that works best in a particular market at a particular time depends on many factors, including:

- customers' propensities to manage or be managed in different ways (and whether there are groups of customers with strong preferences for particular models);
- suppliers' strengths and weaknesses;
- the state of customer management technology.

However, there may be one or two models that work best for most customers—or most of the valuable customers—in a particular market at a particular time. Spotting these models, and making sure that the company can work them well, is a marketing director's responsibility. Where the optimum model does not change much, this part of the marketing director's job is relatively easy. When it requires substantial change, there can be a substantial problem, which in some circumstances can finish the business. It demands the tools of scenario planning to address it.

THE CRM CONCEPT AND MODEL

For years, marketers assumed that established models, such as consumer goods branding, retail marketing and salesforce management, were timeless. However, the CRM concept replaced, or substantially supplemented, these tried and tested ways of doing business. There have been three main factors in this challenge to established theory and practice:

The first is the change in companies' capability to manage customers, occasioned by rapid advances in information and communications technology. This has made a whole range of tasks much easier, typically transforming them from what had been manual or one-off operations into those that could be carried out easily, and sometimes automatically. Examples include:

- Advances in database and data access technology, allowing data about large numbers of customers to be held more cheaply, accessed more quickly and updated more accurately and securely.

- Advances in customer interface technology (e.g. in contact centres, on the web, using mobile technologies, rise of interactivity), enabling interactions with customers to be managed more easily, cheaply and in a more friendly manner, and allowing data arising from the interactions to be transferred to the relevant database more securely.

- Advances in analysis software, allowing the patterns of customers' enquiries, responses and purchases to be understood more easily.

- The web, which allows customers to access companies much more easily, give data about themselves and select products.

The second factor has been the rapid change in customer behaviour prompted by new customer interface technologies; again in contact centres and on the web. Customers have become much more ready to give data, and even update it themselves. But they have also become more concerned about the accuracy of the data and the uses to which it is put. Two main developments have reinforced these trends:

- Media developments, particularly the arrival of new media and fragmentation of existing media (press, TV), giving customers much more choice. This has required companies to know their customers better and understand their behaviour in order to be able to spend advertising money wisely.

- Social trends: more confident consumers demand to be treated better, and are less loyal because exit is easier.

The third factor has been learning by both sides of the market (customers and suppliers) about what is possible, how to make it happen, and how to avoid dealing with companies or customers with whom one does not want to do business.

The problem that these three factors pose for marketing directors is the knowledge that CRM is simply another model of customer management, used in many different ways by different types of company in different sectors. It is not the final answer. Further iterations and developments are likely. A company should therefore keep under review the different models of customer management that may not, but could, exist in their market, or that are currently minority models. They should try to discover:

- Why technological, sociological or market conditions might lead to one or other model (or combination of models) of customer management being more or less favoured.
- Where their own company stands in relation to this model or these models—how its current model(s) compare with it and the company's ability to change to other models.
- How it might change to use one or more new models—including using the resources of business partners, possibly involving outsourcing.

To do this, a company needs to understand the wide range of models of customer management that already exists.

MODELS OF CUSTOMER MANAGEMENT

1 CRM

CRM is the use of a wide range of marketing, sales, communication, service and customer care approaches in order to:

- identify a company's named individual customers;
- create a relationship between the company and its customers that stretches over many transactions;
- manage that relationship to the benefit of the customers and the company.

This definition, while technically a good one, is a little lacking in feeling. Marketing should define a concept or technique in terms of what customers think or feel: a definition that could even be given to customers. So a company could describe CRM to its customers as:

CRM is how we:

- *find you;*
- *get to know you;*
- *keep in touch with you;*
- *try to ensure that you get what you want from us in every aspect of our dealings with you;*
- *check that you are getting what we promised you... subject of course to it also being worth while to us.*

CRM originated in business-to-business marketing (a combination of account management and customer service). Even companies who do not sell to consumers find CRM disciplines very useful in managing intermediaries (conventionally known as "trade marketing").

2 One to One

This is the ideal suggested by consultants Don Peppers and Martha Rogers. Here, as far as possible, most aspects of the marketing mix are actively attuned to the (changing) individual, based on information given by the individual before or during contacts, perhaps supplemented by other data about the individual (e.g. inferred). Web-based one-to-one customisation of offers, such as Amazon, is a good example.

However, the idea of the segment of one is static. Some (but not all) customers are receptive to this approach as they have different propensities to respond, in terms of returning more value. Also, the payback on the large systems and data investments required for one-to-one marketing are not clear and reliable, though there have been some successes.

However, the principle has been successfully applied to large customers, whose value justifies the degree of customisation implied by this approach. Thus, the relationship between a grocery food company such as Unilever or Procter & Gamble, and large retailers such as Wal-Mart, Tesco or Carrefour is probably the nearest to intermediary one-to-one. Although the product supplied is normally standard, the rest of the offer (payment terms, delivery, information, etc.) is usually heavily customised.

3 Transparent Marketing

This is the idea that many customers would like to manage their relationship with companies rather than the other way round (Stone et al., 1998). Customers would like to do this by soliciting information from them, customising the offer made to them (content, timing, etc.), but this is often not permitted to. Where this is possible (e.g. via the web or advanced call centres), some customers are very responsive. However, many companies do not offer anything like this, and often waste much money guessing at customer requirement, based on poor information.

4 Personalised Communication of a Standard Offer

This is very common. It grew out of good practice in direct mail and telemarketing, especially in campaign selection and packaging of the offer. It involves good use of customer data and good management of data quality. It can produce high response and conversion rates and savings in communication costs. It may involve tens, hundreds or even thousands of cells in a large mail campaign, in which the offer made to each customer is selected from one of many (often modular) offers, according to the customer's profile, and presented to the customer using personalisation. In its most advanced form, data given by the customer at the point of contact (e.g. contact centre, web) is used to create or modify the profile and hence the offer made.

5 "Top vanilla"

In this, leadership is gained by offering excellent customer management (before, during and after the sale), but to standards available to everyone in the target market rather than just selected customers. In some cases, this is combined with one of the other approaches for one or more small segments of highly valuable customers. Some of the most successful practitioners of this (sometimes with some personalised communication) are intermediaries.

In the UK, Viking Direct (office supplies) and RS Components (electronic parts) are good examples of providers of a very high standard of service to all their customers. This top vanilla approach is characteristic of companies (often intermediaries) who manage their customers entirely by direct marketing techniques, e.g. telemarketing, direct mail, the internet. Their strength lies in the simplicity of their business model, which is shown in simplified form in Figure 5.1.

6 Spot-Sell

This has three different manifestations.

Within Managed Roster

Some customers, in some or all of the products they buy, prefer to get the best deal (value for money, not necessarily lowest price) at the time of purchase, but only from a selected roster of suppliers. This is common for heavy buyers of fast-moving consumer goods or shopping goods, but also for many industrial

Figure 5.1

The Simple Direct Intermediary Model

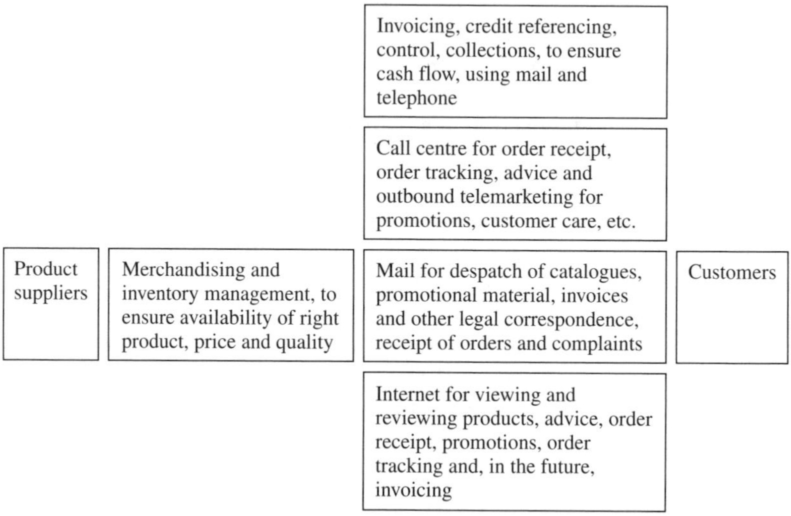

Product suppliers	Merchandising and inventory management, to ensure availability of right product, price and quality	Channels	Customers
		Invoicing, credit referencing, control, collections, to ensure cash flow, using mail and telephone	
		Call centre for order receipt, order tracking, advice and outbound telemarketing for promotions, customer care, etc.	
		Mail for despatch of catalogues, promotional material, invoices and other legal correspondence, receipt of orders and complaints	
		Internet for viewing and reviewing products, advice, order receipt, promotions, order tracking and, in the future, invoicing	

products, where a roster of suppliers is used to optimise variety, product quality and service. Branding is often a critical determinant of inclusion in the roster and also of the share of the customer's business obtained by each company on the roster.

In intermediated markets, final customers may have a roster of products/brands and a roster of intermediaries. In this model, marketing focuses on getting on the customer's roster, and providing best value when compared to other companies on the roster. Top vanilla service can add a competitive edge. CRM can be used to reinforce the supplier's or intermediary's position in the roster, though it may not help to gain "share of wallet".

Managed by Agent

Drawing up the roster can be a complex task, so customers may feel they need the help of an agent; whether for expert advice, bargaining expertise or even just to delegate some of the transaction management. Also, some types of purchase may require the customer to sign on as a registered customer (e.g. buying via telephone or the web), but the customer may prefer to register with an independent agent rather than with the original product or service supplier.

If the customer appoints an intermediary to draw up the roster, agent marketing becomes a key to success for the product supplier and the final customer has less influence on the purchase. Choice is delegated to the agent, so the supplier may use CRM techniques to influence agents. This approach can often be combined with top vanilla service for final customers and agents. In an increasing number of cases, the agent may be web-based. For example, auctioning of airline seats or hotel rooms is undertaken by web agents, with customers specifying price limits. This may be combined with a roster limitation. A contrast with this slightly adversarial idea of agents spot buying on behalf of customers is the idea of partnership customer management.

Pure Spot-Spell

Here, the customer rejects all relationships, and buys, whether from original supplier or intermediary, purely on the basis of current perceived value. Here, buying is strongly influenced by classic marketing mix variables—brand, perceived product quality, price (including promotional discounts), availability, customer service, etc. Good examples of this are purchase in the newly deregulated energy market, the direct banking short-term savings market and web-based auctions (although if a favourite auction website is used it is similar to appointing an agent). To avoid being drawn into this situation, suppliers must seek to differentiate their offer such that the customer realises that pure spot-buying is risky.

7 Channel Partnership

This is a model that seems to have a good pedigree, but is quite difficult to implement. It works where both supplier and intermediary have strong visibility of, and to, the final customer, as in the automotive industry or in financial services. The general ideas behind the model are as follows:

- If both supplier and intermediary (the "partners") use CRM techniques on the final customer, then both will gain.
- For them to work together in this way, a true partnership approach is needed.
- This approach normally also requires business-to-business CRM techniques to be used between the supplier and intermediary. For example, intermediaries are managed according to their current and potential future value, their propensity to work in partnership, exchange data, etc.
- Partners need to accept that customers will decide which relationships, if any, they want to have with which partners, and it is up to the partners to decide which relationships they would like to have and how to motivate customers to take them up. Customers do not classify themselves as "owned". Also, in many cases, customers decide which of their needs (or wants) they want

to meet through which channels, based on the value they perceive that each channel delivers.

- If this approach is taken, it cannot work tactically, as this will lead to conflicts caused by the fact that differences in objectives and requirements have been sorted out. It needs to work strategically. For example, if intermediary or supplier decides to make increased use of CRM techniques with final customers, then the results for both will be better if they plan to work together on this from the beginning.

- If supplier and intermediary are not working in partnership, both sides need to determine potential partnership objectives (e.g. deepening the relationship with the existing final customer base, or broadening the customer base).

- Whether for existing or potential future partnerships, rules and rights in managing the relationship must be determined, as should the way in which the policy processes of each partner should correspond.

- The key to success is trust between organisations involved, and that is often hard to achieve.

- The overall success of a partnered CRM programme will be in the hands of final customers, and they will chose to access and compare an organisation's propositions through different means if they have access to them. They will measure the organisation through all of these.

8 Classic Marketing Models

There are many classic marketing models where customer management is not specified explicitly but there is a strong implicit model of customer management. These include:

- Retailing.

- Salesforce management (especially in business to business, where the oldest model of relationship marketing was born, based on ideas of key account management, industrial buying centres, quality and customer service).

- Mail order (the source of the earliest and in some ways still the most professional ideas of mass relationship marketing, e.g. customer value, customer retention and dismissal).

- Consumer product and company brand management.

- Business product management—closely related to technical innovation models.

CREATING AN OPTIMUM STRATEGY USING CHANNEL AND CRM FACTORS

Obviously, these models overlap, and companies may find they need to combine them in different ways to manage different customers, and different products. However, each has characteristic and very different patterns of investment and return. The choice is affected by such factors as:

- State and rate of change of product technology. This can lead customers to require uncertainty reduction—available through relationship or agents. But it can also create big differences in spot value.

- Underlying production and distribution techniques and costs (e.g. costs of variety, economies of scale).

- Rate of entry of "new to category" customers, which affects role of experience.

- Market structure fundamentals (e.g. patterns of competition or regulation).

- Transfer of learning and expectations of customers between different paradigms of customer management that they experience.

- Customer behaviour and psychographics (or more simply, what they think and feel, how they buy, their need to give or take control, and associated lifestyle and life-cycle issues).

- Timing issues (how quickly customers' needs can be identified, and how quickly they can be responded to).

- Customer expertise: whether customers are good at identifying their own needs and if so, how long it takes, and associated learning issues.

- Sector (strong tendency in some complex business to business relationships for customers to prefer CRM-managed repertoire with spot-buying).

- State of intermediation: type of intermediation (e.g. by agents, web-based) and amount and type of value added by intermediaries.

- Relationship between risk and value.—For example: Do customers have high risks (e.g. credit, insurance) attached to them as individuals? What is the balance between good and bad customers and between good and bad customer characteristics?

- Data issues (quality, legal issues).
- Staffing: current skill levels, possibilities of recruiting new skill sets, training options, etc.
- Systems culture of the supplier. For example: Are managers able to cope with the latest call centre and web-based technology?

THE PARADOX OF TECHNOLOGICAL PROGRESS

The improved ability to capture, manage and use customer information, and to interact with customers, does not imply that CRM automatically becomes a more appropriate model. Technological progress also makes transparent marketing and spot-selling easier, in ways that may reduce customer loyalty.

Example: Utilities—Buying Energy under the New Supply Arrangements
In newly deregulated markets such as the UK, the model for electricity or gas supply is that the individual has a relationship with the supply company. The customer signs on and agrees to buy power from that company. The company proceeds to buy electricity via the best route. This can lead to a CRM model (cross-selling of different power sources and associated household and financial services) or personalised standard marketing. However, in some countries, customers can easily switch supplier according to price fluctuations. This can be agent-managed spot-selling, with the agent possibly web-based. In its extreme form, of course, the consumer would set the computer to do the task, setting control parameters so that the source could be switched without human intervention.

Example: Buying a Telephone Call
Gone are the days when a customer had access to only one form of telephony. Today, a higher value family might have four or five telephony providers, e.g. PTT (e.g. BT), cable, a low-cost supplier (usually requiring an access code to route the call off the local PTT or cable route), and one or more mobile providers. In theory, customers could make each call by choosing the supplier with the best rate. Indeed, this can be done automatically using software, and as the multipurpose handset becomes common, consumers may come to expect this. This is roster spot-buying.

Customers' attempts to do this may be slowed down by the price confusion strategies employed by incumbent telephony operators. However, for specific types of call (e.g. to friends and family overseas, repeated and/or lengthy long-distance calls to the same number), some customers will be motivated to do the comparison and select. In fact, using a process called "carrier preselection", customers in some countries can buy their local telephone service in precisely the same way as they do other utilities, irrespective of who owns the local network. (This development is due to European Union competition law.) In this case, customers may move away from spot-buying towards the utility situation, with contractual spot-buying from a roster (annual or even shorter period contracts with a number of suppliers). However, this may also lead to the selection of several suppliers according to relative rates for different destinations or types of call (data, video or voice).

Example: Short-Term Savings

The invasion of retailers (Sainsbury, Safeway, Tesco) and different financial services suppliers (Standard Life Bank, Prudential Egg, ING) using direct marketing (mainly call centres but also the web) has caused large numbers of customers to switch their savings away from traditional retail banks. Effectively, consumers line up one or more companies on their roster (stepped interest rates—and family group interest rates—make it likely that most will have only one provider at a time). They then switch money to and fro according to the amount of spare cash they have (or expect to have). However, they have a very specific product objective in doing so.

Example: Cross-Selling in Financial Services

Financial services markets are characterised by generally low levels of cross-buying (and suspect profitability of much cross-selling as most companies practice it). This indicates that most consumers are happy to use the variety of channel/marketing/IT options available to them (direct mail response, call centre—often stimulated by direct response TV) to choose each supplier based upon perceived value for money. Also, because consumers' timing is hard to predict for life-cycle products (e.g. life, pensions), it is more difficult to cross-sell to the consumer.

This is why many life and pensions companies, who still get much of their business through intermediaries, are shocked when they get their first data warehouse and realise the low value of their cross-selling ratio. Some companies have now developed a more targeted approach to cross-selling. In some cases, based on best practice, software that works on the basis of products being marketed to customers according to customers' propensity to buy, rather than customers being selected according to the probability that they will help the product manager to meet targets. However, success rates are usually fairly low because, as customers become more aware of the different offers, they are more likely to follow a roster spot-buy policy—and call centres or the internet make this much easier.

Example: Grocery Food Buying

This is the classic roster spot buy. Here, there seems to be much evidence that the more a consumer buys of a particular category, the wider the roster goes, and spot-buying (between brands, and to some extent between stores) takes place within this. In fact, much retail buying is determined by the geographic catchment area, but we can already see the situation developing in which retailers post their price lists and special offers on the web, the consumer applies a standard template shopping list and works out which store offers the best deal.

Interestingly, in this world, brand suppliers are finding ways to develop relationships with their final customers. Most have very active websites, designed to capture customer information and draw their customers' attention to their latest offers. However, classic direct mail approaches also work. Where a manufacturer works closely with a retailer that has a strong loyalty scheme, such as Tesco(see Case Study 5.1), data sharing and vending approaches allow both sides to increase sales. However, the balance between retailer and manufacturer can also change dramatically, such that the retailer becomes the expert in category buying patterns, rather than the manufacturer.

CASE STUDY 5.1 TESCO

UK-based Tesco is one of the world's leading retailers and the UK's largest. Once known for its down-market ethos of "pile it high and sell it cheap", since the 1980s it has undergone a renaissance to the point where it has become a retailing phenomenon, taking £1 out of every £8 spent by UK shoppers. In the year to February 2005, it had profits of £2 billion from sales of £37 billion.

Tesco's reinvention has become a textbook case of how a strategic use of customer knowledge and insight can help a company to streak past once-powerful competitors. While the company had already developed an enviable reputation for innovation throughout the 1980s and early 1990s, it was the launch of the Clubcard in 1995 that really propelled the retailer into its currently unassailable position.

This was the UK's first customer loyalty card, rewarding shoppers with vouchers that could be used for future purchases. By 1997, 80% of Tesco's revenue was spent by Clubcard holders. By 2005 there were over 11 million active cardholders. It is the way in which the company has exploited the information garnered from the Clubcard to segment customers, however, that has created a new model of marketing.

This has given its enormous competitive power in terms of understanding not only about its customers, but about customer potential. It has done this by committing time, effort and resources into mining the extensive information in its customer database to segment customers in advanced and unprecedented ways.

For example, its research showed that families with babies who shopped for childcare products at Tesco spent much more than similar families who didn't buy these products, although this latter group bought an equal amount of other products. However, its brand wasn't as trusted in this sector as much as that of Boots, the leading retailer of healthcare products. To build up its brand and entice more customers to come to Tesco for baby products, the company set up the Baby Club (now the Baby and Toddler Club) which offers tailored magazines, money-off coupons, advice and parking spaces close to the entrance. It has now outstripped its rival in this part of the market.

Its Insight Unit encompasses a broad range of research disciplines and is the guardian of customer knowledge. It informs all decisions, from day-to-day buying behaviour through to more long-term macro trends.

Tesco's journey into the complexities of data handling and analysis began in 1997, when those at the very top of the company recognised that it had to resolve how to exploit the 1600 million data items a month it collected not just to create targeted offers but to make it the operational heart of the company itself. It did this with the help of the two key external partners behind the development of the Clubcard, data analysts Dunn Humby and direct marketing agency Evans Hunt Scott. Rather than try to use all the data to segment customers—the scale of which would have made it almost impossible to do within any feasible time frame—the analysts came up with an approach that used scenarios for customer behaviour to find samples of segments that could then be reasonably applied to the whole.

It also came up with simple and catchy titles for each segment that could be used throughout the company to make sure that customer understanding underpinned every activity. The strategic use of robust data ensures that Tesco receives insights, not volumes of data, and that shoppers receive a customised experience. The customer data collected is also used throughout the business to guide merchandising and planning.

This has given the retailer a powerful competitive edge, and has kept it both at the forefront of innovation while enabling it to expand into a range of new areas. For example, Tesco.com is the largest grocery retailer in the world, while it is already well established in financial services and telecoms. It is also gaining ground in clothing, books, music and electronic goods. Its unifying theme is that "Every Little Helps".

Gathering data on shopper behaviour and analysing it in relation to customer scenarios has thus allowed Tesco to maintain its leading market position through its ability to react strategically to market changes while maintaining its brand reputation for quality.

This case study is based on the entries marked by an asterisk in the References section below.

THE IMPACT OF WEB-BASED MARKETING

The web has freed consumers from the constraints of physical (i.e. non-virtual) channels of communication and channels of distribution. More informed consumers can construct their own channels from a variety of offers. They can decide to conduct some aspects of their buying direct with suppliers, and in other cases through agents. They may get information from agents and buy direct, or vice versa. The web can also accelerate the processing of business—and put at risk those companies that are slow to react to or anticipate customer needs, new competitors or even new types of competition. At the same time, companies that use the web as an opportunity to give customers more information can save costs and improve customer service (e.g. logistics companies' package tracking services).

THE ROLE OF SCENARIOS IN DISTRIBUTION CRM AND CHANNEL STRATEGY

Scenario methods create pictures of possible futures. They are ideal for capturing complex changes in market structures or detailed market research results. They are particularly useful when there is a need to tackle a fundamental shift in distribution strategy affecting a whole sector. Their contribution to the need to examine different risks and returns on investment to confront fundamental paradigm shifts makes them an essential tool in high-level channel and distribution strategy. The process should be as follows:

1. Review current industry channels and competitive effectiveness. Contrast, objectively, to the firm's position.

2. Research and review the buyer's attitudes to current channels, loyalty, response management standards in the industry and probable innovations. Much of this research must be qualitative to gain the depth of views and feelings behind buyer responses.

3. Objectively examine both the firm's channels and relationship management capability in the light of this research and analysis.

4. In dialogue with informed colleagues, construct scenarios of likely developments in the competitive CRM and channel structures. Socialise these scenarios within the firm and with informed industry observers.

5. Construct a strategy to meet the likely scenarios and calculate return.

CONCLUSIONS

This chapter has shown how the new interactive marketing capabilities change the way in which suppliers and customers "manage" each other. The nature and direction of the change is not always certain, but the effect is often great. This means that marketers need to explore a number of scenarios for customer behaviour before making decisions. This involves three stages:

1. ***Analyse*** customers and their propensities to use interactive marketing technologies and channels to change what, when, how and from whom they buy. If a company has been slow to adopt interactive marketing approaches relative to competitors, then its particular customer base is likely to be skewed towards customers with low propensities to adopt them too. Leaders attract leaders, laggards attract laggards. Being at one end or other of the spectrum is not necessarily good or bad—it depends where the type of customers it wants lie, and whether the marketing proposition is attuned to them.

2. ***Build scenarios*** of model evolution, and consider how the company can achieve competitive domination by being either the faster and/or the best to exploit evolving models. If it is a market leader, consider how it can influence model evolution, and if a challenger, consider how it can use different models to attack incumbents. Keep a close watch on changing propensities and competitive actions.

3. ***Integrate*** this analysis and planning into a business strategy and marketing planning. These are the issues that separate the winners from the losers.

REFERENCES

* Gamble, P. Tapp, A. Marsella, A. and Stone, M. (2005) *Marketing Revolution: The Radical New Approach to Transforming the Business, the Brand and the Bottom Line.* Kogan Page.
* Hunt, T. and Humby, C. (2003) *Scoring Points*. Kogan Page.
* Johnson, M. (1997) "The application of geodemographics to retailing: Meeting the needs of the catchment", *Journal of the Market Research Society*, **39** (1).

Peppers, D. and Rogers, M. (1996) "The one to one future", *Currency*.

Stone, M., Byrne, S., Knight, G. and Thompson, H. (1998) "The future of relationships marketing—towards transparent marketing", *Journal of Database Marketing*, **6** (1), 11–23.

* Tenby, D. (1999) "Changing times in retail", *Admap*, May.

SIX

Scenarios in Brand Valuation and Brand Portfolio Strategy

David Haigh

SUMMARY

This chapter describes the techniques involved in brand valuation, and how the use of scenario modelling for making decisions about brand management can be a powerful tool for understanding the impact of decision-making on both short-term profit and the long-term net present value of the business. It is contributed by David Haigh, Chief Executive of Brand Finance plc.

INTRODUCTION TO "BRAND" VALUATION

Brand Finance plc specialises in valuing strongly branded businesses and their component tangible and intangible assets: in particular, their trademarks or "brands". Such valuations are conducted for highly technical accounting and tax purposes, for mergers, acquisitions, corporate finance and investment transactions, and for internal strategy and resource planning. All these applications tend to focus on the same broad valuation approach involving the determination of expected future "brand" earnings.

To arrive at the expected future earnings of a "brand", it is necessary to decide either explicitly or implicitly which commercial scenario is most likely to occur (and then determine valuation assumptions that are appropriate to that scenario). This means that it is inevitable that the consideration of alternative scenarios, and their probability of happening, are central to the "brand" valuation process.

Scenarios in Marketing. Edited by G. Ringland and L. Young.

WHAT IS A "SCENARIO"?

The word "scenario" is a literary term meaning *"an outline of the plot of a dramatic or literary work"*. While a literary scenario might be credible, it is inevitably imaginary and there may be alternative plots or subplots. Brand planning can be much the same.

The original literary term has been adapted by commerce to describe *"a possible set of future events", "an outline or model of an expected or supposed sequence of events", "a postulated sequence of possible events"*. Because all scenarios describe the future, they are inevitably hypothetical and uncertain. Some postulated scenarios may be quite implausible. To be taken seriously, they must be logical, internally consistent and credible.

In Michael Porter's words, a scenario is: *"an internally consistent view of what the future might turn out to be—not a forecast, but one possible future"*.

Every forecast starts with a consistent, credible scenario of the future, usually postulated by incumbent management based on their knowledge of the recent past and expectations of the future. Usually, a valuer (who could be an internal specialist or independent external expert) relies on the incumbent management's preferred scenario, although specific assumptions and variables may be challenged.

In certain circumstances, an incumbent management's preferred commercial scenario may be discarded in favour of that of an equity analyst, investor or third party manager (for example, in the case of an unsolicited take-over bid, break-up plan, liquidation plan or management buy-in). The "brand" valuer must decide which scenario most accurately fits the purpose of his or her opinion of the valuation and then explore the specific variables and assumptions that flow from the chosen scenario.

WHAT DO WE MEAN BY "BRAND"?

I refer to "brand" in inverted commas because, as an asset definition, the word "brand" is ambiguous. "Brands" can be defined very narrowly as simply "trademarks", more inclusively as "trademarks and associated intellectual property rights" or very broadly as the whole business trading under the trademarks—the "branded business".

Niall FitzGerald, the former chairman and chief executive of Unilever, certainly meant the last of these definitions when he discussed the strategic realignment of the Unilever "brand" portfolio under his now abandoned "Path to Growth" strategy.

When considering individual asset values within a branded business, the International Accounting Standards Board (IASB) recommends reporting accountants to consider three broad asset classes: fixed assets, monetary assets and intangible assets. Intangible assets are further classified by the IASB into marketing, artistic, customer, contract and technology related intangibles. Theoretically, companies could identify and report on many individual intangible assets but, in practice, they tend to group several specific intangible assets under generic headings (for example, "Film Rights", "Mastheads", 'Software', "Patents" or "Brands").

The IASB allows companies to determine the specific intangible assets they want to aggregate under these generic headings. For our purposes, as long as the individual intangible assets operate together to create economic value for the company, and have similar useful economic lives, the reporting company can define the components of "brands" for itself.

In its International Financial Reporting Standard 3 (IFRS 3), the IASB requires that an acquiring company must identify the Fair Market Value of all assets acquired in a business and must record the Fair Market Value of each asset in its post-acquisition balance sheet (see the next section for the precise definition of Fair Market Value). The value recorded in the balance sheet must then be checked for impairment, at least annually. Impairment reviews must be conducted using discounted cash flow (DCF) analysis, which determines the net present value (NPV) of the assets in question based on the expected value of economic benefits arising from the asset in the future.

For technical accounting and tax purposes, we are often obliged to separate out the value of "brands" under one of the definitions noted above. However, for all other applications, the value of the branded business is the critical issue.

THE APPROACH TO BRAND VALUATION

However, whether we are valuing "brands" as separate intangible assets or the branded business as a whole, the approach to valuation is very similar.

Some Definitions

To begin with, there is a general presumption that valuations are based on the Fair Market Value principle, which is defined as:

> *The estimated amount for which a property should exchange on the date of valuation between a willing buyer and a willing seller in an arm's-length transaction after proper marketing wherein the parties had each acted knowledgeably, prudently, and without compulsion.*
>
> *International Valuation Standard 1 (IVS, 2005)*

In arriving at a Fair Market Value the valuer has to use expected earnings based on the Highest and Best Use (HABU) of the asset in question. The Highest and Best Use is defined as:

> *The most probable use of a property which is physically possible, appropriately justified, legally permissible, financially feasible, and which results in the highest value of the property being valued.*
>
> *International Valuation Standard 1 (IVS, 2005)*

Alternative Approaches

Assuming that we are determining the Fair Market Value based on the Highest and Best Use, it is then necessary to select one of the alternative valuation bases recommended by the International Valuation Standards Committee. These are:

- *Cost approach.* This considers what the "brand" would cost to create or recreate. However, cost to create or recreate is usually a poor indicator of the value attributable to a unique "brand".

- *Market approach.* This considers whether there is an active market from which a valuation opinion can be directly determined. Again, there are few if any direct market comparables for unique "brands".

- *Income approach.* This considers the value of the economic benefits arising from the asset in the future. Being specific to the future performance of the 'brand' in question, this tends to be the most common approach to valuation.

As a result of the shortcomings with the 'cost' and 'market' approaches, the vast majority of technical valuations rely on the 'income' approach. The income approach is also the way external investors and internal strategic planners generally determine value for their purposes.

In the case of external investors, equity analysts construct intrinsic valuation models of the branded business to determine the target value of the enterprise, and by deduction the target value of each share. In the case of strategic planners, there is a constant endeavour to maximise the value of the enterprise by identifying the optimal portfolio of activities, and then allocate resources to achieve the highest overall enterprise value. Both external investors and strategic planners attempt to forecast expected future earnings and express them as a net present value.

As a result, all three interest groups tend to base their valuations on Fair Market Value, assuming the asset is employed in its Highest and Best Use and all tend to base their opinion on a forecast of future economic earnings, discounted to a NPV using DCF valuation models.

HOW DO WE DETERMINE 'EXPECTED VALUES'?

Whether for technical, corporate finance or strategic planning purposes, it is therefore necessary to determine the expected level of future revenues and earnings produced by the branded business. The starting point is a credible and internally consistent scenario describing how the branded business will develop in the future. Several approaches can be used to determine "expected values" attributable to the chosen scenario.

1 Single Explicit Forecast

The first approach is to identify one explicit set of forecasting assumptions determining 'most probable' sales, earnings and cash flows over the forecast period. These are then discounted back to arrive at the expected NPV. This is straightforward but subjective, although the forecaster implicitly considers alternative assumptions and outcomes before settling on the 'best estimate' for each individual assumption used in the valuation. In other words, only one set of forecast assumptions is developed in detail. In my experience, even this apparently one-dimensional approach to expected value analysis involves detailed discussion and review of many assumptions.

2 Multiple Explicit Forecast

A second approach to valuing the chosen scenario is to produce several alternative forecasts based on flexed assumptions and then attach probabilities to each, thus producing a 'probability weighted' estimate of future earnings. (Flexing is where assumptions are adjusted upwards and downwards in increments to identify the value effect of each incremental change in assumption.) This is more transparent and robust than the first approach, but determining how many outcomes to explicitly forecast and the probability of each occurring is inevitably subjective. However, setting out various explicit forecasts makes it easier to challenge the outcomes and the ultimate expected value.

3 Comprehensive Simulation Forecast

Finally, it is possible to flex all assumptions to determine a 'bell curve' of 'expected values' in the forecast model. In practice, ***Monte Carlo*** simulations (a statistical modelling technique) and similar multiple forecasting techniques tend to be complex, mechanistic and intuitively less comprehensible than single or multiple explicit forecasts. However, they thoroughly explore all possible outcomes under the chosen scenario.

Existing Use to Existing Owner

It should be noted that whether the forecasting approach is single, multiple or comprehensive, all start with a preferred management scenario for the branded business being valued. In valuation terminology such a scenario is often referred to as: *"existing use to existing owner, without hope value."* (Hope value is having an idea about something that may occur but is by no means certain.)

A good example of 'existing use to existing owner' can be seen in the hotly contested acquisition of Rowntree by Nestlé in 1988 (Case Study 6.1).

CASE STUDY 6.1 NESTLÉ ROWNTREE

Before any external bid, a valuation of the Rowntree brands would have been based on the incumbent Rowntree management's preferred scenario and assumptions for its brands. That scenario would have assumed existing and planned products, raw material contracts, factories, distribution channels, personnel, marketing campaigns, pricing, licensing, new product development plans and so on.

To arrive at a Fair Market Value, it would have been necessary for the valuer to challenge and test specific assumptions and variables before arriving at an opinion about the expected value of the brands in existing use to the existing owner. But the preferred management scenario would have been the most probable outcome for the brands in the absence of a new owner. This would have been regarded as the highest and best use for the brands and anything else would have been considered 'hope value' and ignored.

However, if the valuer had prepared the valuation based on a Nestlé commercial scenario, the Fair Market Value opinion would have been quite different. Why? Because Nestlé had plans for different product variants and had access to different raw material supplies, factories, distribution channels, personnel and new product development capabilities. Many of the valuation assumptions might have been the same (e.g. product selling prices, personnel costs and raw material costs etc), but the difference in the Nestlé preferred scenario created a radically different forecast and NPV. This explains why the eventual take-over price per share leapt to over £ 11 compared with a pre-bid share price of less than £ 5.

When briefed to value branded businesses or 'brands', it is very common to flex assumptions and outcomes within a single management scenario—and then provide a probability weighted value outcome. It is not common to base a valuation on two or more completely different management scenarios—which are then probability weighted. Nor is it usual to average two or more quite different scenarios when arriving at a Fair Market Value opinion. The start point for 'brand' valuations is usually a review and agreement that one particular scenario should be relied upon.

KEY ASSUMPTIONS, VARIABLES AND VALUE DRIVERS

One of the reasons it is most common to choose a preferred scenario and then explore specific forecasting outcomes within it is that there are many assumptions, variables and value drivers that may need to be flexed even within one agreed scenario.

Even a single scenario forecast involves forming an opinion on a wide range of key assumptions, variables and value drivers. Forecasts are usually constructed for an initial 'explicit' valuation period of five years. So the forecaster or valuer must form an opinion at least five times (for each year) for each of the key assumptions, variables and value drivers. In addition, DCF valuations usually involve forming a view on the probability that the final, explicit year forecast will be sustained 'in perpetuity'. An 'in perpetuity' opinion must be formed on each key assumption, variable and value driver.

It will be seen that this process could involve a minimum of 30–40 opinions in each year of an explicit forecast and at least another 30–40 opinions for the remainder of the 'in perpetuity' period.

Why should there be so many separate opinions? A branded business valuation model typically involves a forecaster or valuer forming a view (either implicitly or explicitly) on each of the following (for the five explicit forecast periods and for the 'in perpetuity' period to infinity):

1 Key Market Variables

- Population of product or service users
- Average consumption per product or service user
- Subject brand's number of loyal customers
- Subject brand's customer acquisition and lapse rates
- Product or service life-cycle and obsolescence rate
- Size of the whole market and key segments in volume terms
- Size of the whole market and key segments in value terms
- Average market prices
- Relative competitor prices.
- Number of competitors in the market
- Number of distribution channels and outlets

- Subject brand's penetration of each channel and outlet
- Competitor brands' penetration of each channel and outlet
- Channel listing costs and trade discounts
- Subject brand's market, segment and channel share in volume terms
- Competitor brands' market, segment and channel share in volume terms
- Subject brand's market, segment and channel share in value terms
- Competitor brands' market, segment and channel share in value terms.

2 Key Profit Variables

- Subject brand's cost of sales and direct production costs
- Competitor brands' cost of sales and direct production costs
- Subject brand's overhead and personnel costs
- Competitor brands' overhead and personnel costs
- Subject brand's marketing and sales costs
- Competitor brands' marketing and sales costs
- Subject brand's trading margins
- Competitor brands' trading margins.

3 Key Intangible Asset Variables

- Number of key intangible assets in the branded business
- Contribution of key intangible assets to demand and profitability
- Percentage of earnings fairly attributable to each separate intangible asset
- Market royalty rate for each separate intangible asset.

4 Key Cash Flow Variables

- Customer payment days

- Supplier payment days
- Stockholding days
- Capital expenditures

5 Key Economic Variables

- General and market specific inflation rates
- Bank base rate and commercial interest rates
- Equity cost of capital and equity risk premium
- Market average debt to equity ratios
- Income and other tax rates
- Economic growth rates into perpetuity.

Some complex industries may demand that an opinion is formed on an even wider array of key assumptions, variables and value drivers. It will be seen how complicated it can become exploring so many variables for a large number of different scenarios.

SENSITIVITY ANALYSIS

When preparing a forecast valuation it is quite common to flex each of the assumptions one at a time to demonstrate the impact of changes in each variable on the valuation result. However, this is a simple mechanical exercise intended to show the assumptions to which the valuation is most sensitive. It is not a scenario-forecasting technique, but simply an expression of what happens to the NPV of the scenario if one lever is pulled rather than another. The valuer's dilemma lies in trying to determine which of the key assumptions is most likely to change, and how.

THE 'VALUER'S DILEMMA'

It will be seen from this, a forecaster or valuer is obliged to form a view on many individual pieces of information before finalising a single scenario valuation model. Even in a relatively simple valuation, several hundred separate opinions have to be formed before finalising an overall opinion on 'expected value'.

One problem is that key assumptions, variables and value drivers often affect one another. For example:

- If population demographics change faster than expected, the volume, value and precise mix of products or services demanded in a market may change in unexpected directions.
- If either economic or stock market performance diverge significantly from expectations, inflation, taxation and cost of capital may adversely affect consumer confidence levels and therefore demand.
- If excise duties rise significantly faster than inflation, the volume of demand for products like petrol, cigarettes and alcohol may change unexpectedly, particularly where alternative forms of transport or self indulgence become available.

Predicting what will happen out to a one-to-five year forecasting horizon, and beyond it into perpetuity, is the valuer's perennial dilemma. The reality is that most companies only produce detailed forecasts for the following budget year, and possibly for one additional forecast year. Beyond two years, detailed management forecasts are often replaced by long-range strategic forecasts. These are often no more than statements of intent by non-operational planning departments, rather than detailed attempts by management to forecast accurately.

CASE STUDY 6.2 LASTMINUTE.COM

The valuer's dilemma is best exemplified by the sort of valuations that emerged in the dot.com boom. Lastminute.com was a clever concept that captured the public imagination. One of its founders, Martha Lane-Fox, became the figurehead of the dot.com generation and expectations of what Lastminute.com might achieve over a five-year explicit valuation period and beyond became quite ridiculous. When the company floated in 1999 its implied enterprise value rose to over £ 800 million.

This wasn't bad for a loss-making company with virtually no assets or sales. The whole 'value' of the business lay in the assumptions being made about future value drivers in over-heated valuation models. Inevitably, the market value dropped back significantly post-initial public offering (IPO), leaving many disgruntled investors sitting on massive losses. The commercial scenario, as described by Martha Lane-Fox and co-founder Brent Hoberman, could never be realised in the financial valuation model implied in the float.

A number of techniques are available to the forecaster or valuer to improve the robustness of short-, medium- and long-term forecasts.

- ***Short-Term Consumer Research Predictions.*** This involves using short-term consumer usage, attitude and brand price trade-off research to predict market demand and relative market shares. The problem is that it assumes that effective research methods can be designed to predict short-term consumer behaviour. Even when true, this technique suffers from the fact that conditions rapidly change, making it hard to predict consumer behaviour reliably beyond the very short run.

- ***Short-Term Trade Research Predictions.*** This is about using short-term trade behaviour and stockholding research to predict market demand and relative market shares. However, similar issues arise as with short-term consumer research predictions.

- ***Medium-Term Predictions Based on Statistical Analysis of Past Trends.*** This involves using statistical analysis or econometric analysis to determine market and market share trends. It assumes that the behaviour of key independent variables, tracked historically, will remain constant or predictable. However, in practice, this is seldom true beyond the very short-term.

- ***Long-Term Predictions based on Industry Desk Research.*** This uses a variety of industry reports from sector trade organisations, governmental bodies, specialist research consultancies and investment analysts to predict market demand and relative market shares. While it is a helpful way of determining the consensus view in an industry, consensus views are often incorrect.

- ***Short-, Medium- and Long-Term 'Delphi' Predictions.*** This method uses facilitated 'focus group' meetings or specialist software to capture and test management's best opinions of likely market demand and relative market shares. It is a helpful way of determining the consensus view of management. However, management views are often incorrect.

Although all of these techniques are used to help determine the valuer's opinion on assumptions and variables, they are all imperfect. This is why it is helpful to explore alternative outcomes, and then weight them according to probability.

REDUCING FORECASTING COMPLEXITY

Given the large number of key assumptions, variables and value drivers which may vary, it is common to fix as many as possible: for example, population numbers and demographics, average consumption per consumer, product life cycle, number of competitors and distribution outlets, product cost structures, gross margins, terms of payment, inflation rates, interest rates, tax rates and so on.

Fixed assumptions tend to be in areas where there is a general consensus. This approach limits flexing of assumptions where there is general agreement.

HYPOTHESISING BRAND SCENARIOS

In arriving at the preferred management scenario for a brand, there may be significant debate, brainstorming, disagreement and research. In some cases there are fundamental disagreements within management ranks as to what constitutes the preferred scenario for a brand. In such circumstances, the valuer may construct alternative valuation models built on quite different scenarios (as in Case Study 6.3).

CASE STUDY 6.3 COURVOISIER

In 1999 there was a debate within the global brand management group within Allied Domecq as to whether the Courvoisier brand should be classified as a 'core' brand or whether it should be divested given its poor financial performance and declining NPV?

The problem was that the previously preferred scenario for the Courvoisier brand was based on it being a high-end cognac product, sold to high net worth individuals in Asia, Europe and East Coast USA, using traditional marketing and distribution, at a premium price. Given the high cost of production, high stockholding costs and low rate of sale the brand had a low and declining NPV.

Market research indicated that lower-end cognac, sold in different bottle sizes, to mid-market ethnic consumers in the heartland of the USA with contemporary marketing techniques, would radically change the value of the brand.

The two scenarios were modelled and the latter approach indicated a higher level of profits and cash flows, with lower capital investment, and a faster rate of sale.

Variables were flexed but even allowing for changed assumptions, the NPV of the two scenarios were quite different. This led to a change in brand strategy and a rapid improvement in financial performance of the Courvoisier brand. In the recent acquisition of Allied Domecq's brand portfolio by Pernod Ricard, Courvoisier was referred to as a key brand.

In this example the two scenarios for Courvoisier implied radically different capital values for the brand, the higher of which was actually realised when the altered scenario was implemented.

CREATING SCENARIOS FOR BRANDS

It is the responsibility of brand managers to continually postulate and explore alternative scenarios for their brands. Such scenario analysis starts with a coherent and consistent story line and ends with a valuation model which financially elucidates the value impact of an alternative scenario.

For example, a brand manager might postulate the following scenario:

Subject brand is repositioned from fifth player status in the super-premium category to first player status in the mid-market segment. Subject brand has failed to compete in the super-premium segment, but is seen to be aspirational in the mid-market segment. The mid-market segment is treble the volume and doubles the value of the super-premium segment.

Mid-market segment average prices are 20% below super-premium but subject brand drops price by only 15%. Subject brand is seen by consumers and trade to be high quality at a reasonable price. Subject brand doubles advertising/sponsorship and share of voice by doubling communications budget. Subject brand hires appealing male and female 'ambassadors' to create strong appeal with both sexes rather than largely with men. Brand management improves terms of business to increase trade distribution from 50% to 80%.

Market share forecast to increase from 25%–35% throwing fourth mid-market player into loss for 12 months. Brand management acquire fourth player after 12 months to consolidate its mid-market position and share. Net margins drop from 25% to 20% for 12 months before market equilibrium returns.

Does the postulated scenario work? Will it consume or free capital? Will it increase or destroy value?

The credibility of such a brand scenario needs to be explored and tested using consumer and trade research, market, marketing and financial due diligence. If deemed consistent and credible, the value impact can be tested with a brand valuation model. If the new scenario implies that greater value will be created than the pre-existing scenario, then it should be actively pursued.

The sort of scenarios that brand managers have probably explored using valuation models include, for example:

- Extension of Green & Black's chocolate brand into ice cream products.
- Licensing of the Virgin brand into new mobile phone, airline and financial service products.
- Divestment of "redundant" Unilever brands like Mazola.
- Rationalisation of the Vodafone national brand portfolio into one global brand.

- Acquisition of Gillette brands by Procter & Gamble.
- Investment of substantial advertising budgets behind the Mastercard brand.

SITUATIONS WHERE SCENARIO PLANNING CAN REDUCE BRAND RISK

There are many situations where brands have become stale or old fashioned and need to be repositioned to recapture consumer appeal and return to financial viability. In other situations a brand may be highly successful but, if new strategic options are taken, the brand may significantly increase in value. Scenario planning is an ideal technique for identifying and then testing such strategic options.

Repositioning

Brylcreem had been a 'must have' brand of hair cream in the 1950s and 1960s. But by the 1990s it was a 'granddad' brand. It still sold reasonable quantities but to an ageing demographic. The brand was literally dying off. The brand owners proceeded to reposition it as a contemporary brand by relaunching the original product and extending the range to include other, more contemporary products, such as hair gel.

Repositioning the Brylcreem brand against a new range of products and a younger, target demographic implied high risks to existing consumers and sales, which needed to be carefully explored before launching the new strategy. The key issue was to retain the core brand equities and maintain the existing audience while attracting a new generation of users. Different repositioning strategies, together with their probable effects on consumer response and business value, would very likely have been researched and modelled before the relaunch.

Redesign

BMW bought British Leyland and inherited the Mini car brand. The Mini had been launched as a small, functionally but stylishly designed, budget runabout car in the 1960s. It was an icon of the 'swinging sixties'. Although designed by an Italian for Leyland, it had been positioned as quintessentially British and sold to young, fashionable people.

By the 1990s it retained strong emotional loyalty but the product was long out of date. BMW designed a whole new car, which combined high performance with high style. The build quality and performance were far higher than the original Mini. The retro image picked up on the resurgence of 1960s Brit Pop fuelled by films like Austin Powers. The new Mini is more of a highly priced 'hot' car than a functional runabout. Various scenarios were no doubt created and explored prelaunch to identify the highest value-adding strategy.

Rebranding

In 2000 and 2001 Vodafone acquired a raft of strong national mobile phone brands with a view to creating the first truly global mobile phone network brand. Brands such as D2 (Germany), Omnitel (Italy), Europolitan (Sweden), Click (Egypt), Airtel (Spain) and Panafon (Greece) had different levels of consumer and business awareness and preference and were more or less sensitive to brand change. In each territory the value at risk from rebranding varied significantly, as did the optimal time period over which brand change might be effected.

In Germany, local animosity to Vodafone was initially high because Vodafone had taken over Mannesmann, the popular German owner of D2. More needed to be done in Germany and over a longer period to ensure that the economic impact of rebranding was favourable rather than unfavourable. Various alternative rebranding strategies and investment levels were modelled, balancing investment, return and value at risk.

Relaunch

The Commodore computer was an iconic brand of PC which reached its high point in the 1980 s. But it engaged in a vicious price war with Atari and other brands and by the early 1990s was in serious financial difficulties. It stood for reasonably priced, open platform entertainment. The brand was bought by Tulip computers of Holland but the brand ceased production in the late 1990s.

In 2005 the Commodore brand was bought and relaunched by a new owner. It is now developing a range of mobile media and communications devices and associated content. The questions for Commodore are how far the brand can be stretched into new areas, and how far will the trade and consumers support the new brand offerings, and at what prices.

Scenario modelling techniques thus allow a number of alternative product and pricing strategies to be explored to identify which parts of the business mix are most vulnerable to the relaunch.

Reallocation of budgets

Mastercard, Visa, Amex and Diners all promote their payment formats in every country of the world to maximise card issuance, card acceptance and card usage levels. Many cardholders carry multiple cards in their wallets but tend to use only one. Persuading them to switch habitual use from one card to another and to increase the number and average value of transactions can have a significant effect on the value of the business. Similarly, different cardholders affect the business model differently. International business travellers attract higher interchange fees, transaction fees and foreign exchange fees but little interest and no delinquency fees. Low-income local users by contrast attract high-interest charges and fees.

Reallocating marketing budgets from card issuance messaging, from promotion of card acceptance levels or from targeting one demographic group to another can significantly affect business value.

Scenario modelling, incorporating a valuation model with detailed value driver analysis, market research and statistical analysis to model the financial impact of alternative marketing spend patterns is vital to optimise the marketing budget. Scenario modelling is used extensively by card companies to determine the optimal budget size and its allocation between territories and competing messages and user groups.

Revision of Price Point

Grey Goose vodka is a recently created, super-premium, import vodka distilled in France. It is a recent entrant to the US market and competes with, for example, Absolute, Finlandia, Smirnoff and Ketel 1. When entering the market, Grey Goose wanted to demonstrate its pedigree and quality by setting its wholesale and recommended retail prices at a significant premium to the rest of the market. But how far could the price be pushed without choking off demand?

Pricing research and a scenario valuation model allowed the owner to estimate the optimal pricing level and the optimal volume growth trajectory, and to calibrate this over time. After a very few years, the brand sells in excess of 1.5 million cases at a significant premium and has now been sold by its owner for more than $2 billion.

CONCLUSION: FINANCIAL IMPLICATIONS FOR BRANDS

It will be seen from the foregoing examples that financial and market research modelling are vital tools in brand management decision-making. It is all very well having a creative or marketing idea and believing it will work, but it is far more powerful to understand the likely impact of a strategic decision on both short-term profit and the long-term net present value of the business. Scenario modelling goes hand in hand with profit analysis and discounted cash flow modelling to determine shareholder value.

Some critics argue that DCF stands for 'Deceitful Computer Forecasting'. They rubbish values determined by DCF techniques largely because they argue that financial outcomes are uncertain. Of course, their comments have to be taken with a pinch of salt because they are often 'value' investors, preferring to buy distressed shares at knock down prices. On the way in they naturally talk down DCF valuations and focus on tangible assets. I expect their enthusiasm for DCF valuation techniques grows when they are preening businesses for sale or IPO and focusing on valuable intangible assets.

However, it should also be noted that doubts about the accuracy of forecast earnings valuations can be valid because all forecast valuations are based on someone's judgement of a preferred or 'best' scenario. A large number of assumptions also need to be made and the result is inevitably somewhat subjective. A valuation represents an individual opinion at a point in time based on the realisation of a particular scenario and the accuracy of various detailed assumptions. It may be persuasive but can never be scientifically 'accurate'.

Nevertheless, stock market analysts, investing institutions, bankers and corporate planners do take DCF valuations seriously and make decisions on them—if those valuations are professionally and credibly constructed.

In fact, in my view, DCF valuations are a way of telling a commercial story in numbers and values which match a business story told in words. They form an integrated 'scenario'. They are both ways of convincing investors, lenders and colleagues that if the story line is true, value will be created. This is why all branded business and brand valuations depend on a preferred 'scenario' actually happening.

Brand managers need to be aware of this and become comfortable with the process of taking a verbal or conceptual brand scenario, testing it against other scenarios and expressing each in a financial valuation model. Both are creative exercises, one in creative brand management and one in creative accounting. Fluency in making both work together will put brand managers in a strong position to raise finance or obtain resources to achieve their ambitions.

REFERENCE

IVS (2005) International Valuation Standards (7th edition). Appraisal Institute.

SEVEN

Marketing Communication: Radical or Rational Change?

Don E. Schultz

SUMMARY

There's little doubt that marketing communication, as we have known it since the development of mass media in the early twentieth century, is undergoing change. The questions are: Will that change be radical, as some have suggested, or, will it be rational and perhaps evolutionary, rather than revolutionary? Those questions are plaguing the entire marketing communication industry. In this chapter, we explore how and in what way industry managers might use scenario planning to address the potential changes.

This chapter was written by Don E. Schultz, professor-emeritus-in-service of Integrated Marketing Communications at the Medill School at Northwestern University. He is also president of the consulting firm, Agora, Inc.

BACKGROUND

A brief history of what and why the changes are occurring in marketing, communication, branding and promotion will set the stage for the development of possible future marketing communication scenarios for the next decade or so.

It All Begins with Technology

Technology has commonly been one of the primary generators of change in marketing and marketing communication. Various technological changes provided the impetus for the transportation models that enabled newspapers and magazines to transition from purely local to regional and then to national media forms.

Scenarios in Marketing. Edited by G. Ringland and L. Young.

Technology was clearly the underlying factor in the development and distribution of radio, and later, television.

Today, technology is enabling the new media forms such as the internet, world-wide-web, telecommunication and even the iPod. Thus, marketing communication has always been involved in, and the result of, some type of transition. New media systems have emerged, older forms adapted and ultimately, evolved. And, from those, marketers have developed new methods and approaches for reaching and convincing customers of the value of their products and services.

The Challenge of Media Fragmentation

In the past, technology has been used primarily to aggregate greater numbers of people for marketers to address. In other words, the focus has been on audience consolidation and concentration. Radio created massive national audiences. Television created hemispheric ones. Today, the web and internet have created instantaneous global audiences, but not in the same form and format as those before. Today's electronic audiences are interactive and integrative, not just passive recipients of the promotional monologues developed by marketing organisations.

Thus, the technological developments of today are not focused on aggregation and consolidation. Instead, they are being designed to separate and identify more individual audiences. Today audience fragmentation is the driving force in media. More importantly, developmental attention is on audience differentiation rather than audience homogenisation. As a result, the management challenge for marketing communication is vastly different than it has traditionally been for the past 50 or so years.

A Shift of Marketplace Power

The addition of an almost unlimited numbers of new media forms and formats as developed by media organisations, ranging from personalised media such as mobile telecommunications to electronic sales promotion to formalised word-of-mouth have given the marketer greater message distribution opportunities, but with a cost. So, while this panoply of media forms has given the consumer a wider choice of information and entertainment vehicles, it has also provided more means of escape from the ever-increasing crescendo of marketer communication. Clearly, what is occurring is the shift of marketplace power from the marketer to the consumer. Today and tomorrow, the marketplace will be one of consumer choice. The marketer can only hope that the media he or she has chosen as a delivery vehicle is the one selected by the potential consumer.

Today, the consumer picks and chooses between a broad array of media and communication alternatives, no longer held hostage by the transportation-based, and time-specific traditional media forms. Consumers time shift, media-shift, up-load and down-load media in all forms and formats at their leisure. That's why the pressure is now on marketing organisations to catch up with consumers and their actions.

As the consumer gains more media freedom and information resources, the marketer is challenged with new types, methods, forms and formats that are not always friendly and familiar. That pressure is being exerted not just on marketers, but on media, agencies, research and measurement firms—in short, everyone involved in the marketing communication field.

How will the marketing organisations respond? What are the possible scenarios open and available to them? How can they make the changes? All these are questions addressed in this chapter, and some answers are also provided.

THE ROAD AHEAD

The format for this chapter is first to sketch out the apparent scenario under which most marketing organisations are operating today. This is based on the implied assumptions that underlie current marketing communication planning, development and distribution. We then identify the most disruptive factors challenging these current systems. That is followed by the four possible future scenarios of how marketing communication may develop, which are:

- The status quo, where only minor changes and adaptations occur.
- Further development of market and customer segments.
- A consumer-dialogue scenario where interactive communication is the norm.
- Finally, a consumer search scenario in which the consumer has total control of the system and the marketing organisation simply responds to customer demands.

We speculate on the impact of each of these scenarios and finish with some conclusions and forecasts.

THE CURRENT MARKETING COMMUNICATION PLANNING SCENARIO

Because there is no, single, well-defined theoretical base for marketing communication planning or development, it's difficult to clearly define the current scenario under which most marketing organisations are operating. Each marketer, each agency and each media organisation appears to have separate and unique approaches and methodologies. Yet, there are some identifiable, commonly understood assumptions, which seem to underlie most current practices. Those are described below.

1 Assumptions of the Current Marketing Communication Planning System

Owing to the lack of formalisation in marketing communication planning, this discussion is based primarily on some commonly used, industry assumptions.

- All marketing communication is developed by marketing organisations and their agencies and is delivered by independent media organisations to audiences those media have created. Thus, all marketing communication is outbound and one-way: from marketer through the media to the audience. Thus, it is a system of marketer-delivered monologues directed to marketer-determined audiences.

- Marketing communication is controlled, in terms of amount and content, by the marketing organisation. Thus, the marketer is free to develop and distribute communication through almost any media form and in almost any volume desired or available. This is done through financial allocations. Consumers have little or no input into the distribution of messages. They can only accept, ignore or avoid.

- A corollary is that most marketing communication activities are based on an interruptive model—that is, the media organisation gathers audiences through content development. Marketers are then "rented" exposure to these audiences by the media owner. Consumers come to the medium primarily for the content, not the marketing communication. Therefore, almost all marketing communication interrupts the flow of content, which is something consumers seldom appreciate.

- All marketing communication is based on an underlying behaviourist psychological model called the Hierarchy of Effects. This model, developed in 1961, posits that marketing organisations, through the distribution of marketing communication messages, move consumers along a continuum from awareness to eventual product purchase. This is done through repeated exposure to the marketer's messages. The essence of the concept is a conditioned-response model which the marketing organisation controls. The premise is illustrated in Figure 7.1.

  As shown, it is assumed that the more messages the marketer sends out, the more rapidly the consumers move through the Hierarchy. Thus, marketing communication investments are considered to be one of the key elements

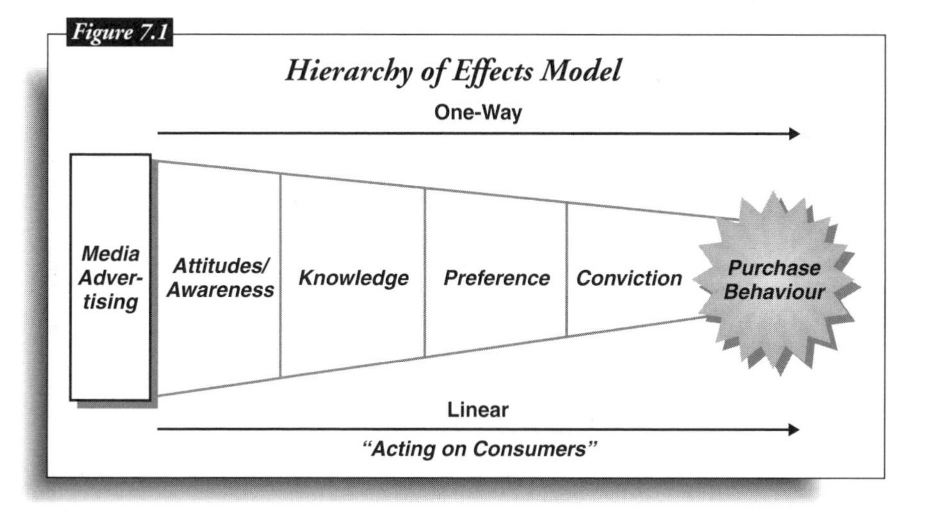

in marketplace success. While the model is intuitively appealing, there is little hard evidence to support the assumptions, i.e. there is scant evidence that consumer advertising exposures at some point result in a consumer behavioural response.

- Following from the Hierarchy of Effects model, most marketing communication planning is based on the efficient delivery of consumer messages or incentives. By assuming that all marketing communication messages are equally persuasive, and thus effective regardless of the media form through which they are delivered, the more messages the media forms can deliver, the better. In short, today, marketing communication is based on media tonnage or output, not a consumer-driven response model.

- The media efficiency planning model is supported by measurement of changes in consumer information acquisition, storage and recall, i.e. knowledge, attitudes, etc. (see the Hierarchy of Effects model in Figure 7.1). While the model assumes some type of behavioural response, most measurement is based only on communication effects, not behavioural change. It is therefore almost impossible to connect most media advertising programs to marketplace sales results.

While there are a number of other assumptions driving current marketing communication planning, these are key ones. These assumptions are supported by a large number of service and supplier organisations committed to the Hierarchy

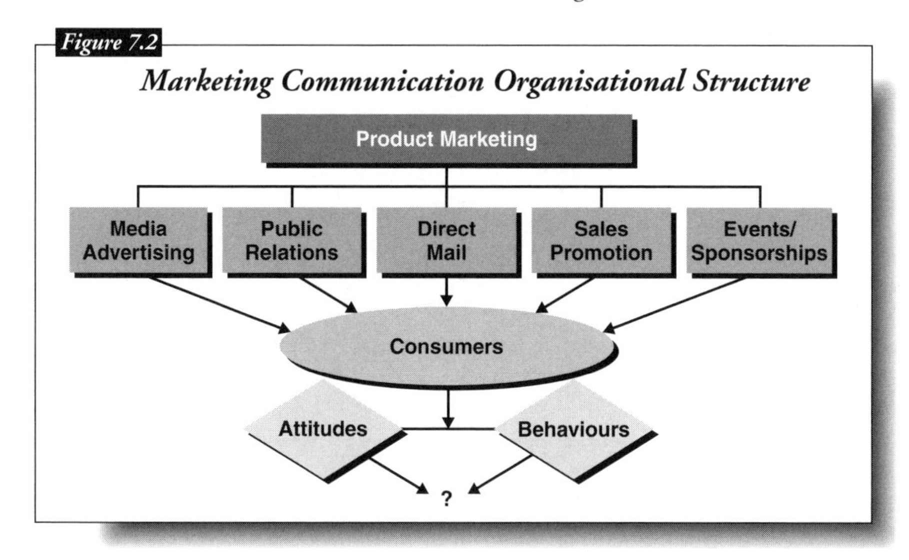

of Effects model. Thus, the model has a number of both internal and external adherents.

2 Embedded Systems Support Marketing Communication Assumptions

The assumptions described above have been in place for at least 50 years, ever since the commercialisation of television which became "the" mass medium of choice for marketing organisations. Marketing firms have built their organisational structures around these assumptions and suppliers have developed their product array as well. The current typical organisational structure of a major consumer product marketing organisation is illustrated in Figure 7.2.

As shown, each marketing communication activity is planned and developed separately and independently within the organisation. Each is assumed to be unique and independent, even though most marketers understand that consumers take in, process, use and respond to combinations of marketing and communication activities over time. Many vendors and suppliers tacitly support the Hierarchy approach and have developed methodologies to support the existing marketing communication system. Many of these are directly wedded to the Hierarchy of Effects model described earlier. These range from television commercial testing organisations and the media audience measurement groups to advertising production companies and research firms that gather data on consumer needs and wishes.

Obviously, these support firms, since they are embedded in the system, are reluctant and resistant to change. Most marketing communication management has, therefore, a fairly myopic view of the marketplace, the consumer, the media forms being used and the impact and effect of their marketing communication investments. This has an impact on how they view and respond to the marketplace drivers that are influencing marketing communication development now and into the future.

3 Change at Little or No Cost to Consumers

Interestingly, for the most part, the media and marketplace changes occurring commonly come at little or no cost to the consumer. They have no investment in new marketing communication approaches such as sponsorships, events, public relations, sales promotions, etc. The cost has all been borne by the media and marketing organisations. In addition, any change in how marketing communication is developed and delivered in the future will also likely be at the expense of the marketer, not of the consumer. Marketers will pay more and consumers will benefit only if one assumes that an overcrowded marketing communication marketplace is of value to anyone except the media firm.

This "no-cost to consumer" paradigm raises additional spectres of substantial consumer change with little or no apparent benefit to the marketing organisation, although there will be potentially higher conversion costs. This is probably not an area that senior management of marketing organisations will cherish.

4 An Assumption of Marketplace Maturity

Marketers generally believe that current marketing approaches and methodologies will continue to diffuse throughout all established and developed markets. Thus, it is assumed that emerging markets such as China, India, Russia, Brazil and others will develop along the same path as those currently existing in the United States, the United Kingdom, Japan, Canada and Australia. Thus, it is assumed that, over time, the system we presently see in the established markets will either develop, emerge or be implanted in developing markets and that those systems will be similar to those that currently exist.

This assumption seems to ignore the rapid diffusion and consumer acceptance of new technologies such as telecommunication, mobile, etc., in these emerging countries. Even though it is increasingly clear that some markets will "leapfrog" traditional communication development forms, the common wisdom of the marketing communications community is that an orderly transition will occur—a view not supported by the facts or evidence.

With this brief description of the marketing and marketing communication management assumptions supporting the current scenario, we can now turn to the factors that will likely influence change, whether it is wanted or not. Those are listed in the next section.

DISRUPTIVE MARKETPLACE FACTORS MAY CHANGE THE CURRENT SCENARIO

Five major emerging factors will likely change the existing marketing communication scenario. They are:

1 A Clear Power Shift to the Consumer

As before, the rapid deployment of technologies being used to create new marketing communication forms and formats will be the primary drivers of scenario change. The rapid adoption of mobile, electronic, web-based and other forms of consumer information delivery, and the easy access to that by all levels of consumers, makes their dependence on marketer-originated communication systems less and less important. With their new-found information power—for example, the ability to "Google" any topic, product or marketer—consumers will find less and less need for traditional marketing communication approaches. They will become more selective in their access to and use of traditional marketer practices.

2 Increasing Marketing and Communication Costs

As fragmentation increases, the cost of marketing communication will continue to escalate for marketing firms. Where once audience aggregation and consolidation enabled marketers to deliver messages and incentives efficiently to prospective customers, with the increase in multiple media systems it simply costs more to effectively reach the same people. For example, only a scant 25 years or so ago, a marketing organisation in the USA, through network television "roadblocking" (placing a commercial simultaneously on all three major networks) could reach 75% or so of the entire adult population. Owing to media fragmentation, those methods have been superseded.

The result is that marketing costs are escalating while traditional marketing audiences are plummeting. In addition, in many consumer product organisations, marketing costs now account for 30% or more of the firm's total financial outlay. Senior management is therefore much more interested in marketing expenditures than it has been in the past.

3 Increasing Demands for Accountability

With marketing expenditures increasing and audiences decreasing, senior management is naturally much more concerned with accountability. Much of that is being driven by increased management dependence on various quantitative methodologies such as Six Sigma, Balanced Scorecards and the like. Unfortunately, marketing communication management's inability to measure the financial returns on the organisation's marketing communication investments subjects the expenditure to increasing senior management scrutiny. With that scrutiny comes accountability and the demand for better investment and return measures. This is an area in which marketing communication management has been notoriously weak and there is little visible help on the horizon.

4 Above-the-Line/Below-the-Line Controversy

Historically, marketing communication budgets have been allocated on an accounting basis, commonly termed "above-the-line" (ATL) or "below-the-line" (BTL). Spending in support of activities that have some perceived long-term organisational value such as advertising and branding are considered ATL. BTL are those activities perceived to have only a short-term impact, usually with little long-term value. Those include such areas as sales promotion and direct marketing. While both are expenses, ATL is viewed differently inside the organisation and traditionally has had more senior management support.

As increasing amounts of marketing communication budgets are shifted from above-the-line programmes to the more consumer action-inducing below-the-line programmes in an attempt to achieve short-term incremental sales increases, changes in the traditional marketing communication methods and approaches are inevitable. The question is, of course: What new marketing communication management model will emerge? That is still under development.

5 Rise of a Communication Planning Function

Historically, marketing communication planning for many marketing organisations was relatively simple. The prime communication form was advertising and the prime media choice was television. All other media and promotion forms revolved around that initial decision. The premise was: "Buy the most television time possible and support that with other media forms, primarily BTL and then watch the profits roll in".

With the increased breadth and depth of communication alternatives, there has been an increasing need for new and different forms of marketing communication planning. In many cases, new, supposedly "media neutral" planning organisations are emerging. (Media neutral has come to mean not starting with television advertising, but, not much more). These media-planning organisations take a much broader view of the marketplace and attempt to include and involve many of the new forms of marketing communication bursting on the scene.

These new groups, sometimes allied with traditional advertising agencies but increasingly independent, provide a new voice in the marketing communications arena. They think differently. They plan differently. They operate differently from the traditional advertising agencies and their internal media planning structures. There is, therefore, more external pressure on how marketing communication is planned and bought than there has been in the past.

Given the five drivers in the previous section, we can now construct a set of potential new marketing communication scenarios for the years ahead.

POTENTIAL MARKETING COMMUNICATION SCENARIOS

While it is possible that a number of permutations and variations of marketing communication planning, implementation and measurement may develop, the four most probable are detailed below.

1 Managed Evolution

The most obvious scenario is that not much will change. In other words, the status quo will be maintained, but, with some slow evolution to other scenarios. The marketplace will continue to be driven by marketers who will use familiar mass communication marketing approaches, i.e. primarily above-the-line advertising, delivered through mass media channels. Marketing organisations will continue to control the communication systems in terms of advertising and promotion volume and content based on their investment levels.

While the media forms may morph and adapt to the new technologies, many consumers will continue to be content to accept or ignore the messages and incentives the marketers distribute. Thus, customers will continue to use traditional media forms in large enough numbers so that marketers can convince themselves that they are efficiently delivering communication messages. The result? Marketers will, in essence, ignore or resist any power shift to the consumer.

For many consumer marketers, television in its various forms and permutations will continue to be the dominant marketing communication delivery system. Other marketing communication activities will continue to be adapted and applied to support the TV campaigns. Thus, while costs of communicating will likely rise, marketing organisations can continue to argue that efficiency is being achieved through the number of messages distributed.

Accountability will continue to be an issue, but marketers will still focus on message distribution and attitudinal change. They will be supported by media firms and other vested promotional organizations. Measurement vendors will continue to provide methods of measuring marketing communication impact using traditional tools. Since there will be no incentive to change the current system dramatically, any improvement in accountability will be slow, tedious and expensive.

There will be some additional shift of above-the-line expenditures to below-the-line and an increasing blurring of the concept. Marketing communication will, however, continue to be planned and implemented, function by function, and measured in the same manner.

This scenario does assume change, but not radical change. The "Big Idea" will continue to dominate most marketing communication planning and implementation approaches. This will continue to be based on the assumption that there is some "magic message" or "silver bullet creative" that, if delivered often enough and in the right form and format, will drive consumer behaviour in the marketplace. Traditional advertising agencies will continue to be the primary developers of marketing communication although media planning will continue to evolve. Thus, communication planning will continue to be done piecemeal, i.e. multiple agencies developing multiple message programmes, all based on their functional expertise.

In this scenario, marketing and communication managers will continue to place their faith in the Hierarchy of Effects model, or some variation of it. That means that marketing communication will still be focused on a behaviourist psychological model where it is assumed that consumers move through some type of measurable process on the way to purchase. The role of marketing communication will continue to be viewed as one that helps to move consumers towards purchase regardless of the communication tools used.

2 Increased Market Segmentation and Communication Customisation

In this scenario, marketers will increasingly use customer data to create identifiable and marketable consumer population segments that can then be addressed with much more refined and targeted marketing communication activities. In some instances, marketers will be able to create the long-promised "one-to-one" marketing distribution system based on the use of various forms of interactive communication. This scenario assumes that current consumer data acquisition systems will continue to be relatively open and free and that government regulations or controls will not substantially increase.

In this scenario, it is probable that the marketers' communication costs will continue to increase as more emphasis is placed on data capture and analysis, but, since returns-on-investment will continue to rise as a result of less waste, the offset will be enough to satisfy senior management. The development of closed-loop communication systems by the marketers, as illustrated in Figure 7.3, will provide the marketers with increased accountability.

As shown, as a result of knowledge of the consumer, the marketing organisation will be able to place a financial value on a customer or group of customers. By knowing that value, the marketers can then make managerial decisions as to how much to invest against that or those customers in various forms of marketing communication. By being able to then measure the increased value of the customer or customer group over time, i.e. the value that is increased by marketing communication, the marketers can then "close the loop" on their investment: Thus, the marketers will be able to determine the actual financial return on their marketing investment. In this scenario, this type of analysis by the marketers will become commonplace.

Increasingly marketers will move away from measures of consumer attitudinal change to newer approaches based on actual consumer behaviours. As this occurs, marketing accountability will be enhanced, and, thus, some of the pressure from

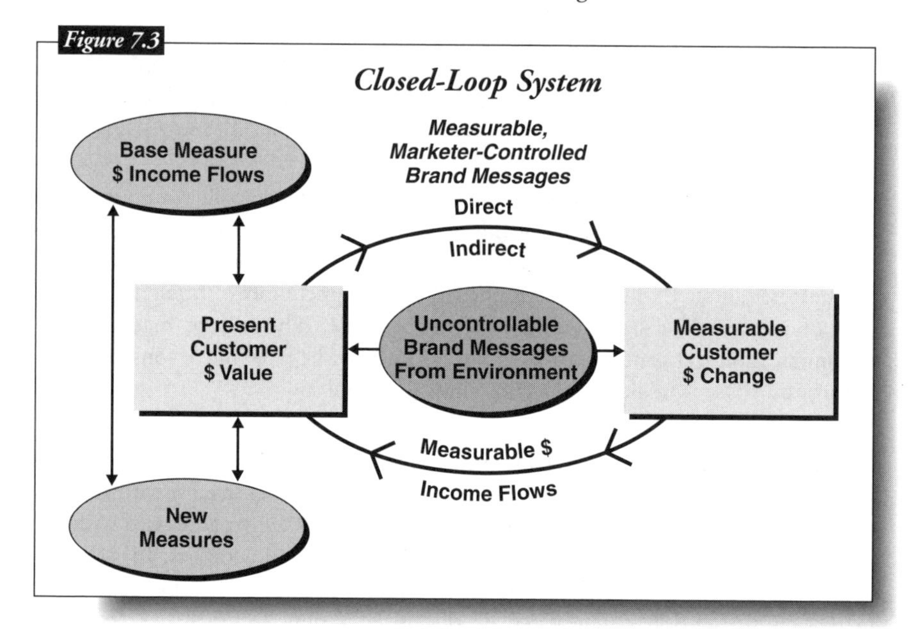

senior management for accountability relieved. In some cases, using these closed-loop systems, it may even be possible for the marketing organisation to develop ongoing profit and loss statements on individual customers or customer groups.

Above and below-the-line considerations will continue to blur as the marketers seek to develop combinations of marketing activities that provide the most profitable returns. Internal marketing communication groups will likely continue to exist, but their primary focus will be on developing the increasingly specialised marketing communication programmes required. They will, however, not drive the systems as they have in the past.

Marketing communication planning will increasingly be developed by a group of market and media generalists who will know and understand how the various marketing tools can and should be used in various combinations. These analyst/planners will, over time, replace traditional advertising agency media planners and buyers. They may well be located in specialised marketing communication planning firms.

In this scenario, marketers will eventually abandon the traditional Hierarchy of Effects models and focus primarily on observable consumer behaviours that will be tracked and measured by retailers. There will be closer relationships between retailers and traditional manufacturers with the power tilting to retailers in terms of how marketing communication programmes are developed and implemented.

Figure 7.4

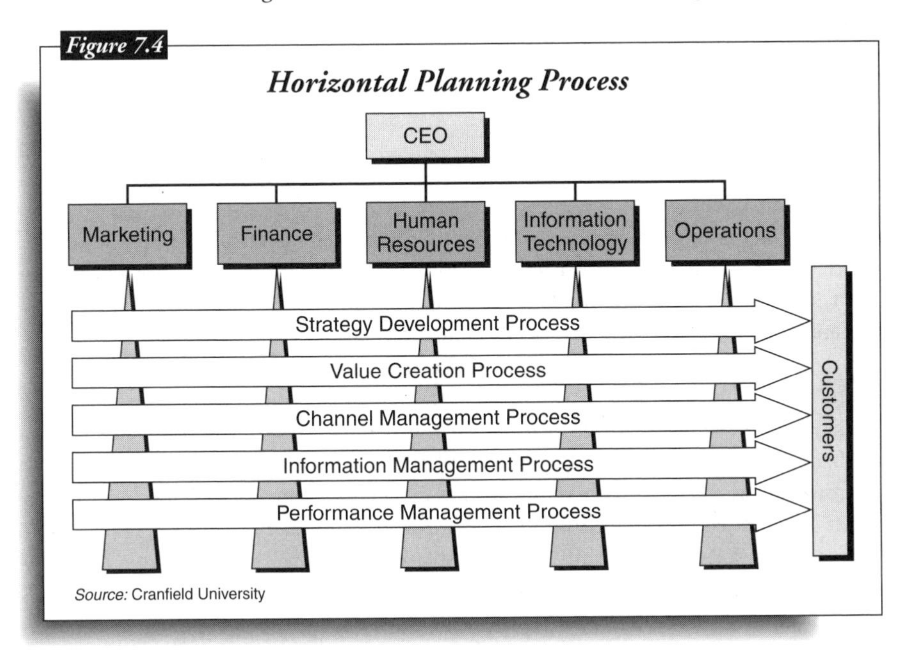

Source: Cranfield University

These new alliances will drive much of the marketing communication planning and allocation in the future.

While the marketers will still exert some level of marketplace control in this system, that power will slowly but surely shift to the consumers. Consumers will be increasingly hard to reach and harder to influence.

The marketing organisation will begin to consider marketing and marketing communication as an organisational activity, not something that only a few marketing people or marketing departments do. As that occurs, the marketing organisation will begin to shift from a vertical, functional structure to one that is more focused on horizontal planning and implementation, as shown in Figure 7.4.

In this scenario, the development of holistic marketing programmes will become quite common. Marketing departments will change from those of marketing developers and implementers to marketing coordinators as marketing becomes something the organisation does, not something a functional department does. Thus, the skills and capabilities of the marketing manager and the relevant direct reports will change from the development of tactical activities to those more related to strategic planning and the overall management of the marketing communication programmes the organisation originates.

This scenario suggests a more pronounced evolution from today's established methods with some revolutionary elements also developing. The evolution will probably be slow but steady, taking five or more years to occur.

3 Marketing Communication becomes a Dialogue between Buyer and Seller

In this scenario, marketers and consumers become equal partners in developing reciprocally beneficial marketing and communication programmes. Both parties make investments in the marketing communication process and both expect to benefit. The concept is illustrated in Figure 7.5.

As shown in the figure, both the marketer and the consumer have inputs into the system and both derive benefits. The system works when both parties believe they are receiving equal value for their investments of time and money. In short, this envisions a system of cooperative relationships where marketers seek input from consumers as to their wants and needs and then provide the products and services desired to which consumers accordingly respond.

In this scenario, the shift of marketplace power from the marketer to the consumer is clearly evident. The marketers no longer dictates the marketing communication messages but seeks to determine what the consumers wants to hear and then delivers those messages in forms and manners that best suit the customers. This cooperative approach will be quite challenging to marketing managers accustomed to developing and delivering marketing communication

Figure 7.5

The Relationship Framework

Measuring and scoring customers/prospects on both dimensions yields Relationship Strength

Value of the Customer to the Brand
(Continuing income flows and margins along with brand loyalty over time)

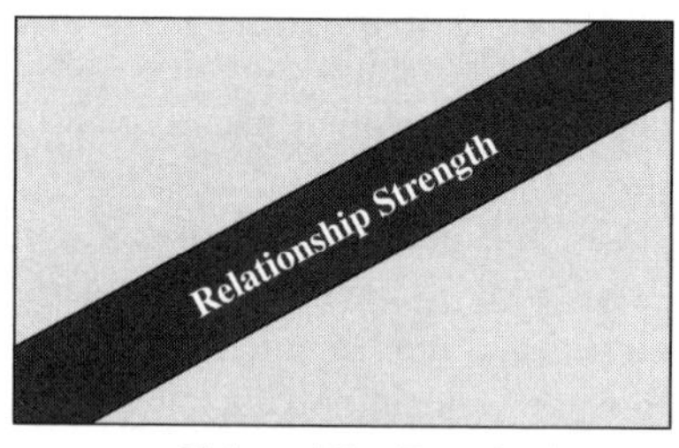

Value of the Brand to the Customer
(Value of the product or service in solving customer problems or providing benefits at a fair price)

monologues based on the needs of the marketing organisation rather than on the needs of the customer.

One of the primary challenges in this scenario will be the radical changes required of most traditional marketing support organisations. As the marketing organisation moves from "talking" to consumers to "listening" to them, new types and forms of marketing research will be required. The same will be true of media organisations, which will be required to treat readers and viewers as equals, rather than as audiences. Most of the methodologies currently in place will have to be changed. That will result in increasing demand for training programmes that will be required to educate current marketing communication personnel to the new requirements.

In this scenario, marketing communication costs will begin to decline for the marketing organisation as consumers begin to share the cost of the communication process. Sensing that there is true value to participate in a dialogue, consumers will become more willing to invest their time and resources to create interactive systems with the marketing organisations since they will see real benefits to themselves from the process. Thus, using this shared-cost approach, marketing communication costs may increase for the consumer, but they will probably decline for the marketer.

For this reciprocal system to develop, however, dramatically new marketing communication forms must emerge. Traditional outbound systems such as television, radio, magazines, newspapers and the like will be replaced by interactive systems driven by various forms of electronic communication. The traditional media will not disappear, but their form and format will change dramatically and their power and influence in the marketplace will diminish substantially. Media owners may well become involved and engaged participants in the marketer–consumer interactions.

Accountability will change dramatically as marketers begin to understand customers as business partners with reciprocal interests. Thus, the measure of marketing communication success will be based on the customer relationships developed. This will result in long-term rewards for both parties rather than the current focus on short-term marketing returns, which are the norm for today's organisations.

The above- and below-the-line accounting view of marketing communication will become a thing of the past. In a reciprocal marketplace, the concepts themselves become irrelevant. Most likely, marketers will move to a marginal cost and marginal return view of marketing communication. Continuous measurement of marketing returns will allow the organisation to begin treating marketing communication investments as marginal costs of doing business, and invest and measure returns accordingly.

Perhaps the most dramatic difference in this and the two preceding scenarios is that communication planning will move back into the marketing organisation. Since customer relationships will be the stock in trade of the marketing organisation, putting some external organisation in charge of those relationships will make little sense. Thus, the marketing organisation will begin to treat its customers the same way it currently treats its tangible assets by, for example, assigning senior managers the responsibility for protecting and managing the asset value of customers.

This will require a total review and change in traditional marketing management structures. Marketing will therefore move from being a functional activity designed to generate short-term returns to one of the primary strategic activities of the organisation. The focus will be on managing customers as assets and their income flows as the primary resources of the organisation. In this scenario, marketing moves from being a middle-management initiative to the primary activity for the senior management of the firm.

4 Marketing Communication to Facilitate Consumer Search

This is the most radical of the four scenarios for it portends the demise of marketing and communication as it has been developed and practised for the past century. This scenario will be neither well received nor accepted with much enthusiasm by current marketing professionals who will probably resist the development and implementation of this approach, but market forces will prevail.

In this scenario, the consumer gains complete control of the marketplace to the extent that marketing organisations are totally beholden to and subservient to their needs, wishes and desires. Marketers move from being developers and initiators of new products and services to becoming primarily vendors and suppliers. The premise supporting this scenario is that all products and services become totally commoditised with no differentiation between them, except through price and distribution. While brands will continue to exist, they will be based primarily on the nationalist feelings of the consumer as there will be no practical difference between the actual physical products.

In this situation, consumers dictate what is needed and the marketing organisations are forced to focus on delivering what is required at the lowest possible cost and within the least amount of time. Economies of scale and logistical excellence become the key elements in marketplace success. Thus, marketing communication becomes more a form of continuing response to consumer requests and demands than one of persuasive value.

In this scenario, the cost of communication shifts completely, with marketers now in a response mode, i.e. consumers indicate what is needed and marketers bid to supply those needs. For example, the eBay-type model of availability will dominate the system. Consumers will signal their needs and marketers will respond, or post availability of products which will then be auctioned off to the highest bidder. Communication will shift from outbound to inbound, from persuasive to responsive.

The key element in marketing communication becomes the firm's ability to respond to consumer requests. This means that the marketing organisation treats marketing communication more as a sales function, and thus tries to become as efficient in response as possible. Marketing and distribution/logistics become inexorably entwined with as much emphasis on delivery and distribution as on manufacturing capability.

Accountability is built into the marketing system since the focus is on driving consumer access to the firm's contact facilities where it can respond. Thus, it is possible to track each and every customer order and relate that directly to the cost of acquiring that order. As a result, the focus of the marketing organisation becomes one of trying to be everywhere the customer or prospect wants or would like to obtain products or information.

In terms of communication planning, the key will be to determine how and in what ways consumers would like to interact with the marketing organisation. The firm's goal will be to make those facilities and resources available as conveniently and as accessible for consumers as possible. It is likely that the most successful marketing firms in this scenario will be those who have the widest marketplace net, that is, the most available places for customers to interact with them.

Most traditional marketing concepts become things of the past. Marketing managers become product or service managers, trying to respond to consumer needs. This requires a much closer interaction between the contact organisation and the manufacturing/distribution functions within the firm. Marketing really becomes the order generator and receiver for the organisation, which takes marketing almost 180 degrees from where it has traditionally been and impacts marketing communication in the same way.

Which one of the above scenarios is most likely to develop? In the next section, we speculate a little on what is likely to occur.

WHICH SCENARIO WILL PREVAIL?

Of the four scenarios listed above, which is most likely to succeed? The answer is *all four*. but for different reasons than one might expect. All the above scenarios assume one standard, monolithic marketing communication approach. What will most probably occur, however, is that different scenarios will emerge in different geographies—for example, one scenario in the USA., another in China and another in Ghana. As the marketplace fragments, and as consumers gain control, much will depend on what the various cultures and economies want and will accept. The marketing communication scenario of the future is not and will not be in the hands of the marketing organisation or even the media organisation. It will be in the hands of the consumer. That is, and likely will be, the most radical change of all.

If it is probable that all these scenarios will develop in various markets and in various product categories, what should the marketing communication manager do? The answer is to focus on developing massively improved market research capabilities: capabilities that are based on forecasts of the future, not an analysis of the past. This is an area that likely needs the most immediate attention.

We will look at the impact of scenario planning in the marketing and communication area in the final section of this chapter.

WHAT ABOUT THE FUTURE?

Given our previous discussion, two questions naturally arise about scenario planning and marketing communication: (a) if the organisation has already developed a set of potential corporate scenarios, should the marketing communication manager employ those in developing marketing communication strategies and tactics for the firm, and/or, (b) should the marketing communication manager separately develop a set of marketplace and communication scenarios to help to guide and lead the organisation through its marketing communication development?

Clearly, the answer to both questions is a resounding "Yes".

Isolation of the marketing and communication function has been all too common in many organisations, as described earlier. Silos abound and marketing communication is often believed to be something that a department or group of people do, not what the organisation does Thus, marketing and communication managers have too often developed plans, programmes and initiatives that, while seemingly creative and innovative, are not supportive or reflective of the scenarios the firm has identified or is following.

In too many instances, the marketing and communication people seemingly are "marching to a different drummer" when it comes to corporate strategy. They develop programmes that the organisation cannot or is not willing to support. The most obvious example is the advertising campaign that promises high-sounding solutions to customer problems and then learns that the firm cannot support those promises or are in conflict with the overall corporate scenario the firm is following.

Clearly, the best path is for the marketing and communication manager to be knowledgeable of the various corporate scenarios that senior management or the strategic planning group is considering or employing. That means that marketing and marketing communication must be considered as one of the strategic alternatives available to senior management, i.e. something that can and, if used properly, should contribute to the overall success of the employed scenario(s). Going forward, marketing communication must be thought of as something that can and will make a difference in the success of the firm, not simply a group of tactics that are turned off and on at the whim of management.

For this to happen, however, the marketing and communication people themselves must become more managerially oriented. They must have broad business skills, not just communication capabilities. That will require training and development on an ongoing basis.

Similarly, it is critical for the marketing and marketing communication group to develop a set of marketplace scenarios that can be considered by senior management. By being closest to the customer, the market and the communication systems, the marketing communication managers should be able to construct a set of strategic, marketing and communication-based scenarios of how and in what way those areas might be used to support various corporate initiatives. As the speed with which marketing and communication systems develop and change—as customers evolve, as competitors develop new initiatives, as the entire system becomes more globalised and new demands develop that the organisation must either respond to or initiate—marketing communication scenario planning, that is, the clear identification of a set of situations, developments and initiatives, becomes critically important for the entire organisation.

The question, of course, is whether or not marketing and marketing communication managers are capable of either responding to and/or implementing programmes to support the current corporate scenario assumptions or are sufficiently skilled to develop a set of scenarios like those contained in this chapter. In too many instances, the answer, unfortunately, is likely to be negative.

And that will continue to be the case as long as marketing communication is considered to be a tactical activity of the firm which has little long-term impact on the business. Thus, training of current and developing marketing and marketing communication managers becomes a critical issue within most firms. Hopefully, this chapter will contribute to the initiation of those development programmes.

CONCLUSION

The twenty-first century organisation can no longer isolate marketing and marketing communication in a department or group, and can no longer assume that marketing communication is something the organisation can choose to do or not to do. The world has changed. Scenario planning is one proven way of recognising and attempting to accommodate that change.

EIGHT

Scenarios for Fast-Moving Sectors

Andrew Curry, Lloyd Burdett and Crawford Hollingworth

SUMMARY

This chapter introduces the use of scenarios in fast-moving sectors, and discusses the circumstances in which purpose-built scenarios, using existing scenarios, or qualitative cross-impact approaches, work best. It is contributed by Andrew Curry, Lloyd Burdett and Crawford Hollingworth of Henley Centre Headlight Vision.

INTRODUCTION

Scenarios can be used effectively in fast-moving sectors. They can help to understand strategic issues, to identify potential market spaces, to spot innovation opportunities and to test for potential future risks.

It is possible to imagine that this is not the case—that in a business that has to respond to frequent and short-term changes in consumer demand, the longer-term perspectives implied by scenario work are not appropriate. But this would be a mistake, for four reasons:

1. Many of the significant issues that affect the success of fast-moving companies and sectors are long-term. These include regulation, talent, environmental issues, technology, property, logistics systems and regulation. In all of these areas, for most companies, "inevitable surprises" are waiting in the woods (see Schwartz, 2003).

Scenarios in Marketing. Edited by G. Ringland and L. Young.

2. The use of shorter term scenarios (for example, on a five-year time frame) can help to understand the way consumer markets are likely to change and help to ensure that an organisation, or even a department, will have the capacity and capability to deliver. Sometimes this can be a valuable health check; even if it shows that the overall strategy is right it can identify places where there are critical delivery weaknesses.

3. Many of the techniques used in scenario development are also useful in helping to think about changing customer needs, about product and marketing innovation, and about risk. Building the skills for strategic futures work inside the company helps many areas of the business, not just the strategy department.

4. The use of scenarios also encourages people to be more outward looking, going beyond the confines of a single brand or category and providing a vehicle that encourages thinking across multiple brands, categories and sectors.

It is also worth noting that one of the benefits of shorter-term futures or scenarios work is that rather than pointing you towards a range of alternative possible futures, they are more likely to steer you towards a range of developing market opportunities. Several of the scenarios that are identified in such work are likely to play out at the same time in different parts of the market. This means that they can help you to identify both the spaces where you can be competitive, given your capabilities, and the spaces where you will flounder. The key is to understand what technique to use, and when, and why.

This chapter will look in outline at three techniques which are either scenario-based or use strategic futures approaches:

- Creating purpose-built scenarios.
- Using pre-existing scenarios.
- Qualitative cross-impact analysis.

To help to understand when the different tools are best applied, we have used a simple matrix, as shown in Figure 8.1. On the vertical axis, what is the primary purpose of the scenario's work? Is it more strategic, or is it concentrated on marketing, innovation or proposition development? The time scale is on the horizontal axis—with shorter time scales (2–5 years) to the left, longer ones to the right.

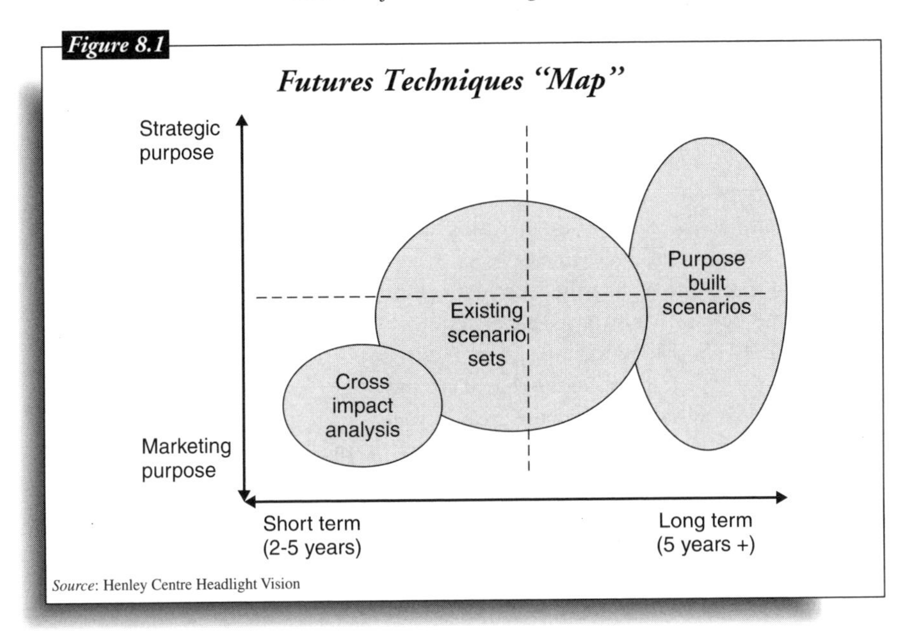

Source: Henley Centre Headlight Vision

The sections that follow draw on work done by Henley Centre Headlight Vision, both for internal knowledge development and client project work. Much of this is in the public domain. In some places, we have disguised material to protect client confidentiality.

DOING SOMETHING IS BETTER THAN DOING NOTHING

Most of the futures work in fast-moving companies is typically done within the research, insight or innovation departments. These areas tend to have a reasonable capability for scanning consumer trends.

In practice, the circumstances in which such companies are willing to make the investment and commitment required for a piece of substantial additional futures work are fairly rare. More often, these organisations prefer to work with individual trends for innovation purposes, and also to use more traditional techniques based on official (or 'desired') visions of the future, to inform their corporate strategy development.

For these reasons, the best way to address futures work inside fast-moving companies is often to help them to think about the range of drivers of change, and about the unpredictability and uncertainties these create for the organisation's market and operating environment.

Innovation-oriented futures work has a different emphasis from more strategic or risk-based analysis. If the latter needs a robust analytical approach, together with a greater sense of transparency and plausibility, the former is more directed towards providing creative stimulus to help to identify and understand new, and sometimes disruptive, areas in which new product, service and marketing propositions could reap rewards. In the words of Art Fry, the 'inventor' of the Post-It note: *"You have to kiss a lot of frogs to find the prince. But remember, one prince will pay for a lot of frogs."*

Sometimes there is benefit in using a "quick and dirty" process to get a snapshot of an issue, particularly when using futures work primarily as a spur to innovation, rather than the lengthier commitment involved in developing the richer and deeper futures space generated by full-scale scenarios.

Similarly, for risk management purposes, some organisations believe that more provocative "What if?" scenarios, based around a high-level examination of trends and their manifestations, have the greatest value.

An important common thread, however, is the need to look outside the organisation to identify changes in the external environment, before starting to think about their internal impact. It's important to build a sufficiently good picture of the world outside before getting down to the consideration of the particular operational or strategic issues that might arise for an organisation or brand as a result. Missing this stage means that you can never be sure that your view of the future isn't being clouded by internal concerns.

The French futurist Gaston Berger said, *"Looking at the future disturbs the present"* (Berger, 1967). In our experience, using some futures techniques to help to think about the present is better than doing nothing. It is worth trying out these techniques for yourself. For this reason, this chapter includes a number of short exercises to enable you to do this.

CONNECTING SCENARIOS TO ACTION

One of the risks of futures work is that its techniques and methods are not always well understood within the marketing and the market research communities. Yet, because of the clear connections between futures, insight and consumer behaviour, it is often the marketing or the intelligence department that is expected to seek support for a futures process.

A Note of Caution

As a result, people who could spot someone making an implausible claim about a segmentation technique or a qualitative research method at a hundred metres find themselves in an area which they understand less well. Therefore, it is often a lot harder for them to assess what's going to be useful for the company or department, and what is not.

One of the key reasons why strategic futures techniques such as scenarios are not more widely used in business is that, in the wrong hands, they can promise more than they deliver. Futurists sometimes get into this line of work because they are interested in narratives about the future, and forget that scenarios and other futures techniques are simply tools for informing *decisions* about the future.

Business managers, on the other hand, have to show that the work has led to a business development or outcome of some kind; and that it has been a productive use of managers' time. Depending on the purpose of the work, this might be a better, more future-proofed strategy—a new product or marketing innovation, the identification of promising new market opportunities or a better risk management strategy.

Businesses also need a level of confidence that their planned course of action is the best one in the circumstances. Again, this can produce a clash of expectations. Having a futurist explain—even for the best of theoretical reasons—that there are multiple possible futures and that none is more likely than any of the others is not always understood as being helpful. A client of ours, who had sponsored a strategic futures process within her department, admitted at the end that she'd initially expected it to lead to "a lot of intellectual pontificating", and not much else. Thankfully, at the end of the project, she was pleasantly surprised at the level of insight and action-oriented thinking that had been generated through the work.

In practice there are a range of powerful tools, some adapted from management and strategy, to help to reach the stage of an action plan. It's not possible to be prescriptive, since the actual mix of the tools depends on the culture of the organisation, the futures techniques that have been used during the process, and the business issue being addressed. The important thing to keep in mind—especially at the start of the process—is that a futures process needs to have an end as well as a beginning, and that afterwards it will be judged internally more on the quality of the output than on the quality of the input (see Box 8.1).

BOX 8.1 GETTING THE PROJECT OFF ON THE RIGHT FOOTING

There are a number of key lessons that result from the above in order to begin a piece of futures work off on the right footing. For example:

- Be clear on why you're starting the work at the beginning: what business question is being addressed through the strategic futures process, and why?

- Be clear that there is commitment to the process being used—even if it's not fully understood within the business.

- If you hire external support, make sure that they have in hand tools and techniques that can help you to translate the futures insight into outputs that are usable by the business and fit with its processes.

BUILDING SCENARIOS

This section uses the example of a set of Henley Centre scenarios about obesity to show the process that can be involved and the way in which strategic implications can be extracted from scenarios work. The obesity work below is in the public domain (Curry and Kelnar, 2004). The description below starts with framing a futures question, then looks at identifying and prioritising drivers. It then describes the scenarios, and finally explores the way in which strategic implications emerged from the scenarios.

Scenario processes have been described in detail elsewhere in this book. In the obesity scenarios, which were built using a drivers-based scenarios method, we went through six stages.

- First, we defined the question.
- Second, we identified the long list of drivers.
- Third, we filtered the drivers for importance and uncertainty.
- Fourth, we identified a set of axes.
- Fifth, we developed the scenarios.
- Sixth, we tested the scenarios for their strategic and product implications.

Space doesn't enable us to review the process in full here. Instead, we will look at the places where there is specific learning for fast-moving sectors. It's also worth saying that a number of these steps are valuable, even without doing a full-blown piece of scenarios work. For example, the task of identifying possible drivers of change, and then assessing them for importance and uncertainty, can often generate insight on its own, even if the work ends at that point.

However, all futures projects, in our view, benefit from clarity about a 'scoping' question (and we've seen problems when this hasn't been done properly).

Identifying the Question

Futures work typically starts with understanding drivers and trends. There is more discussion below about what we mean by this, and how to assemble an initial list of drivers. But, before starting work, there is an essential first step. Good futures work isn't done in a vacuum; it's about identifying prospective changes in a particular "system". The system is defined by the strategic or policy question being asked by the company or organisation. So a futures project is defined by an initial question, which is the basis of the subject, the scope and the time scale (Exercise 8.1).

For example, a futures question for a company in a fast-moving sector in the UK might be: "How will the shape of demand for soft drinks in the UK change over the next five to eight years?"

EXERCISE 8.1 DESIGNING THE FUTURES QUESTION

To help you to think about the likely scope of a piece of futures work, the first exercise is to design a futures question.

- Write down a futures question that is relevant to your company or organisation (or other body in which you are involved).
- Your question should identify the scope of the work, the geographical area, and the futures time scale (how many years out?) under review.
- Answering the question will be likely to identify interesting or challenging strategic issues for your organisation.
  - — Too general, and the answer will be too broad, and therefore hard to connect to your organisation and its issues.
  - — Too specific, and the answer won't help you to think in a strategic way about your challenges.

The framing question for the obesity scenarios was: "What will increase or reduce the levels of obesity in the UK between now and 2014?"

Working with Trends and Drivers

As with all credible futures work, the best place to start is by understanding the drivers and trends that will influence your world, and the relationships between them. Don't rush to judgement yet about the robustness of your brand, products or strategy in the face of the drivers. That comes later in the process. The first stage is to get to a clear view of the possible changes to the wider environment in which you are operating. You need to understand this better before assessing where your brands and products stand.

Some Definitions

We regard "drivers" as forces or factors that are likely to accelerate or slow down change, in the system defined by the question. Different types of language are used by different futurists. Historically, futurists used to focus on the "big picture" drivers, such as globalisation, increasing affluence, ageing population, and so on. We've found that drivers of change that involve shifts in values, attitudes and behaviour are as important and as revealing as these widely recognised "macro" drivers, since they reflect changes in people's inner and local worlds, and can therefore produce significant and sustainable shifts in behaviour relatively quickly. In addition, the company is more likely to be able to see how to respond to

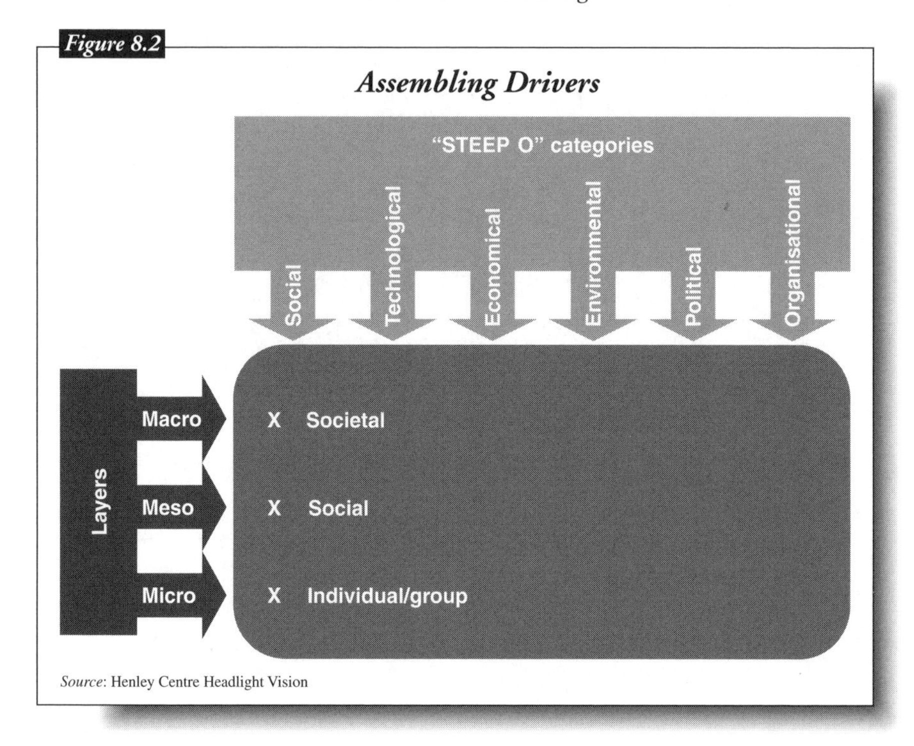

Source: Henley Centre Headlight Vision

these shifts. We often find that the most interesting changes come when drivers at different levels collide.

Typically, when gathering drivers at the start of a project, we'll use a grid, which looks something like that in Figure 8.2.

It looks at social, technological, economical, environmental, political and organisational forces (STEEPO) on the one hand and the impact at different levels on the other. At the macro level of these layers are the "big picture" trends, with their long-term impact. Globalisation might be here, for example, and it is also possible that different expressions of it will be found in the different "STEEPO" categories. "Increasing global competitiveness" might be in the Organisational column; "Increasing influence of multi-lateral organisations" (the World Trade Organisation, for example) might be in the Political column; "Increasing volume of world trade" might be in the Economical column; "Increasing migration" might be in the Social column; and so on.

At the micro or bottom level are changes in individual behaviour, attitudes and values. Thus, in the Social column, we might see "Increasing hostility to 'Brand America' brands", or, in the Economical column, "Increasing visibility of fair trade products".

The meso level, in between, captures group expressions of the drivers. In the Political column, we might see "Rise of Make Poverty History movement", or "Increasing counter-globalisation protests".

Even if drivers seem completely certain, the form in which they are expressed can still be volatile. "Globalisation" can be considered "a fact" (although this is itself controversial), just as the ageing of the European population is "a fact", but the *outcomes* of both of these are very uncertain.

It's also essential to remember that drivers and trends often produce counter-trends, and you also need to be alert to these. It's when trends collide, or combine, that they become interesting, and create turbulence, opportunity and threat. For example, in the obesity project, the long-term drivers that had contributed to the emergence of obesity as a public issue included rising affluence (a macro driver), time shortage (a micro driver) and the rise of convenience culture (a meso driver).

There are, however, counter-trends at all three levels: time shortage leads to individuals feeling short of energy, and being willing to change their lifestyles a little to correct this imbalance, through eating better, exercising more and generally taking better care of themselves (and through drinking enough Red Bull to make its founder a billionaire). Increasing affluence has been matched by an increase in the desire for well-being, which is (at least sometimes) about things that money can't buy.

And two drivers that are more associated with public engagement also come into play: the public health costs of an obese population, and a moral concern (driven by a rights-based public culture) for the prospects of young people who may be big consumers of fast foods, but are clearly poorly informed about the effect of this on their long-term health prospects.

BOX 8.2 DRIVERS, TRENDS AND MANIFESTATIONS

Some people, especially in fast-moving markets, find it more useful to think of drivers as happening at three levels: drivers, trends and manifestations, as in Figure 8.3.

As you move through the layers of drivers, trends and manifestations, you effectively filter them for their relevance to the strategic futures question.

This has disadvantages and advantages. It is easier to link them to the world of consumers, marketing and brand behaviour. (Trends tend to link most closely to factors changing consumer behaviour, while manifestations tend to capture expressions of branding and marketing in response.) On the other hand, it creates a one-way flow of thought, almost too tidy, which means that you can miss some of the bigger changes that are happening, and the connections between them.

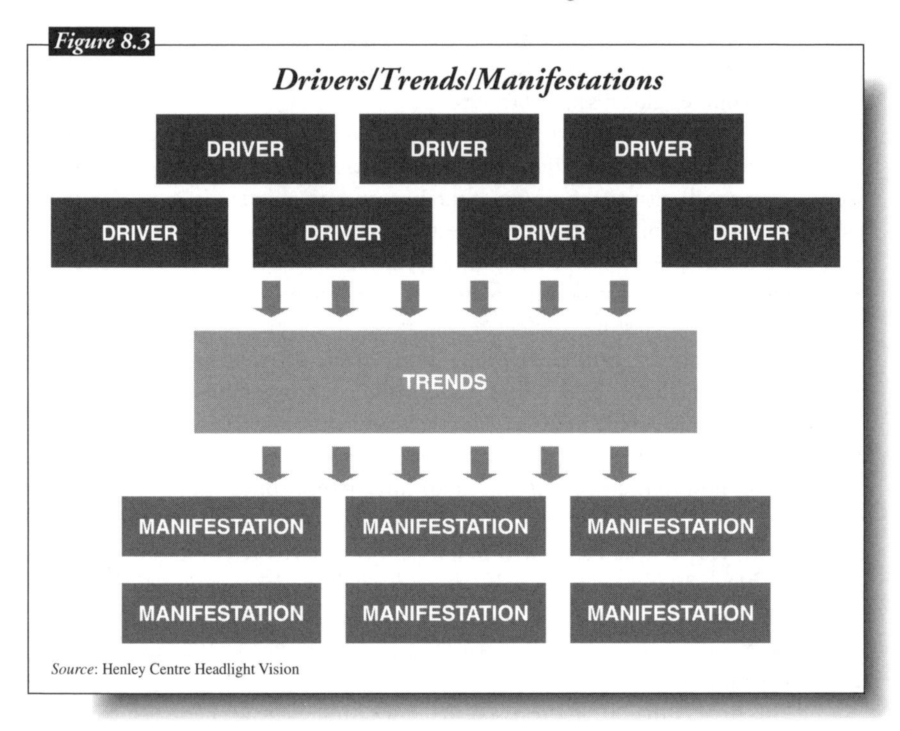

EXERCISE 8.2 THINKING ABOUT THE EXPECTED DRIVERS OF CHANGE–AND THE UNEXPECTED

This exercise is designed to help you to start thinking about drivers of change, and to test the assumptions that are made about change in your business or organisation.

- Draw three columns on a piece of paper.
- In the left-hand column, write down between three and five common assumptions held in your organisation about customers, suppliers or regulators.
- Now, in the middle column, write down drivers or trends that support this assumption.
- In the right-hand column, write down drivers or trends—or other evidence—that might make a challenge to the typical assumptions and to the evidence that is offered to support them.

Here's one example to start you off:

1. ***Assumption***: "You'll never get consumers out of their cars."

2. ***Trends in favour***: Car mileage continues to increase. Rate of increase in the cost of private car use remains much lower than the cost of public transport.

3. ***Possible trends against***: Increasing awareness of connection between car use and climate change, some indication that some consumers are reducing car use because of this, public bodies looking to follow London's example and introduce congestion charges.

In completing this exercise, you may uncover different trends, and counter-trends that could lead to alternative and diverse views of the future—in other words, alternative, but equally plausible, scenarios. Some of these may challenge the most commonly held assumptions in your organisation, and thereby lead to the identification of hitherto unforeseen (and therefore potentially costly) risks, or new (and therefore potentially fruitful) opportunities.

The Scenarios for Obesity

In the project on obesity, the assessment of the drivers led to two axes: "Whose weight is it anyway?" and "Approach to change". (Figure 8.4).

'Whose weight is it anyway?' is about where the responsibility for managing obesity lies. At the "my weight" end of the spectrum, the emphasis is on individual responsibility for weight and lifestyle. There are potential social divisions between those who can afford to help themselves and those who cannot. At the other end of the axis, "our weight" reflects a far greater degree of social responsibility for the obesity problem and for lifestyle issues in general.

On the vertical axis, 'approach to change' is about the speed and depth of response to change. "Quick fix" captures the fast solutions to obesity, at both the individual and social level. Speed increases the likelihood of unintended outcomes. "Slow fix" encapsulates longer term solutions to tackle obesity, which also attempt to address the issues at the level of the system (of which obesity is only a symptom). There are questions here about whether the rate of change is quick enough.

The scenarios are summarised in Figure 8.4. In outline, moving clockwise from the top left, they range from: a future that is dominated by individual short-run consumer and corporate responses to obesity; to a future where political and public intervention is more acute, even if short-termism is still prevalent; then to

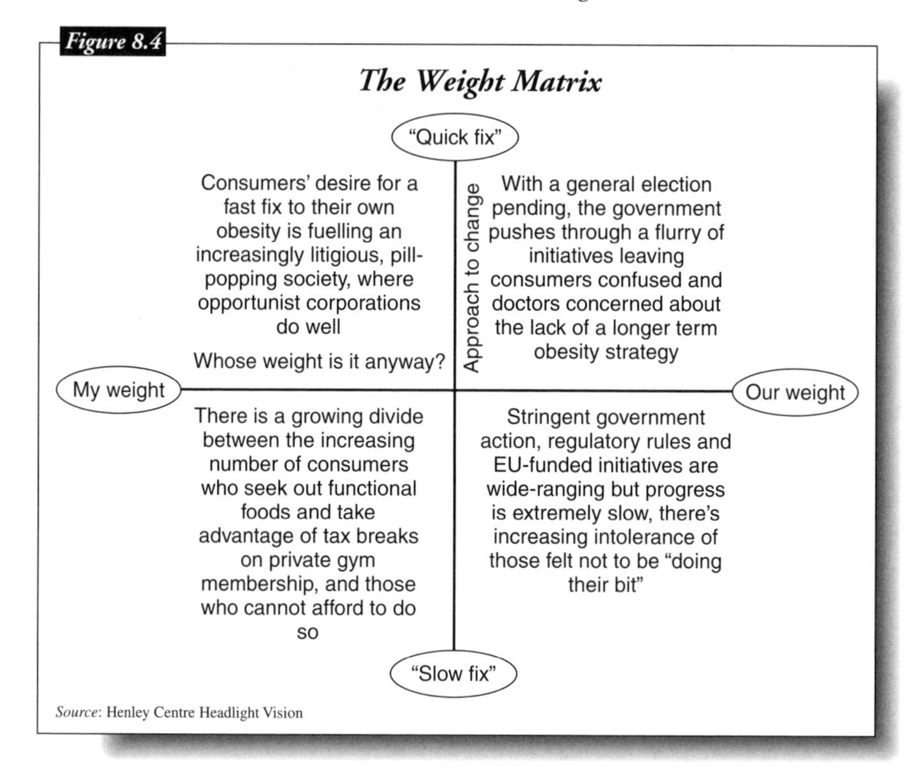

Figure 8.4 ***The Weight Matrix***

Source: Henley Centre Headlight Vision

a future involving sustained political pressure and relatively high degrees of social intervention; and, finally, to a future in which consumer and local activist organisations, including non-governmental organisations (NGOs), use the corporate social responsibility agenda to ensure that companies take a longer term view.

FROM SCENARIOS TO STRATEGIC ASSESSMENT

As we said earlier, the purpose of a scenario set is not simply to develop some interesting stories about the futures; it is to improve clarity about what one has to do in the present. Assessing the strategic implications of a set of scenarios is the most valuable part of the process.

There are two important parts of the strategic assessment. The first is looking across all the scenarios and identifying strategic issues that will emerge no matter which scenario evolves.

The second is looking at each of the scenario spaces as market opportunities and identifying those in which one has a competitive advantage, either actual or potential, and the changes one might have to make (either internally or externally) to sustain that advantage.

The Overall Implications

Quite a long list of overall strategic implications emerged from the assessment of the obesity project. We'll take one here, and explore it a little further.

> *In all of the scenarios, the market is extremely volatile. To prosper, companies will need significant organisational agility.*

If markets are volatile, then companies certainly need to be better at listening to signals from markets and consumers. But one of the reasons for the volatility is because the food and drink market has become politicised, so companies also need to be better at reading political signals, and not just in Whitehall, Brussels, or Washington. Pressure groups need to be on their radar too.

Market volatility is also likely to lead to shorter production runs and a weakening of market control. This would have implications for product development, logistics and production. Some of the innovation possibilities this affords are revealing: if markets are volatile, and there is social and public pressure against fats, salt and other additives, this should create an opening for traditional brands with a simple promise and straightforward provenance (in effect, the strategy that Bird's Eye has adopted). But it also creates opportunities for food brands that aren't good for you; the "nice but naughty" products.

Looking at a Particular Scenario

When looking at a particular set of scenarios, a critical assumption is that it should be possible for a company to make money in any of them, provided it has an appropriate business model, an appropriate brand and the right set of capabilities. It doesn't follow that any one company will prosper across *all* the scenarios; strategy is about choosing what *not* to do, as well as choosing what to do.

To take one of the obesity scenarios as an example of the type of companies that would prosper, the top left quadrant ("quick fix/my weight") conjures a market opportunity where individuals are responsible for their own weight, and products and services to assist them are readily available. Demand for such products may be stimulated by the removal of public services (e.g. health care) from the obese. At the poorer end of the market, customers may be desperate. As with the personal finance market, such a combination will attract both responsible and less responsible providers.

Successful providers who want to retain a public reputation will probably need to offer a combination of products (such as appetite reduction pills) and services (which may involve both interventionist surgery and counselling), and have strict codes of conduct enforced by a producers' association. Success here will require high-quality customer care. Such companies would support charities that helped individuals whose weight-related behaviour was causing them personal or social problems.

WHEN TO USE EXISTING SCENARIO SETS

It is generally not a good idea to pick up a set of scenarios generated for another purpose, and adapt them to your question or your issue. Good scenarios are developed in response to a specific strategic or policy question, and it is often not possible to find out what the question was for an existing set of scenarios.

There are some other problems. It can be difficult to work out which drivers have been left out of the assessment process. The reported accounts of the scenario process are often obscure or opaque about the actual process, so it's hard to be confident about how robust they were. Sometimes the axes are constructed in a way that makes the future worlds rather one-dimensional.

There are, however, exceptions. We have used other scenario sets on occasion for clients who need to stretch their thinking quickly, and need a framework for their challenge or simply want something to use immediately as a creative stimulus for idea generation and innovation.

The types of scenarios that work well for this sort of work are usually generic to a sector or a region, or both. One example is the longer-range Foresight scenarios on "Brain Science, Addiction, and Drugs" (www.foresight.gov.uk), which can be used to test the future of the pharmaceuticals sector (see Andrew Curry's article on www.shapingtomorrow.co.uk).

A similar "framework" set of scenarios which have a direct application for the retail and fast-moving goods sector is the set originally developed for The Store of the Future project by WPP's The Store, with Henley Centre, to understand the future of the retail space. The axes are shown in Figure 8.5. They capture the level of engagement of the supplier on the horizontal axis, and the level of engagement of the consumer, or end customer, on the vertical axis.

- In the top right (high engagement by supplier and customer) one tends to find "identity" retailers such as The Body Shop or L'Occitaine or Lush.

- In the bottom right one sees (high engagement by supplier, low engagement by customer) one finds companies with outstanding logistics but lower customer commitment (leading supermarket chains would be here).

- In the bottom left there are retailers with a functional approach and a price-led proposition (invidious to suggest names).

- In the top left there are, mostly, online spaces, which appear to be highly engaged with their customers, but in fact just build a software frame which is then actively populated by its engaged customers (Amazon is an example).

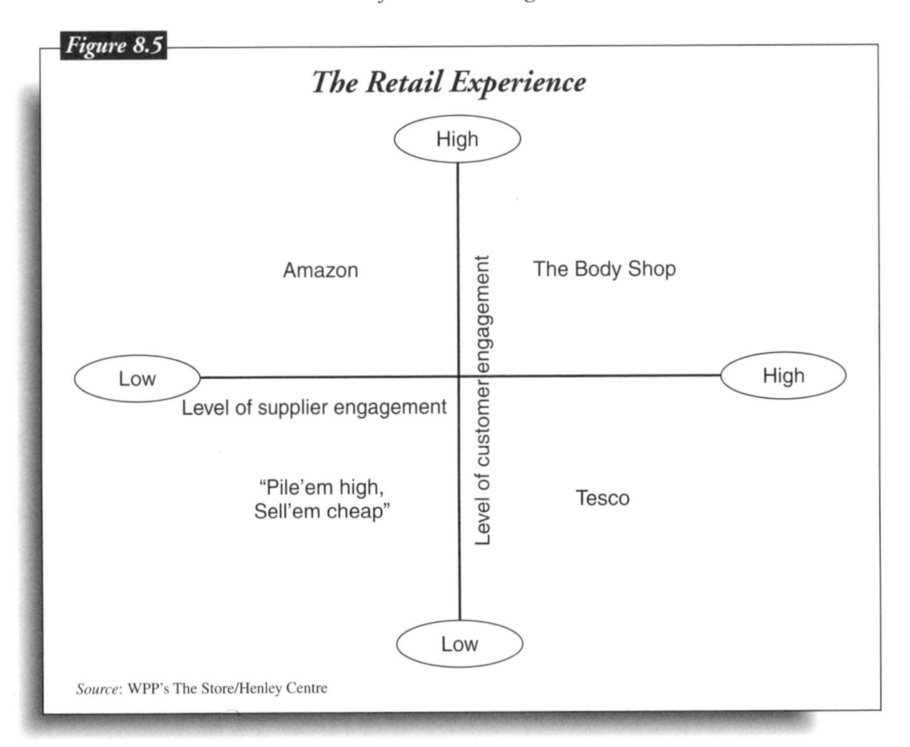

We used this scenario set with a health products firm as the basis for a competitor analysis. It turned out that all the quadrants were densely populated companies in the sector, except for "online" space in the top left. (The internet was less well established then than it is now.) This then led into a discussion of what the barriers were to the development of a proposition in this quadrant, and what capabilities would be required.

EXERCISE 8.3 ASSESSING IMPLICATIONS

This exercise is designed to allow you to practise and understand how scenarios can help you to think through strategic and marketing implications.

- First, take a consumer sector with which you are reasonably familiar.

- Then, populate each quadrant of The Store of the Future scenarios above with examples of companies from that sector which are operating in each quadrant (one or two per scenario).

- Briefly identify how each company positions itself to its customers. What are the important parts of its product and range, and the core capabilities needed for it to ensure continuing success in that quadrant?

- What can your business or organisation learn from one or more of these companies?

Having understood this, you may then want to assess how easy it would be to adapt your existing business model, products, services, overall marketing strategy or brand positioning to take account of the learning from these other companies, to create a new value added proposition.

SNAPSHOTS OF THE FUTURE: CROSS-IMPACT ANALYSIS

Simpler tools can help to get to the kind of insight that is needed when current thinking needs shaking up, or to provide additional stimulus for future innovation or idea generation, as is often the case for fast-moving consumer-facing companies and brands. They can also help to create a basis for thinking about the future within the organisation which opens up the possibility of more rigorous and robust approaches. One such tool is qualitative cross-impact analysis.

Using Qualitative Cross-Impact Analysis to Understand Tourism Innovation

Cross-impact analysis sounds complex—and it certainly was when it was first developed in the 1960 s by the RAND Corporation. It was originally designed as a quantitative mathematical model to calculate the likely probabilities of future events. Qualitative cross-impact analysis is far simpler, although the interpretation can require care.

It does more or less what it says on the tin. If a small group of trends that are relevant to a particular question have been identified, cross-impact analysis is a way to open up the "spaces between the trends" to get to the unpredictable.

We were asked by the UK's Tourism Management Institute to review the critical trends affecting domestic tourism over the next seven years, and help them to identify emerging spaces in the marketplace. The most relevant trends were identified as follows:

- The rise in well-being.

- The increase in the experience economy.

- The rise of "entitlement" (public policy about greater equality of aspiration).
- Changing social structures (social fragmentation, ageing).
- The fragmentation of leisure.
- Increasing awareness of environmental impact.
- The urbanisation of culture (urban renaissance, more technology based culture).
- Increasingly networked society.

We constructed a matrix, with these drivers of change along the side and the top. Each box was filled in by asking the question: "What happens if the driver on the left-hand side impacts on the driver along the top?" Some squares produced uninteresting results. Those that produced recurring themes, or unexpected outcomes, were highlighted for further discussion.

To take two examples: the impact of the experience economy on the urbanisation of culture was summarised as: "The city experience. Urban safari. Trading places for a day." The impact of social fragmentation on experience economy was: "More places to meet. Shared moments. You've got a friend." And so on.

The whole process takes time (all the drivers have to be tallied against all the others, so maybe a few hours), but the work is stimulating. In fact, the analysis itself often provides ideas and stimuli which feed the later discussion.

In the case of domestic tourism, the approach identified four potential areas of innovation, two of which—supported by other analysis in the cross-impact analysis—are hinted at above:

1. ***Naked City (or Urban Safari).*** Experience the city as the natives never do, going deep into its cultures and its subcultures, with expert guides. There's a variant, which is city-as-backdrop to gaming or treasure-hunting experiences, using technology to knit participants together (who may never have met face to face).

2. ***Illicit Pleasures.*** Increasingly there are—and will be more—things that we are not allowed to do in public places. Foxhunting is already on the list. High-noise activities (such as quad biking, for example) are likely to follow. This scenario is about holidays in which private land and locations are used for socially disapproved-of activities.

TABLE 8.1 WHICH TECHNIQUE WHEN?

Technique	Use for	Risks/Disadvantages
Full strategic scenarios	• Corporate strategy/future direction • Systematic risk management • Future proofing major planned investments, and decisions • Analysing key specific more "strategic business" futures and uncertainties—e.g. future of a sector, market, category, brand or business	Time/resource required
Existing scenario sets	• A stretch/challenge to the assumed future/current thinking • Identifying high-level uncertainties for further consideration • Future proofing new products • Analysing strengths vis-á-vis competitors • Analysing future opportunities	Lack of tailoring to specific purpose/ question/uncertainty
Cross Impact Analysis (Qualitative)	• Identifying potential market opportunities—new market spaces, growing market spaces, new brand positioning, new marketing and communications opportunities • A creative stimulus to innovation and ideation—new products, marketing, etc. • Identifying potential risks/blind spots within current strategy	Less systematic risk/strategic analysis

3. ***Deep Peace.*** Well-being taken to its logical conclusion; mental or psychological asceticism is added to the physical cleansing found in spa offers. Location matters; quiet matters; but this may well be combined with learning and personal development.

4. ***Glastonbury without Fences.*** The big free public festival, or public event, likely to be rooted in the distinctive traditions of the place. La Tomatina, in Spain, or the German Oktoberfest, are examples. They're likely to get bigger. They're about celebrating the things that make places distinctive.

The output of a cross-impact process is best thought of as a way to test thinking about possible innovation spaces. It helps you to identify those areas that emerge where trends collide. Once this is done, they still need to be developed further, to be brought to life, and explored to see if they can produce revenue streams, if the organisation is well placed to compete there, and so on.

CONCLUSIONS

People sometimes say they haven't got the time, or the budget, to do futures work. But the cost when corporate projects fail, in terms of both time and money, is enormous. And the literature on this suggests that some of the reasons why projects go wrong are reasons that are addressed by good futures work. The research of the American academic Paul Nutt has analysed the causes of failure of several hundred substantial projects across the commercial, public, and NGO sectors, and suggests that half of all projects fail, and for four main reasons (Nutt, 1999):

- The decision is taken too early, and as a result information that supports the decision is endorsed and the information that doesn't is discounted.

- The context in which the decision is taken is too narrow.

- There is insufficient participation in the decision by employees and partners of the organisation.

- The decision-maker misunderstands how significant stakeholders will respond.

All of the above, in their different ways, are failures of perspective, and they can all be mitigated by futures work. The future is already here, as the science fiction writer William Gibson observed. It's just unevenly distributed. It doesn't take very much effort to find it.

REFERENCES

Berger, G. (1967) *Etapes de la prospective*, PUF, quoted by Michel Godet (2004) *Scenarios and Strategies: A Toolbox for Problem Solving* (3rd issue). LIPSOR.

Curry, A. and Kelnar, R. (2004) *Fat is a Strategic Issue*. Henley Centre; available from Henley Centre Headlight Vision.

Nutt, P. (1999) *"Surprising but true: Half the Decisions in Organizations Fail"*. *Academy of Management Executive*, **13** (4), 75–89.

Schwartz, P. (2003) *Inevitable Surprises*. The Free Press.

NINE
Conclusions

SUMMARY

In this chapter we relate some of the concerns of marketers to the chapters in the book that can help to address them.

Scenario planning has been a tool of corporate planning for some years. It has been used at the top of leading companies, world wide, and as ways for governments to explore the future. The case studies in this book are based on SAMI Consulting's work with their clients, and by many other organisations.

Marketing people are continually debating how they can get board level influence. *Scenario Planning* is a tool with Board appeal. Marketers can gain influence by understanding it and getting involved at Board level.

They can also use it effectively within their own function.

Scenario planning contributes to many aspects of the marketing function in crucial ways, bringing both creativity and discipline: *creativity*, through using the "memories of the future" described in Chapter 1, and explicitly in driving innovation, as in Chapter 4; and *discipline*, through systematically exploring the space of possible futures, as illustrated in Chapter 8.

Scenarios have helped to make strategy more visionary and creative. Marketing can be more motivating and long-term focused using scenarios. Chapter 3 describes the use of scenarios in strategy.

Many marketers have been side-tracked into focusing primarily on cheapness. The real role of marketing is not to "pile 'em high and sell 'em cheap" but to build ongoing relationships with customers, based on shared values and mutual

Scenarios in Marketing. Edited by G. Ringland and L. Young.

trust. Chapter 5 describes the use of scenarios in customer relationship marketing, and Chapter 7 discusses possible futures for marketing communications.

Scenarios should appeal to marketing people, as they are challenging, visionary and stimulate creativity. It may be that some of the glamour of media can be overlaid on the scenarios process—for example, in developing screenplay and even "soaps". Chapters 4 and 8 describe the use of media in scenarios work.

Scenarios can be useful in developing brand strategy. They can be used, for instance, to test the sustainability of a mega-brand (McDonalds, Nestlé) compared with product or segment brands (as favoured by Unilever, Aviva, etc.) in different future marketplaces. Chapter 6 discusses the use of scenarios in valuing brands.

Scenarios can be used with focus groups to test reactions to different products in varying future contexts. Focus groups tend to assume that the future will be substantially similar to the present. The use of scenarios, as described in Chapter 1, to create physical environments, helps to focus groups to "live" in the future.

Marketing thrives on differentiation in competitive markets. Too often the "marketing mix" choices follow the herd, e.g. price cuts. Scenarios can uncover a wider range of choices than those perceived by competitors, facilitating customer preference and longer term relationships. Scenarios explore uncertainty and can help to anticipate and allay the deeper concerns of customers. The use of scenarios in fast-moving sectors is discussed in Chapter 8.

In conclusion, we hope that you find this book helpful. If you do, tell your friends—if not, please tell the joint editors, Gill Ringland or Laurie Young.

APPENDIX ONE

Building Scenarios

Scenario planning has been a tool of corporate planning for many years. It has been done at the top of leading companies, world wide, and as ways for governments to explore the future.

Marketing people see themselves as one rung down from this level and are continually debating how they can get board level influence. Scenario Planning is a tool with Board appeal. Marketers can gain influence by understanding it and getting involved. They can also use it effectively within their own function.

The process described in this appendix is extracted from Scenario Planning (2nd edition), by Gill Ringland. The process it describes is generic across a range of time scales and type of project when major decisions are to be made based on them. Chapter 8 discusses when to build scenarios and when to use existing, prebuilt scenarios and Chapter 4 (on innovation) describes a workshop approach to "quick build".

The generic scenario process is divided into five stages:

1 Project Startup

It is fair to say that this stage is the most crucial for a project's success. Matters agreed at this stage should include:

- Appointment of an Advisory Board in the client organisation, to discuss the project as it proceeds: and in addition the formal reporting requirements for

Scenarios in Marketing. Edited by G. Ringland and L. Young.

budget and progress. These should be documented and copied to all team members.

- Defining the scope of the project (topic, time scale).
- Definition of the team. We prefer to work in a joint team with the client, to ensure transfer of learning.
- Appointment of a Project Manager, a Client Manager and a Technical Consultant with separate roles—for budget and time scale, to keep the client informed, and to advise on methods.
- A realistic timetable needs to be set depending on the time available from team members, reporting requirements, Board meetings, etc.
- Agree a format for exchange of documents, Powerpoint slides, etc., and categorise information sources already to hand (hard copy, web portals, data sources, e.g. OECD).
- A one-day walk through of the stages of the project for the entire team to ensure that everybody understands the role of each stage of the process.

It is also desirable to have an event—even if only a lunch with a briefing—to "launch" the project.

Figure A1.1

The Typical Overall Process

Step 1 Month 1	Step 2 Months 2–4	Step 3 Month 5	Step 4 Month 6	Step 5 Month 8
Startup:	Diagnosis:	Issues (expert) Workshops:	Scenarios Workshop:	Options:
Scope Team Budget Time scale Reporting Information exchange	Interviews Analysis Synthesis Research Feedback	External Market Internal	Trends Uncertainties Clusters Names Storylines Timelines	Triage: "just do it" More work No Action plan Feedback
Launch				Team celebrate

Reproduced by permission of SAMI consulting.

2 Diagnosis, or Identifying the Focal Issue

Interviews

After the client has specified the scope of the scenarios, for instance the insurance industry in 2010, the foundation of the process is interviews of respondents, chosen by the client for their knowledge of the area to be studied, and for the likelihood that they will have meaningful insights into the forces shaping its future. The interviews should encompass all the important constituencies within the client organisation and reach external participants whose contribution may be important both individually and as a whole.

We often recommend an initial pilot study. In a pilot study there should be at least 12 interviews to create a meaningful range of issues; a complete study will typically have some 40/60 interviews.

Interviews are carried out using SAMI's "Seven Questions" technique (Table A1.1), which is very open-ended and flexible, leaving the respondents to set their own agendas. The questions can also be used with groups, or using electronic bulletin boards. These questions provoke the interviewees to "know what they did not know they knew".

The need to ensure that the rich harvest of material is captured fully and accurately makes the use of two interviewers advisable. One is normally from the client, to give continuity. Interviews will last as long as the respondents wish. It is normal to allow about 11/2 hours as some respondents will produce their deepest thoughts late in an interview—the thoughts are unattributable—see below.

Analysis

Once a small number of interviews have been completed the issues within the material will be brought out and ordered for further processing. This is done by preparing a 'trial agenda' of issues, ordered within three main areas:

- external issues
- the business interface
- internal issues.

Each item in the 'trial agenda' will be numbered so that interview scripts can be broken down into the appropriate item number. When the 'trial agenda' has been stabilised it becomes the 'natural agenda' for the study.

When all the interview scripts have been marked up, they can be sorted by computer to produce a breakdown of the interview material under 'natural agenda' headings. When sorting, all respondent names are removed to ensure that views are not attributed to individuals.

TABLE A1.1 SEVEN QUESTIONS

Start with an invitation to the contributor to talk about what he/she sees as "important for the future of the enterprise". When he/she finishes speakup, use the questions as a set of "triggers".

Over a relevant time horizon:

1 Clairvoyant

If you could spend some time with someone who knew the outcome, a clairvoyant or oracle if such existed, what would you want to know? (i.e. what are the critical issues?)

2 An Optimistic Outcome

Optimistic but realistic. If things went well, how would you expect the organisation to perform and what would be the signs?

3 A Pessimistic Outcome

How could the environment change to make things more difficult? How could the organisation itself go wrong?

4 The Internal Situation

From your knowledge of the culture, organisation, systems and resources (including people), how would these have to be changed to achieve the optimistic outcome?

5 Looking Back

How did the organisation get to where it is today?

6 Looking Forward

What decisions need to be made in the near term to achieve the desired long-term outcome?

7 The Epitaph

If you had a mandate, without constraints, what more would you need to do?

Synthesis

The report containing the material sorted under the 'natural agenda' is examined to:

- identify the higher order issues underlying the interview scripts;
- pull out conflicting views on issues (for further exploration);
- find memorable quotations to use in workshops and reports;
- reveal significant gaps in the material (for further interviews or research).

The process of synthesis will also begin to reveal the relative importance of different issues in the minds of respondents. This pattern should not be taken "at face value" but may indicate where further evidence is needed or where challenge should be directed.

Desk Research

It will often be useful to use a range of sources, working from the clients' information base or external data via the web, to establish some reference points relating to trends in the external world and the competitive environment.

Feedback

The results of the first stage will be discussed with the clients in order to clarify arrangements for the first conference/workshop, the Issues Workshop. This workshop will examine the issues identified so far, and modify or prioritise the factors considered.

3 Issues Workshops

These workshop(s) have the overall purpose of forcing the teams' thinking into the future by:

- testing the areas of the 'natural agenda' that are likely to have a crucial role in shaping the future;
- understanding the limits to which key factors may be stretched;
- debating key issues about which conflicting evidence has emerged in the interviews;
- identifying and exploring the potential interaction between key factors emerging from the synthesis;
- drawing out the implications for the client organisation of the threats and opportunities emerging from the process, leading to the identification of strategic options;
- identifying further areas where additional research is needed.

The number of Issues Workshops needed will depend on the scope and complexity of the interview material. Issues Workshops are usually focused on related groups of issues under a generic heading, e.g. economic performance, marketing, culture, environment, technology, human resources, trading restraints, etc.

It is useful to plan the sequence of workshops so that the external issues lead on to market issues and both end with internal issues, e.g. starting with economic issues and finishing with internal self-renewal.

4 Development of Scenarios

After the Issues Workshop(s) the forces shaping the future, and those impeding change, will be clearer and the building blocks of scenarios will emerge. New areas for additional research or interviews will also emerge. Finally, a set of factors will become stable as the set to be used in the scenarios.

Some of these factors will be trends, such as demographic or technological factors that form part of any scenario. Others may be factors for decision or factors outside the organisation's control—for instance: Is our business global (which parts, how far), or local/regional?

A Scenarios Workshop is used to bring together a client team to create scenarios. The steps are:

- Sort the factors and rank, using, for instance, the matrix in Figure A1.2.
- Examine the causalities and connections between factors.
- Cluster the factors into as few building blocks as reflects the scope of the study.
- Look for a few combinations of clusters that provide internally consistent and viable futures. These are the scenarios.
- The scenarios should ideally include one ***"Business as Usual"*** or ***"Official Future"***. Others may be "as good as it gets", and one or more scenarios probing elements of change challenging the organisation.
- Where scenarios are not stable it will be necessary to identify possible migration paths and time scales that they may follow to find stability.

The scenarios detail the characteristics of alternative futures and indicate the conditions that may bring them about. They will normally be described through a storyline, possibly with accompanying environmental, competitive or internal data, e.g. "In this scenario, the company grows its labour force by 25% per year". Early indicators of each scenario will be looked for, to identify aspects of each scenario that could be visible soon or even now.

The scenarios will provide significant guidance for shaping policy and, for businesses, to help both to craft strategies and to test them for robustness against different futures.

Figure A1.2

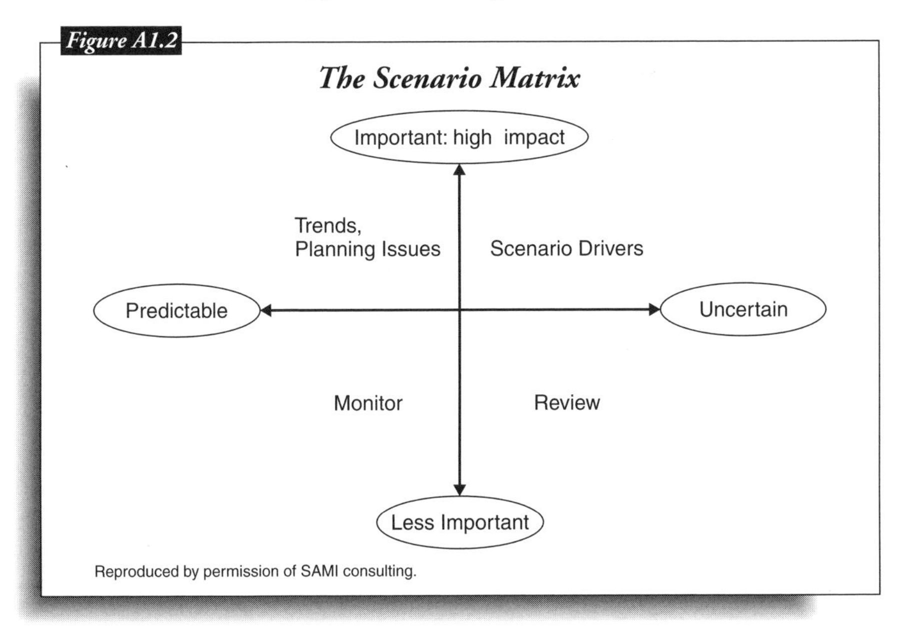

Reproduced by permission of SAMI consulting.

5 Investigation, Development and Evaluation of Strategic Options

The client will probably already be considering a set of strategic options, and the scenarios may suggest additional options. These are often captured in brainstorming mode as part of the Scenarios Workshop. Some may be aligned to only one scenario; others may span two or more.

In evaluating the viability of options for an organisation, it is important to consider both the competitive position of the organisation—can it set a new agenda? And the culture—is it entrepreneurial and risk-taking, or defensive as befits a fast follower? Options chosen by an organisation would tend to be:

- ***Planning in Line with the Most Probable Scenario***
  - Fast follower
  - Organisations not dominant in their market
- ***Planning in Line with the Worst Scenario(s) for the Organisation***
  - Defensive culture
- ***Staying Flexible until a Scenario Emerges, as Evidenced by Early Indicators***
  - Fast follower

- ***Planning in Line with the Best Scenario(s) for the Organisation***
  - Entrepreneurial culture
- ***Planning to Increase the Likelihood of the Best Scenario(s) for the Organisation***
  - Organisations dominant in their market

All organisations, whatever their culture, benefit from more robust planning once they have explored their options under a number of scenarios, and made informed choices. The alternative is driving with a firm view in the rear view mirror, running the risk of going over the cliff.

A fuller description of the process and a wide range of case studies are found in *Scenarios for Business*, ISBN 0-470-84382-9, or *Scenarios for Public Policy*, ISBN 0-470-84383-7 or *Scenario Planning* (2nd edition), ISBN 0-470-01881-X.

APPENDIX TWO
Marketing Tools and their Use with Scenarios

Like other professionals, marketing specialists use a range of concepts, models and tools in their work. Some have their roots in economics, some in corporate strategy and some in historical management fads. This appendix, contributed by Laurie Young, contains descriptions of a number of marketing tools and shows how each can be used with scenario planning techniques. It does not attempt to be an exhaustive review of all the techniques to which marketers can resort nor does it attempt to provide a detailed description, or critique, of each one. It is simply an indication of ways in which scenario techniques might work on the functional level of marketing activities.

ANSOFF'S MATRIX

Application: Strategy Development

1 The Tool

The, now, classic representation of Ansoff's matrix is reproduced as Figure A2.1. It suggests that firms distill their strategic options by focusing their thinking through a review of existing markets, new markets, existing products and new products. As such it is a useful simplification to help leaders to reach consensus during strategy debates.

However, Ansoff's original representation of the concept (Ansoff, 1957) was more sophisticated and was designed to examine diversification options at the corporate level. His work was based on analysis of the diversification activity by American businesses in the first half of the twentieth century. He suggested

Scenarios in Marketing. Edited by G. Ringland and L. Young.

Figure A2.1

The Ansoff Matrix

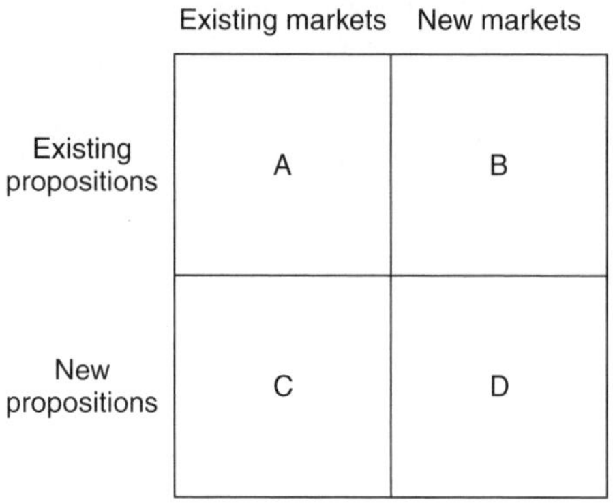

	Existing markets	New markets
Existing propositions	A	B
New propositions	C	D

Source: Ansoff (1957). Reprinted by permission of Harvard Business Review. From "Strategies for diversification" by I. Ansoff, Sept/Oct. Copyright © 1957 by the Harvard Business School Publishing Corporation, all rights reserved.

that there were two key bases for diversification, which he made the axes of his diagram. They were:

- ***Product Lines.*** Referring to both the physical characteristics of the product and its performance characteristics.

- ***Markets.*** For the sake of this analysis he referred to markets as "product missions" rather than buyer segments. By this he meant "all the different market alternatives" or the various uses for the product and its potential uses.

He proposed his matrix as a way of constructing different "product–market" strategies; those "joint statements of a product line and the corresponding set of missions which the products are designed to fulfil". His original diagram is reproduced in Figure A2.2 (π represents the product line and μ the "missions"). Interestingly, this representation of his work puts less stress on market penetration than the popularly used version and details the many strategic options that arise from thinking broadly about the fusion of product and market possibilities.

2 Constructing the Tool

The first step in constructing the tool is analysis of product and market opportunities. This may begin with a simple list of all the existing product/market groups in which the company is established. Then, using market reports, client research and internal brainstorming, it is possible to identify the other opportunity areas.

Figure A2.2

Ansoff's Original Format

Markets / Products	μ_0	μ_1	μ_2 - - -	- - - - - - - - -	- - - μ_x
π_0	Market penetration	← Market development →			
π_1	Product development ↓				
π_2			Diversification		
⋮					
π_x					

Source: Ansoff (1957). Reprinted by permission of Harvard Business Review. From "Strategies for diversification" by I. Ansoff, Sept/Oct. Copyright © 1957 by the Harvard Business School Publishing Corporation, all rights reserved.

Once the analysis is available, the options can either be summarised, using judgement, into the simplified version of the tool or crafted into a more thorough analysis by creating a cell for each product/market match, using the original version. The opportunities can either be discussed by the leaders at this stage or prioritised using agreed criteria. Ansoff himself recommended that, due to the risk and cost involved, firms conduct risk analysis of the more likely strategies. The most acceptable programmes should then be developed into full product, marketing and business plans.

3 Use of the Tool

The matrix helps leaders to think through four different growth strategies, which require different marketing and communications approaches. They are presented below in ascending order of risk:

- Strategy A is ***Market penetration***, or increasing market share with existing propositions to current markets.

- Strategy B is ***Market extension*** or market development, targeting existing propositions at new markets.

- Strategy C is ***Product development***, developing new propositions for existing segments.

- Strategy D is ***Diversification***, growing new businesses with new propositions for new markets

The matrix helps to clarify leaders' thinking and to illustrate the very different strategic approaches needed for each of the four strategies. Ideally, an operational marketing plan should be constructed for each strategic option that is finally approved.

4 Ansoff's Matrix and Scenario Planning

Scenario planning can be used with Ansoff's matrix in three ways. Firstly, if corporate scenarios exist it can be used to assess the risk of each one and to construct relevant marketing strategies. Corporate scenarios can also be used as frameworks within which to identify the potential products and markets. They can act as a constraint, or framework for, the opportunities to be identified.

Secondly, scenarios can be generated by the marketing function based on market research and competitive trends. These can then be used as frameworks within which to develop and test product/market alternatives.

Finally, the matrix can be compiled as Ansoff intended, with a broad, creative view of all product/market alternatives. They can then be reduced into manageable groups by combining them into possible market scenarios.

ARR MODEL

Application: Relationship Marketing

1 The Model

The "actors–activities–resources" model was developed (Figure A2.3) during the early 1980s, by researchers and theorists interested in both business-to-business marketing and network marketing (Hakansson and Snehota, 1995). Yet it appears to be a tool that can also be used in practical marketing within a normal business as well as just pure theoretical research.

The model divides business relationships into three layers:

- ***Actor Bonds.*** These occur when two business people interact through some professional process. Theorists suggest that there are three components necessary for them to develop. The first is reciprocity during the process, ensuring that both sides give something to the interaction, even if one is a buyer. The second is commitment and the third is trust. As people interact they form perceptions of each other about: capability, limitations, commitment and trust. If the relationship develops these perceptions influence the degree

Figure A2.3

The ARR Model

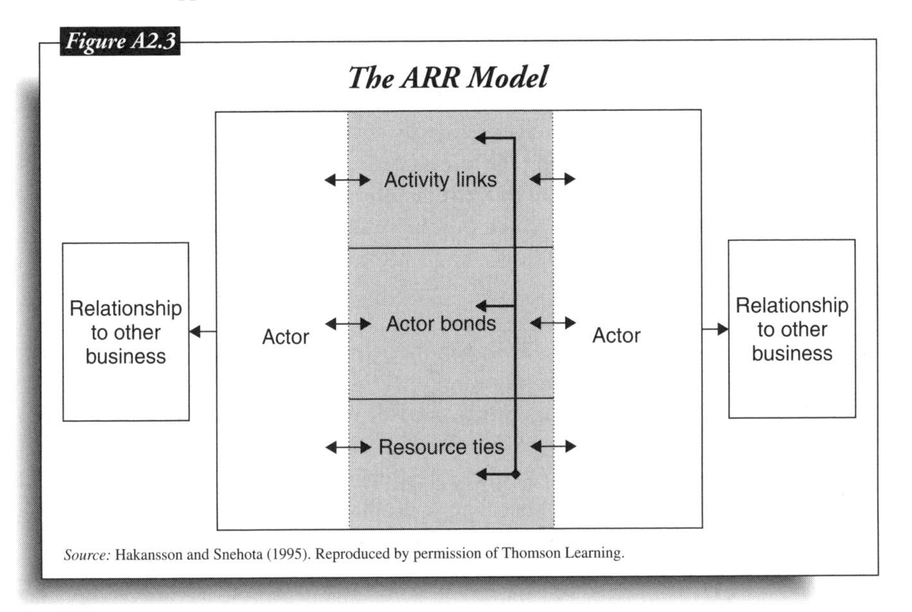

Source: Hakansson and Snehota (1995). Reproduced by permission of Thomson Learning.

and clarity with which the two communicate; and also the degree to which they involve each other in their own professional network. So, for account managers, the way in which they conduct their work influences the trust their customer develops in them and the degree to which they will be invited further into the buyer's organisation, and thus into the possibility of further work.

- ***Activity Links*** capture the work, or other activity, which is involved in the interaction and business process. These vary with the depth of relationship. They range from simple technical projects through to two firms meshing or adapting their systems and business processes to become more efficient. The latter has created exciting business opportunities in areas such as outsourcing.

- ***Resource Ties*** are items used by people during business interactions. Resources might include: software, intellectual capital, skilled staff, knowledge, experience and expertise. People who have resources, or control over them, have greater power in professional networks.

2 Constructing the Model

At its very simplest the model can be used as a basis for discussion with internal colleagues to map relationships in a network. Account managers can be asked to complete formats of their customer relationships using the three levels of the model. Actions arising from discussion (e.g. creating more opportunities for non-task-related exchange or making different resources, such as knowledge available) to strengthen relationships can be put into account plans.

However, the model can be used as a basis of detailed analysis and research. A hypothesis of the professional relationships that exist in a market, and the types of interaction, can be created using the terms of the model. The model can then be used as a guide to designing the research sample and questionnaires. A two-step, qualitative and quantitative research process is likely to reveal powerful insights into the relationships that customers have with the firm and its competitors.

3 Use of the Model

The thinking behind the model will seem intuitively correct to many in sales and marketing. This is its strength, capturing, as it does, the day-to-day experience of many staff. It allows a firm, when needed, to use a common process and terminology in its approach to relationship management. However, it also introduces (perhaps for the first time) a reasonably robust mechanism whereby professionals can analyse and understand in detail what many recognise to be their most important approach to market: relationships with customers.

4 Use of Scenarios with the Model

This model is relatively new and there is little evidence of it being used with scenarios. It could certainly be used, though, within corporate scenarios that set directions in which accounts should be developed. It might also be used as a basis on which to develop scenarios of different segments of customers.

BOSTON MATRIX

Application: Analysis of Business Portfolios

1 The Tool

One of the best known portfolio management tools is the Boston Consulting Group's growth share matrix (Figure A2.4) which was developed around the concept of "the experience curve" (BCG, 1968). The consultancy demonstrated that, over time, companies specialising in an area of expertise became more effective in their market, reducing costs and gaining competitive advantage. A company might be at various points on the experience curve, depending on its maturity and the accumulated investment in its prime area of focus. The ***Boston Matrix***, which plots relative market share against relative growth, was an attempt to give corporate strategic planners a way of evaluating different business units in different markets.

2 How to Construct It

First, the annual growth rate of each business unit, in each market, is calculated. This is plotted on the matrix, depending on whether its growth is high or low.

Figure A2.4

The Boston Matrix

Market growth	High relative market share	Low relative market share
High	"Star" • Defend leadership • Accept moderate short-term profit and negative cash flow • Consider geographic expansion • Consider line expansion • Aggressive marketing posture • Price for market share	"Question mark" • Invest heavily in selective businesses • As for "rising star"
Low	"Cash cow" • Maintain market position • Cut less successful lines • Differentiate to maintain share of key segments • Limit discretionary marketing expenditure	"Dog" • Prune aggressively • Maximise cash flow • Minimise marketing expenditure • Maintain or raise prices at the expense of volume

Source: BCG (1968). Reprinted by permission of The Boston Consulting Group.

(*Note*: The horizontal axis of the matrix is not positioned at zero on the vertical axis but at 10%.) Secondly, the relative market share of each unit is calculated and plotted on the matrix. The turnover of each unit is then represented by appropriately sized circles.

The portfolio of business units is then categorised by the matrix into four groups:

- The ***question marks*** (otherwise called "problem children" or "wild cats") have low market share in high growth markets. A business which has just started operations would be a "question mark" because the ability of the management team to improve on its competence would be unproven. These are businesses with long-term potential that may have been recently launched and are being bought primarily by buyers who are willing to experiment. They need large amounts of cash if they are to be developed to their full potential because the company has to keep adding plant, equipment and personnel to keep up with the fast-growing market.

- The ***rising star*** is a company that has established itself in the market and is beginning to thrive. It is a leader, with high share in a high growth market. It requires significant investment in order to maintain and grow market share. It does not necessarily produce a positive cash flow but stars are usually profitable and can become "cash cows".

- The ***cash cows*** are companies that are well established and profitable. They have high share in low growth markets. They are producing profit but are unlikely to achieve much incremental improvement. They are generally cash positive and can be used to fund other initiatives.

- The final group are known as ***dogs***; they have low share in low growth markets. These are companies who are in decline and worthy of withdrawal. They have weak market share in low growth markets and tend to be loss-makers, providing small amounts of cash if any.

3 Use of the Tool

The matrix can be used to determine strategy for major firms. A multi-business company needs a balanced portfolio of businesses or SBUs (strategic business units) which use cash from the cash cows to invest in other development issues. It is thought that an unbalanced portfolio of businesses can be classified into four areas:

- Too many losers causing poor cash flow.
- Too many question marks requiring too much investment.
- Too many profit producers.
- Too many developing winners.

The matrix is used to develop different business strategies and corporate requirements for each business unit according to its position on the matrix. Objectives, profit targets, investment constraints and even management style are likely to be different according to their position. Strategies set by the leadership are likely to include:

- ***Build***. This means increasing the market share using cash, resources, marketing programmes and management attention.

- ***Hold***. This means maintaining the market share and is appropriate for strong cash cows if they are to continue to yield cash.

- ***Harvest***. This means using resources to get as much cash from a business unit as is possible regardless of long-term effect. It is appropriate for weakening cash cows whose future is uncertain or dim.

- ***Divest***. This means selling or liquidating the business, and is appropriate for dogs and question marks that are acting as a drag on company resources.

Due to inadequate teaching and lack of understanding, some companies have tried to use this conceptual framework to understand the positioning of their individual products or services rather than business units. Managers can be heard to talk of their offers as either being a "cash cow" or a "dog". This misuse of the concept is dangerous because it muddles two different concepts (the experience curve of a business and the product life cycle).

4 Use of Scenarios with the Tool

Properly constructed, the ***Boston Matrix*** gives an objective view of relative position because it is based on actual share and growth figures. It is in the deduction of strategies that there is opportunity to combine it with scenario work. Having decided that a business is, say, a rising star, the marketing team can create scenarios that predict its trajectory. It may decline fast or grow into a cash cow, for instance. The view taken will determine the level and style of investment in the business.

THE CULTURAL WEB

Application: Change Management

1 The Tool

The Johnson and Scholes cultural web (Figure A2.5) identifies the elements of an organisation that need to be taken into account when planning major strategic change (see also Johnson and Scholes, 2004). They are:

- The ***paradigm***. This is the way the organisation views the world. It may have a number of facets such as the sector or segment on which it concentrates, its products or its competitors.

- ***Organisational Structure***. This is the way people interrelate in the firm.

- ***Power Structures***. This acknowledges the authority that people have in the organisation and how they use it. It covers both formal and informal power.

- ***Control Systems***. These are built into the structure of the firm to ensure that objectives are met. They might be processes, systems or measures.

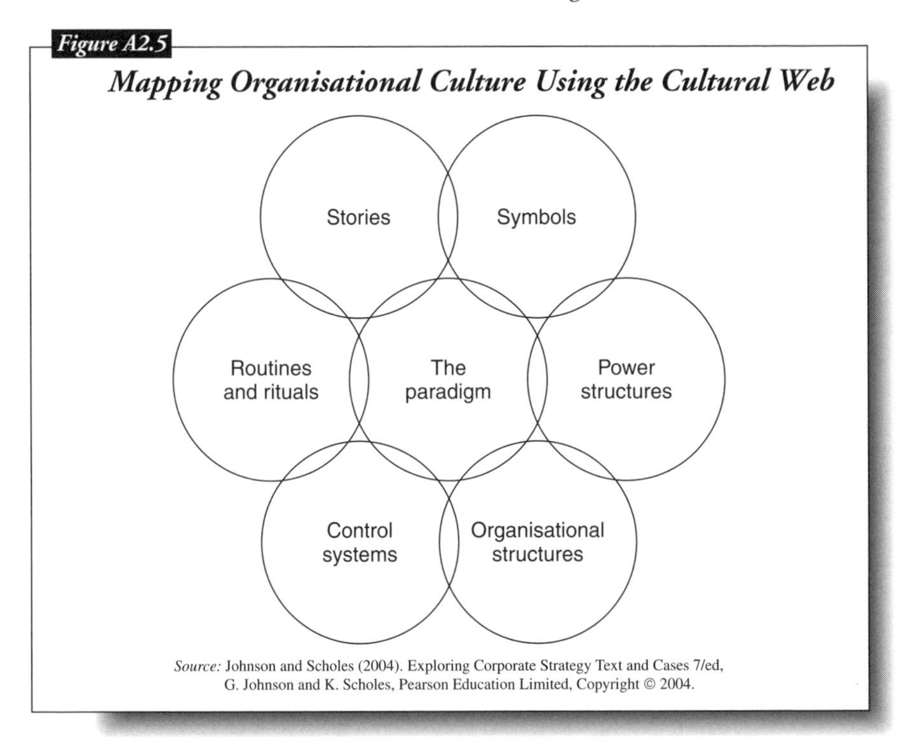

- ***Routines and Rituals***. These may not be overtly described by the firm or part of its acknowledged policies, but they can be very powerful nonetheless. Very often they are the real functions of the organisation.

- ***Symbols***. These are physical evidence of past victories, failures, moments of history or power. They are very influential and can cause deep emotion to be stirred.

- ***Stories***. These circulate in an organisation and affect behaviour.

2 Constructing the Tool

The tool is best configured using internal interviews. Employees can either be shown the tool and asked to contribute, or interviewed on a range of subjects to reveal the components of the web.

3 Use of the Tool

The tool can be used to plan major change programmes, internal communication campaigns and internal marketing. The components of the web indicate the full range of activities that need to be considered if change or communications are to be effective.

4 Use of the Tool with Scenarios

As the cultural web is a tool for major strategic change, it fits well with use of scenarios. Corporate scenarios which require major strategic change can be developed into stories and communication programmes that influence all aspects of the web. The rich pictures created in scenarios can be easily built into clear reasons to change and visions of where the business is headed.

DIRECTIONAL POLICY MATRIX

Application: Business Portfolio Tool

1 The Tool

Another well-known product portfolio technique is the ***Directional Policy Matrix*** (Figure A2.6) developed by McKinsey for its client GE. This was developed soon after the Boston matrix as a result of inadequacies with it. It was typical of several methods of "multifactor portfolio models" which were developed at the time.

This is a way of categorising businesses against markets and is more flexible than the Boston Matrix because it uses criteria created by the management team themselves. As such it is more relevant to the individual strategic position of the company in its marketplace. The grid plots "market attractiveness" against "business strength" and allows management to prioritise resources accordingly.

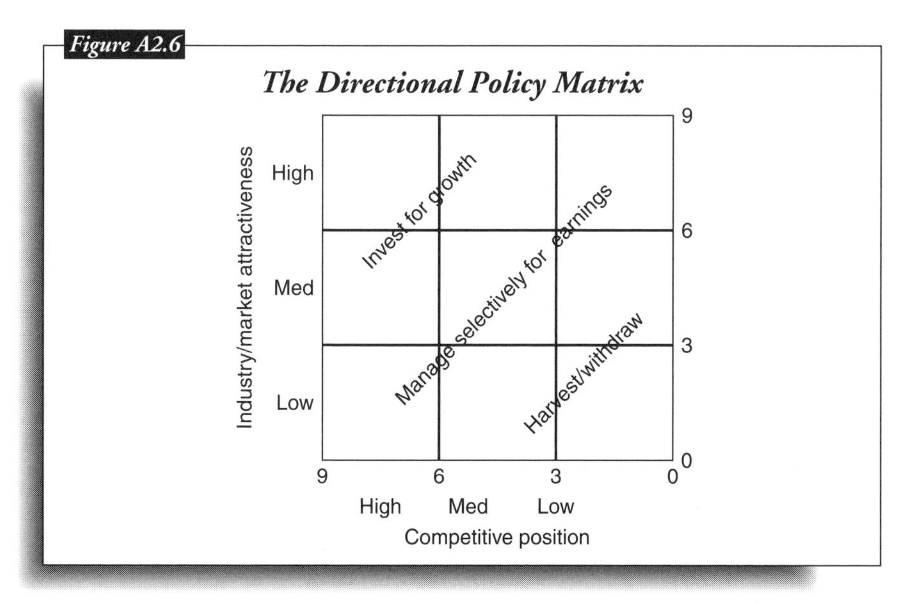

TABLE A2.1 FACTORS OF MARKET ATTRACTIVENESS AND BUSINESS STRENGTH USED IN THE ORIGINAL GE MATRIX

Market attractivencess	Business strength
Size	Size
Growth rates	Growth rate
Competitive intensity	Market share
Profitability	Profitability
Technology impact	Margins
Social impacts	Technology position
Environmental impacts	Strengths and weaknesses
Legal impacts	Image
Human impacts	Environmental impact
	Management

The original GE matrix used the factors of market attractiveness and business position, which are listed in Table A2.1. GE used these key factors because they believed that, taken together, they had the most influence on return on investment. However, this list should be modified for each company according to its own particular circumstances.

2 Constructing the Matrix

There are clear steps in compiling the matrix. They are:

- Identify the strategic business units (SBUs).
- Determine the factors contributing to market attractiveness.
- Determine factors contributing to business position.
- Rank and rate the market attractiveness and business position features.
- Rank each SBU.
- Plot the SBUs on the matrix.
- Represent the total size of the market and the businesses share by a pie chart at the appropriate plot on the matrix.

The two ranking steps involve numerically rating the relative importance of each feature. Multiplying these together and totalling them for each business unit gives a composite score which enables the matrix to be compiled. The total size of each market in which the firm's businesses operate, and their share of each, can be represented by a pie chart centred on each plot. As with the growth/share matrix, the visual presentation enables complex information to be presented in an easily understood form.

3 Use of the Tool

Strategy can be deduced from the matrix as follows:

- Where a business unit scores high or medium on business strength or market attractiveness the firm should maintain or grow investment.
- Those that score low/low or low/medium should have investment depleted. If possible, cash should be harvested from them.
- Units scoring high/low or medium/medium should be examined to see if selective investment should be made to increase earnings.

There has been some critical evaluation of the GE matrix. Many people consider the fact that it uses several dimensions to assess business units instead of two, and because it is based on ROI rather than cash flow, it is a substantial improvement on the Boston matrix. However it is criticised because:

- It offers only broad strategy guidelines with no indication as to precisely what needs to be done to achieve strategy.
- There is no indication of how to weight the scoring of market attractiveness and business strengths. As such it is highly subjective.
- Evaluation of the scoring is also subjective.
- The technique is more complex than the Boston matrix and requires much more extensive data gathering.
- The approach does not take account of interrelationships between business units.
- It is not supported by empirical research or evidence. For instance, there does not seem to be evidence that market attractiveness and business position are related to ROI.
- It pays little attention to the business environment.

It is really powerful, however, as a tool to reach consensus among a group of business leaders. The definition of business units, the agreement of common criteria and, particularly, the joint scoring exercise stimulate debate, which can be very valuable.

4 Use of the Tool with Scenarios

This tool works very well with scenarios. If corporate scenarios have been developed, they can be used as a context for scoring. The scenarios will influence the judgement of those creating the matrix, affecting the scoring and the judgement of business unit success.

The tool is particularly good at dramatising the future direction of businesses. The marketing team can turn market analysis into future scenarios and these can be superimposed on the matrix to predict the likely business direction. Strategy and investment can be deduced from this.

EXPERIENCE CURVE

Application: New Service Development, Competitive Strategy

1 The Tool

This concept, pioneered particularly by the Boston Consulting Group during the early 1960s, suggests that unit costs of a firm fall with experience of operating in an industry and with a company's cumulative volume of production (Figure A2.7). The consultancy invested substantial time into research on many industries (including service industries) and used "the scientific method" to validate the

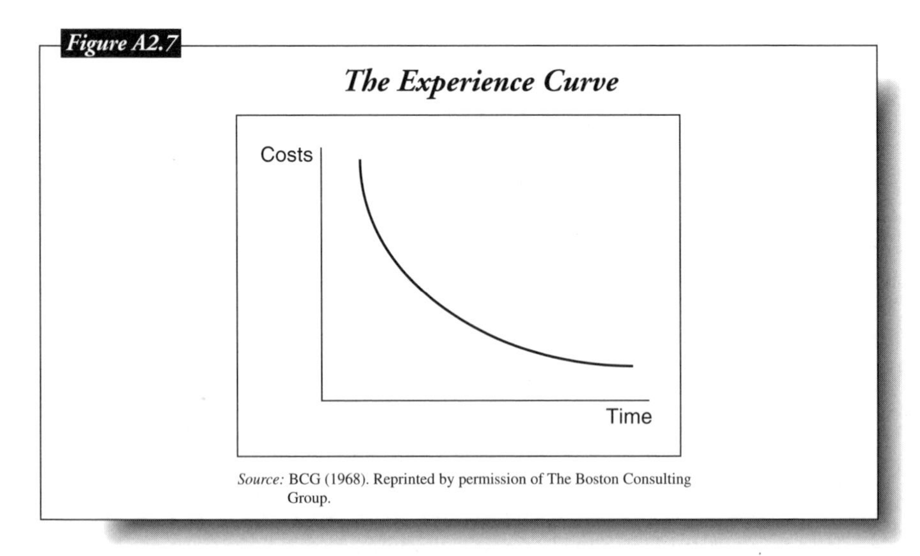

Source: BCG (1968). Reprinted by permission of The Boston Consulting Group.

concept. Although appearing deceptively simple, and intuitively right, the concept can be used to set exhilarating strategic objectives.

Costs decline due to a combination of: economies of scale, a learning curve for labour and the substitution of technology for labour. The cost decline gives competitive advantage because new competitors can face higher costs if not entering with a major innovative advantage. Some have argued that the advantage is so great that established leaders should drive to gain further advantage through actions such as price-cutting.

2 Constructing the Tool

Plot the firm's prices or costs against unit volume, projecting back in time as far as is sensible. The resultant curve should reveal the accumulated gains by the firm.

Note: For the analytically minded, the Boston Consulting Group recommended the use of double logarithmic scales because they show percentage gain as a constant distance. "A straight line... means, then, that a given percentage change in one factor results in a corresponding percentage change in the other... reflecting the relationship between experience and costs and experience and prices" (from *Perspectives on Experience*, BCG, 1968).

3 Use of the Tool

The tool can be used to identify cost gains and advantages compared to competitors. As a result it can become a benchmark by which the firm can set a strategy for business units to improve costs. It can also be used to predict and set prices by giving a directional indication of industry costs and likely competitive responses.

The tool can also be used to plan and sell outsourcing concepts. As illustrated in Figure A2.8, a firm whose business is focused on a particular function is likely to be further down the experience curve than a client's in-house team. If the in-house operations are passed to the supplier, the client gains advantage of the supplier's "experience". When the UK government's audit office first reviewed public sector outsourcing deals initiated by the Thatcher government in the 1980s, gains of up to 20% where found. This sparked the outsourcing trend in much of Europe. Note, however, that further dramatic gains are unlikely and continuing success depends on the nature of the relationship between the two parties. If the relationship breaks down, the client loses the supplier's experience and begins to build cost back into its business.

4 Use of the Tool with Scenarios

This tool works well with scenarios. It might, for example, be used to set detailed internal cost and pricing targets to achieve market positions required by corporate scenarios. It can also be used as a basis for different cost advantages that the business can achieve, which can then be built into market-based scenarios.

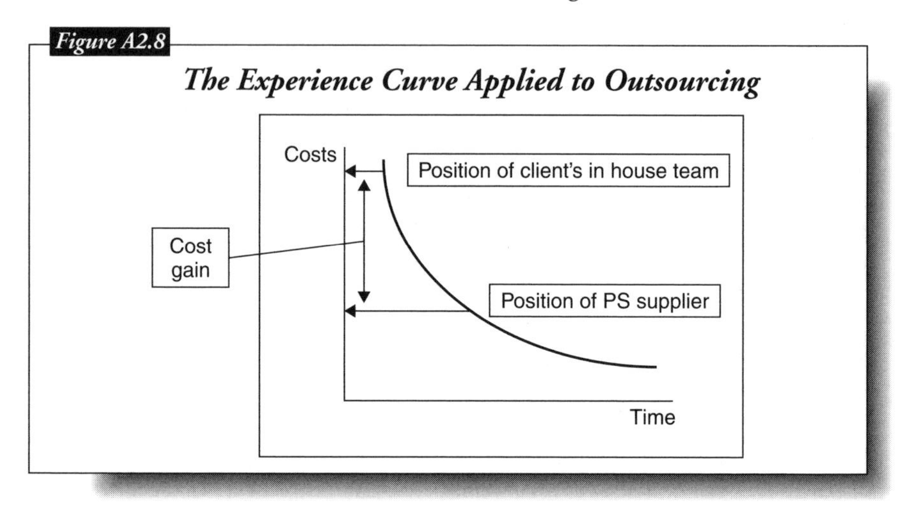

FEATURES ANALYSIS

Application: Service Design

Features analysis (Figure A2.9) is a concept used in product design to proactively plan the content of the offer. It is a development of the suggestion by leading marketing thinker Philip Kotler that products and services are propositions augmented by intangible marketing concepts such as brand and design. It suggests that each product offer comprises three sets of features. They are:

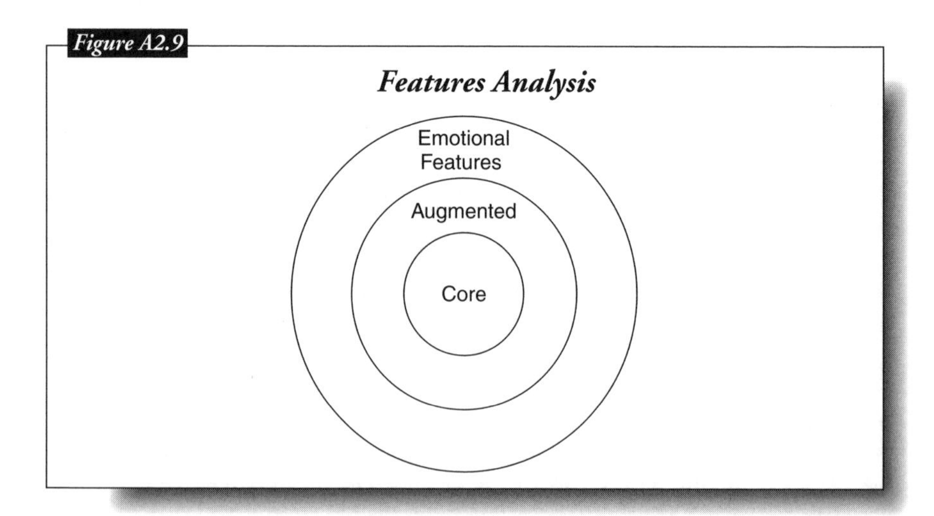

- ***The Core Feature.*** This is the hub of the offer and is the prime benefit to buyers. In the case of a briefcase it will be to "carry documents", in the case of a car it will be for "personal transportation". Experience shows this to be one of the most difficult aspects of product and service design. Service designers find it inordinately difficult to settle on the core proposition.

- ***Augmented Features.*** These are the physical components of the product which the product manager chooses to use to represent the core feature. In the case of a briefcase it would include the choice of leather, latches, nature of stitching, internal construction, etc. In the case of a car it would include the engine, the bodywork, the colour and the physical layout of the car. This is very much the design and assembly of physical components around identified customer need.

- ***Emotional Features.*** These are designed to appeal to the buyers' underlying, often unknown and unarticulated, emotional requirements. These are often the most influential aspects of the appeal of the proposition to the buyer. They particularly affect perceptions of value. Without them many offers become commodities.

Although these are actually offered through the physical (augmented) features, the emotional ring of the planning tool is there to remind designers to proactively plan their presence. They are particularly tied to the firm's brand values. For example, the emotional promise of a briefcase that is labelled "Gucci" will give a different message, for example, than one which is labelled "Woolworths".

Incidentally, the importance of emotion in the planning of a business-to-business proposition is just as critical as it is in consumer propositions. Early writers and teachers of marketing had suggested that business-to-business marketing is more "rational" than consumer marketing because formal buying processes exist. This is nonsense. Business buyers are human beings who experience emotions at work. The degree of risk, personal enhancement or political effort in a purchase, particularly a service purchase, can be decisive.

It is the proactive management of this mix of features that allows managers to design increasingly sophisticated versions of their offer in the light of feedback from markets. This allows the evolution of real choice and the supplier to create profit through the evolution of differentiated offers.

In service businesses, this technique needs to be adjusted to take on board the observation by Lynne Shostack that propositions from companies are neither all product nor all service. Using her goods/services spectrum of offers (as identified in Figure A2.10) the following four models can be used.

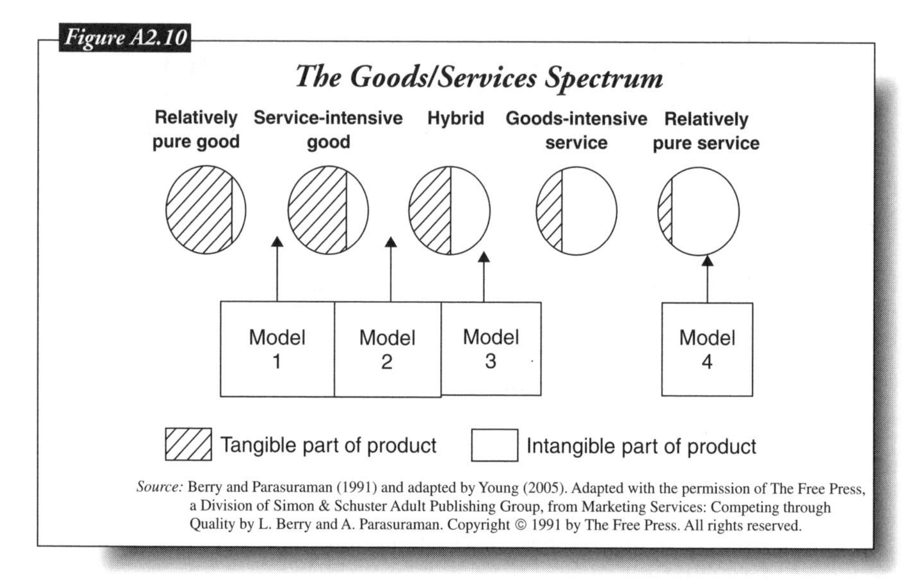

Source: Berry and Parasuraman (1991) and adapted by Young (2005). Adapted with the permission of The Free Press, a Division of Simon & Schuster Adult Publishing Group, from Marketing Services: Competing through Quality by L. Berry and A. Parasuraman. Copyright © 1991 by The Free Press. All rights reserved.

Model One (Figure A2.11)

This represents a proposition where service is primarily an emotional reassurance to a product offer. The core proposition is a product that has been augmented by

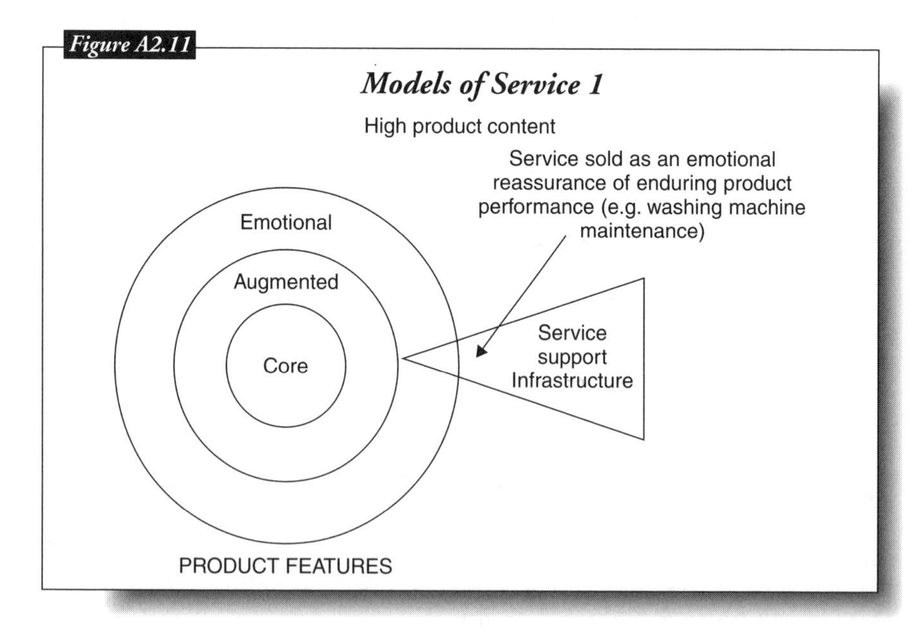

physical features. However, because it is based on new technology, the supplier has accepted, generally, that faults will occur in their product. Service has to be provided as an emotional reassurance to the purchaser of the enduring provision of those benefits. Service is therefore an emotional feature of the product. This has been in evidence with many product offers over the years, from washing machines and cars through to computers and elevators.

Model Two (Figure A2.12)

This represents an evolution in a market where suppliers begin to build service into the product concept. It occurred, for example, in the computer industry during the latter half of the twentieth century. Suppliers began to provide preventative maintenance through a monitored service involving people, procedures and technology. It was sold as part of the product offer so that computers failed less due to self-diagnostic technology and preventative maintenance. (This was an entirely different proposition to the previous maintenance contracts which promised "Don't worry, if it goes wrong we'll repair it quickly".) In this model, service has become an augmented component of the product offer.

Model Three (Figure A2.13)

This represents a position where people are buying a mix of service and product. It is common in industries which offer a high volume, low margin product. The fast

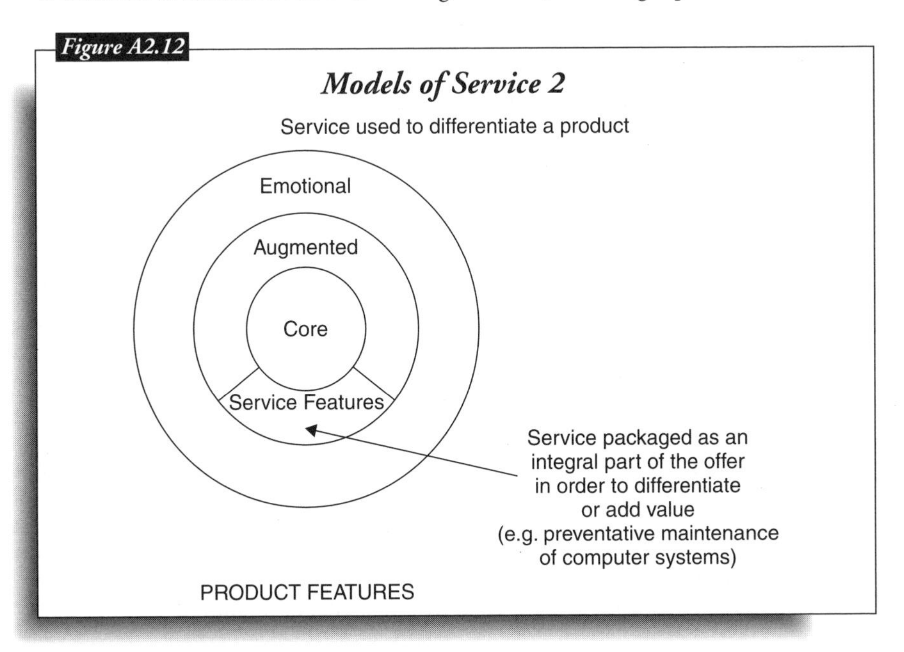

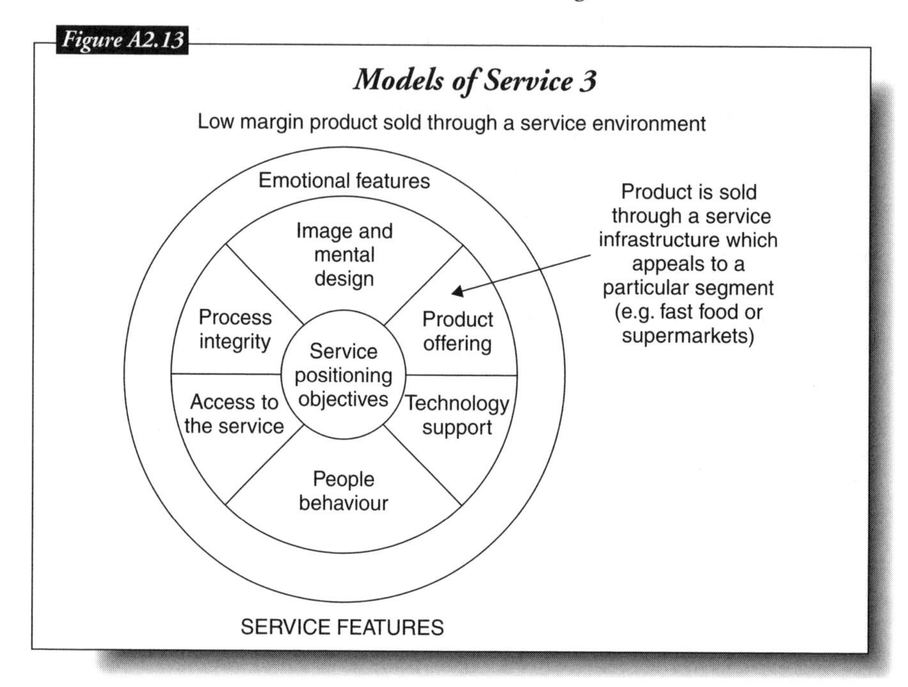

food industry, for example, uses service to sell a cheap product. The brand, environmental design, product range, technology support, people behaviour, method of accessing the service and the process through which the service is provided are all integrated into a holistic experience which people buy. This is the core service of fast food retailers and has evolved over a long period of time.

Model Four (Figure A2.14)

This represents a service offer which applies to many professional service firms. It has almost no physical or product content. An example would be management consultancy where any physical components (e.g. slides or bound reports) are merely an emotional reassurance to the buyer that good quality and high value exist in the offer. The tangible elements are a reassurance of the intangible benefit.

If service designers choose to use features analysis, it is essential that they use the correct design model. It may be, for example, that market conditions have changed and a service which was once associated with a product offer (paradigm 1) can be positioned as an entity which has value in its own right (paradigm 4). In this case, a different features mix must be used.

Use of the Tool with Scenarios

Features analysis allows marketers to design potential product and service concepts proactively. It therefore works well with corporate or strategic marketing scenarios.

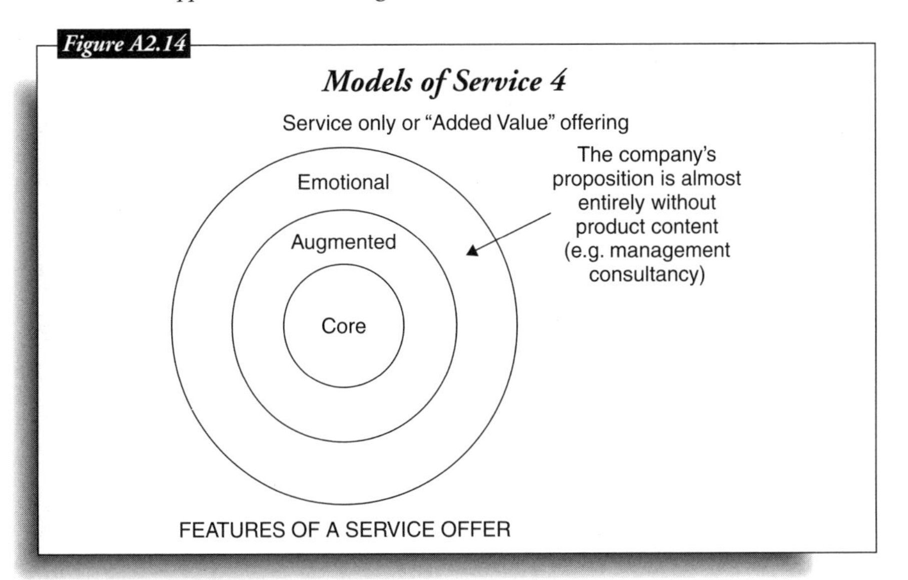

Designers can use the method to create the detailed components of service envisaged by different future scenarios, calculate the cost involved and construct a detailed product or business plan.

GAP MODEL

Application: Diagnosis of Client Service Issues, Development of Service Strategy

1 The Tool

This model (Figure A2.15) was designed and proposed by A. Parasuraman, V.A. Zeithaml and L.B. Berry, a group of academics who specialise in service marketing studies, (Zeithaml et al., 2000). It acknowledges that:

- Buyers find service quality more difficult to evaluate than product quality. They have few tangible clues as to quality, so must rely on other clues.

- Quality is a comparison between expectation and actual performance. Satisfaction depends on the degree to which the two match.

- Quality evaluation by buyers depends on outcomes and processes. Quality can be influenced by technical outcomes and functional or client service outcomes. It can also be influenced by physical aspects of the service and by company image as much as by the interaction with client service staff.

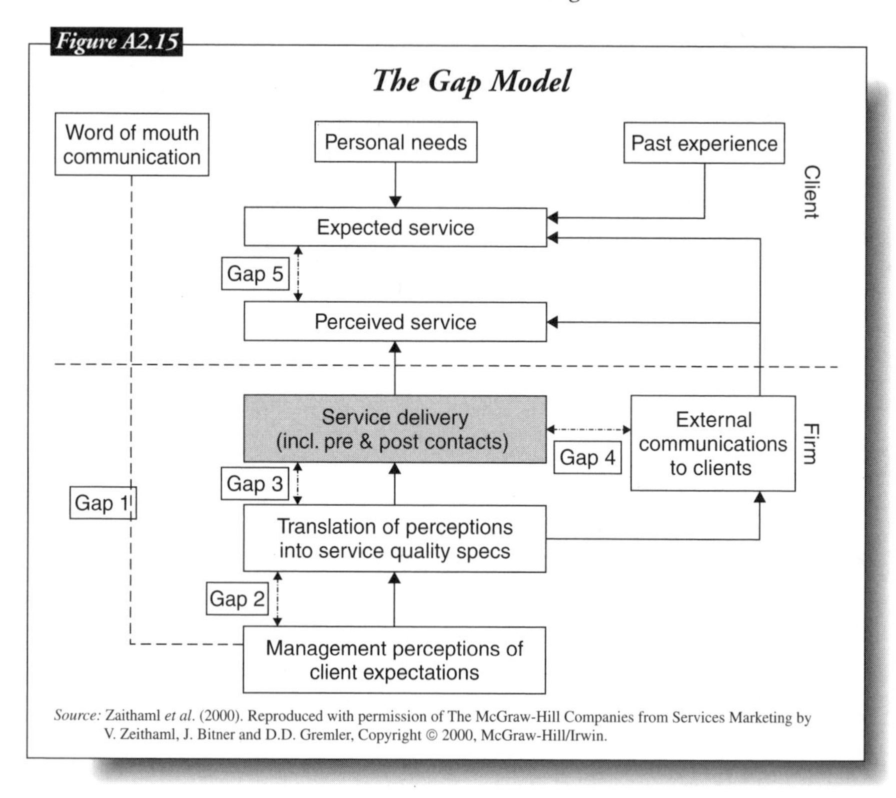

Figure A2.15 ***The Gap Model***

Source: Zaithaml *et al.* (2000). Reproduced with permission of The McGraw-Hill Companies from Services Marketing by V. Zeithaml, J. Bitner and D.D. Gremler, Copyright © 2000, McGraw-Hill/Irwin.

The original investigation to substantiate the model was conducted in financial and product repair services. It has, however, been widely tested and developed since.

The model focuses on five "gaps":

- ***The Management Perception Gap***. This is any difference between management's views and those of clients or the market in general.
- ***The Quality Specification Gap***. This exists when quality standards, strategy or plans do not reflect management objectives or views.
- ***The Service Delivery Gap***. This exists if there is a difference between quality strategy or plans and the firm's delivery to clients.
- ***The Market Communications Gap***. This tracks any difference between marketing communications and service delivery.

- ***The Perceived Service Gap.*** This exists if there is a difference between the service delivery perceived or experienced by clients and their expectations.

2 Constructing the Tool

The representation of the tool above is used as a format for analysis, representing as it does major parts of the firm. Research and data collection needs to be undertaken at the point of each gap to compare and contrast opinion or experience.

3 Using the Tool

In actual business the tool is best used as a diagnostic for the improvement of service strategy. Its analysis brings into sharp relief the differences between various perceptions and experiences. It allows the leadership to construct very specific improvement programmes in all relevant areas of business.

4 Using the Tool with Scenarios

The service issues revealed by the gap tool can be easily turned into scenarios that dramatise the company's competitive service situation. By creating "service scenarios" in this way, the marketing or service specialists can highlight key difficulties that need to be addressed, and alternative investment options with their anticipated impact.

HOFSTEDE'S CULTURAL DIMENSIONS FOR MANAGEMENT AND PLANNING

Application: International Marketing

1 The Tool

Geert Hofstede researched, developed and published a number of dimensions of cultural difference based on studies of IBM employees across the globe (Hufstede, 1980). He grouped, tested and demonstrated the affect of these dimensions on management practice (Figure A2.16). They can be used to guide international strategy and planning. The dimensions were:

- ***Individualism versus Collectivism.*** Some societies are loosely knit where individuals are supposed to take care of themselves and their immediate families. Work, career, economic provision and progress are centred around the individual. Others are more collective. Individuals can expect their relatives, clan or gang to look after them in exchange for unquestioning loyalty.

- ***Power Distance.*** This is the extent to which members of a society accept that power in its institutions is distributed unequally. This attitude affects

Figure A2.16

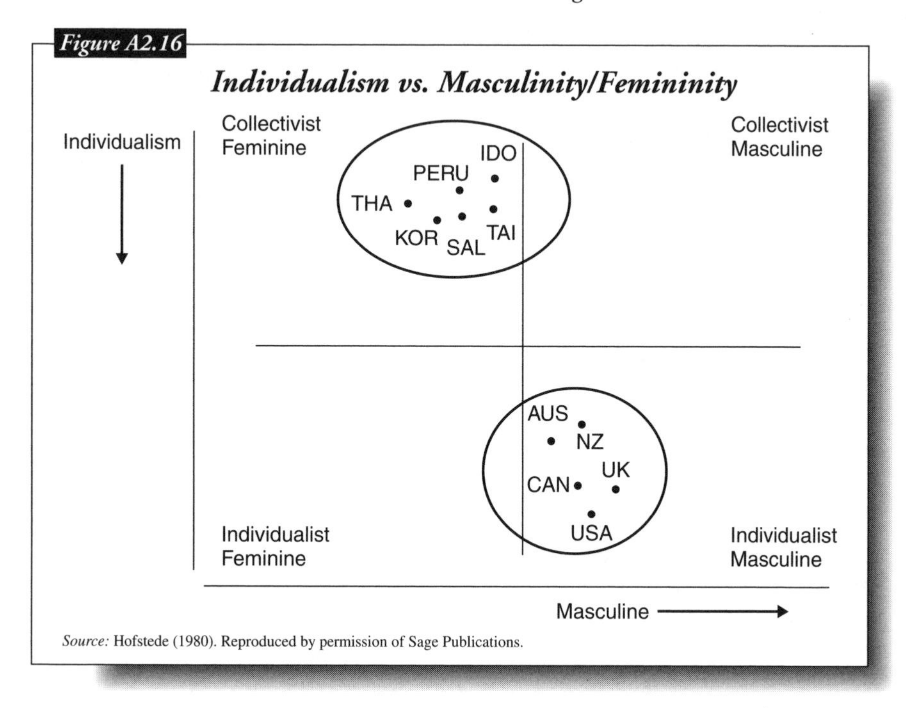

Source: Hofstede (1980). Reproduced by permission of Sage Publications.

the behaviour of those with and without power. Large power distance cultures accept hierarchical order in which everyone has a place; small power distance cultures strive for equalisation. This issue affects how societies handle inequalities when they occur.

- ***Uncertainty Avoidance***. This is the degree to which members of a society feel uncomfortable with risk, ambiguity and uncertainty. Uncertainty avoidance cultures maintain rigid codes of belief and behaviour. They are intolerant towards deviants. Weak uncertainty cultures are the opposite.

- ***Masculinity versus Femininity***. In Hofstede's view masculine cultures prefer achievement, heroism and material success; whereas feminine cultures stand for relationships, modesty, caring for the weak and quality of life.

This work shows how different cultures cluster and are similar under different dimensions. Figure A2.16 above represents just one set of pairings (individualism/collectivism with masculinity/femininity). This clearly shows the clustering of the "Anglo Saxon" influenced cultures of the USA, the UK, New Zealand and

Canada. A proposition built on the assumptions of individualistic masculinity (like high end executive search) is likely to succeed in this group.

2 *Constructing the Model*

Determine the dimensions that have the most profound association with the product service or strategy. Group the firm's existing international operations and any target countries using the clustering on the relevant dimensions. Adjust the programmes to fit key clusters.

3 *Use of the Model*

The model can be used as an aid to almost any international marketing function. It can be used to develop growth and acquisition strategy. It readily reveals compatible cultures that will be low-risk target. It also shows how communications and product or services need to adapted to penetrate different cultures.

4 *Use of the Tool with Scenarios*

The depth of the Hofstede dimensions can be used to create detailed scenarios of potential cultural differences and their appeal to different marketing strategies. They can be used with research to create models of how different strategies are likely to succeed in different countries.

INDUSTRY MATURITY CURVE

Application: Strategic Insight into Market Development

1 *The Concept*

The ***Industry Maturity Curve*** (Figure A2.17) is often mistakenly referred to as the 'product life cycle concept'. Yet the phenomenon occurs in the sales volume of product groups over time, not individual products. There must be multiple suppliers and multiple buyers in markets that develop over time for it to be observed. (Individual products rarely go through the sales history represented in the figure. Most die soon after launch.)

The concept draws an analogy between biological life cycles and the sales growth of successful product groups, by suggesting that they are born, introduced to the market, grow in sales, mature (sales growth stops) and then decline (sales fall). In fact, it represents an iterative learning process between the buyers and suppliers in a market. The cycle is represented by the well-known maturity curve.

At "birth"—the first introduction of the proposition to the world—a new product concept sells poorly. Buyers are unaware of its existence, suspicious of the new idea, or experience problems when ordering (with production capacity, effective distribution or product quality). "Bold" or "innovative" people buy the new product during this stage as a substitute for an existing product or to meet a

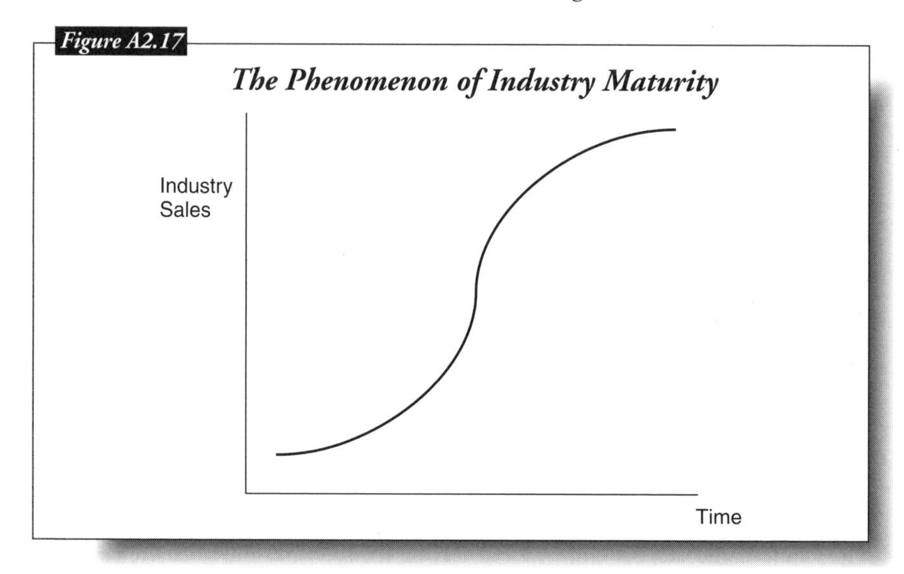

newly identified need. Profits may well be low or non-existent because of the high cost of sale.

In phase two, sales growth develops as a consequence of "word of mouth" communication. Early buyers pass on the good experience of the product to others or repurchase it. Producers and distributors (whether new to the market or well-established) recognise the opportunity and switch over to produce their own version. The market broadens through policies of product differentiation and market segmentation. Profit margins peak as experience reduces unit costs and promotional expenditure is spread over a larger sales volume.

Maturity occurs because all markets are ultimately finite (in time, volume and geography), and the market becomes saturated. Sales growth becomes more or less flat as sales settle down to a level that reflects the regular volume of new buyers entering the market plus repurchase rates. Profits decline because of the number of competitive offerings; cost reductions become more difficult and smaller, specialist competitors enter the market.

Decline occurs as buyers switch to new offers that give advantages or benefits not present in the existing product. Producers therefore initiate a new curve, bringing to an end that of the product group to be displaced. Declining sales are accompanied by falling profit margins as too many competitors fight for the remaining market. Price-cutting is prevalent and marginal competitors move out of the market.

This is a basic description of the industry maturity concept that has been tested, examined, criticised and developed over the past four decades. It was first observed

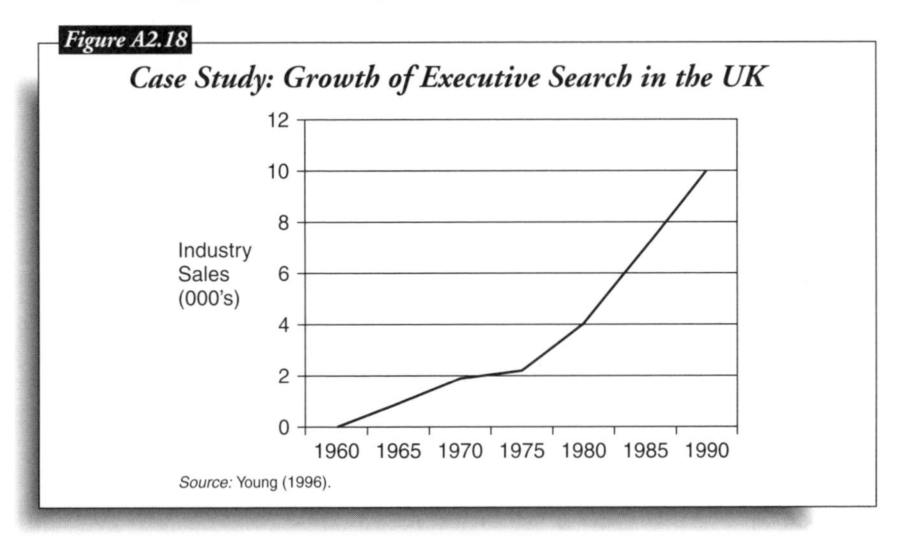

by an economist and then brought to prominence by leading marketing writers. The history of its development gives clues to its usefulness today, especially in service markets.

2 *Constructing the Curve*

Industry sales figures should be collected or calculated in a defined region or country. They should be projected back as far as is reasonably possible. Figure A2.8 shows an actual version for the UK executive search market.

3 *Use of the Concept*

As the phenomenon occurs when there are independent variables (i.e. groups of suppliers and buyers), and rarely applies to individual products, it can be used to create marketing strategy. Many have found that the concept can be used to form a judgement about movements in the category's sales growth curve. They can develop marketing strategies appropriate to each stage in the life cycle.

The concept is also useful in indicating the maturity of a market (i.e. the relationship of the group of customers to the group of suppliers, and the level of maturity of the understanding of the concept). An individual product being offered into that marketplace can then be adjusted in the light and understanding of that relationship. The likely strategies in each phase are summarised in Table A2.2.

Firms can use this concept to understand the position of their firm and service in the light of a total market's evolution. They can then construct their business strategy in the light of it.

TABLE A2.2 STRATEGIC IMPLICATIONS OF DIFFERENT PHASES OF INDUSTRY MATURITY

	Introduction	Growth	Maturity	Decline
Characterist s				
Sales	Low	Fast growth	Slow growth	Decline
Profits	Negligible	Peak levels	Declining	Low or zero
Cash flow	Negative	Moderate	High	Low
Customers	Innovative	Mass market	Mass market	Laggards
Competitors	Few	growing	Many rivals	Declining
Responses				
Strategic focus	Expand market	Penetration	Defend share	Efficiency
Marketing spend	High	Declining	Falling	Low
Marketing emphasis	Product awareness	Brand preference	Brand loyalty	Selective
Distribution	Patchy	Intensive	Intensity	Selective
Price	High	Lower	Lowest	Rising
Product	Basic	Improved	Differentiated	Rationalised

Source: Doyle (1976).

4 Use of the Tool with Scenarios

If companies should take the time to step back and create scenarios of any strategic situation, it is with regard to industry maturity. Numerous industries, from mobile phones and computers to cars and tourism, have found, to their cost, that the growth phase of their market can end suddenly and painfully. Although the concept is well known, managers seem unable or unwilling to acknowledge that maturity has arrived. Yet, if they don't, revenue will decline while costs stay static.

When this occurred in the big systems end of the computer market, for instance, the mighty IBM nearly went down. Scenarios of potential market developments and their implication can easily be modelled in the light of maturity trends by calculating, for example, the penetration of the offer into different potential markets and the rate at which saturation will be reached.

MARKETING MIX

Application: Planning and Influence

1 The Tool

This concept focuses on the aspects of marketing that need to be coordinated in order to influence the buyers. They are the "four Ps" of marketing (Figure A2.19):

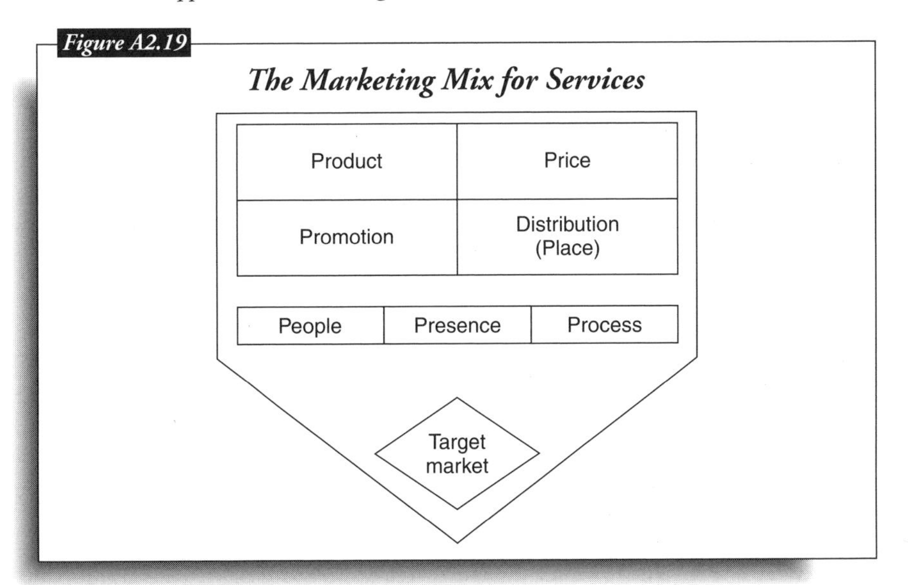

- The **P**roduct; or the offer to clients.
- The **P**rice at which the product is offered.
- The **P**romotion of the product to the target buyers
- The **P**lacing of the product in the market through sales and distribution channels.

Classic marketing training emphasises that all these elements need to planned in order to achieve success. However, there are two other ingredients. The first is a clear knowledge of the target market. Suppliers need to know, in detail, the attributes and benefits that the buyers will value. The second is the "mix" of components that will most appeal to the buyers. These need to be planned and balanced carefully.

In reality, few marketers have direct line responsibility for all the components of the mix. They therefore need to influence these other areas in order to achieve their objectives and create value for their employers. Experience suggests that they will fail to have impact and their work may as well not be attempted if they are restricted to just short-term tactical aspects of one or two aspects of the mix.

The mix for a service business is different. Firstly, the offer is not a tangible product but a proposition, which is likely to be a mix of intangibles and tangibles. This changes marketing dramatically.

However, it is generally accepted that there are three further aspects of the marketing mix for services—three extra "Ps". They are:

- The **P**eople who deliver the service because the buyer often cannot separate them from the value they buy.
- The **P**hysical evidence, or tangible aspects of the offer, designed to help deliver perceived value to the buyer.
- The **P**rocess through which the buyer moves while using or buying the service.

Again, all aspects of the mix need to be designed to match the aspirations of the intended buyers.

There is, of course, complexity behind this concept. Each "P" has many detailed aspects; the "P" of promotion, for instance, represents detailed, carefully managed and interactive marketing communication.

2 Constructing the Tool

In any planning situation simply list the elements of the mix and ensure that they have been considered for the particular target market.

3 Use of the Tool

The marketing mix is most often used in management dialogue or communications. Those involved can use it as an informal checklist to ensure that all aspects of a proposition have been properly considered. However, it can also be used in detailed marketing planning. Once strategy has been decided, a full campaign comprising all elements of the mix should be created for each target market.

4 Use of the Tool with Scenarios

With large, new or risky campaigns, it would be possible to create scenarios of different impact on the target market. These could form the basis of alternative investment decisions.

PORTER'S COMPETITIVE FORCES

Application: Market Analysis, Strategy Development

1 The Tool

Among Michael Porter's impressive and prodigious work on competitive strategy (for example, Porter, 1979) he offered a powerful conceptual framework which works well as part of the market analysis and strategy development process. His "five forces" of competition (Figure A2.20) are a useful checklist for strategists and marketers to work through when analysing a market. They are:

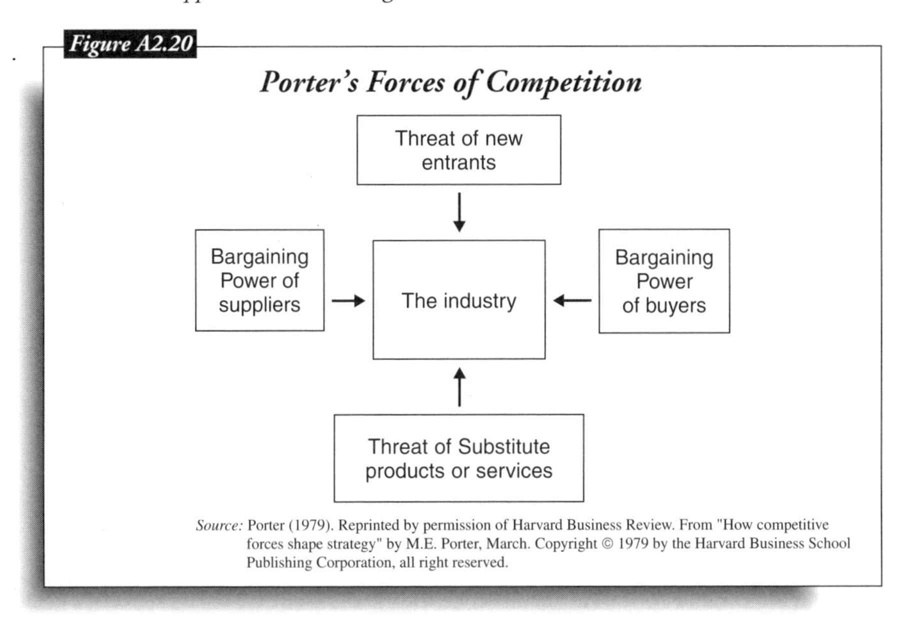

Source: Porter (1979). Reprinted by permission of Harvard Business Review. From "How competitive forces shape strategy" by M.E. Porter, March. Copyright © 1979 by the Harvard Business School Publishing Corporation, all right reserved.

- ***The Power of Buyers***. Buyers can influence a market by forcing down prices, by demanding higher service and quality or by playing competitors off against each other. Porter suggested that there are a number of circumstances when a buyer group is powerful including: if they are concentrated; if buying commodities, or components; if driven to get price cuts; or if the purchase is unimportant to them.

- ***The Power of Suppliers***. Suppliers can execute power by raising prices or reducing the quality of the offer. They can squeeze profitability out of the industry. They are powerful if: dominated by a few; have unique offers; are not obliged to compete; threaten forward integration; or are not part of an important industry to the buyers.

- ***The Threat of New Entrants***. These bring new capacity, the desire for market share and resources. The seriousness of the threat depends on barriers to entry which have six sources (economies of scale, product differentiation, capital requirements, cost advantages, access to distribution, and government policy).

- ***The Threat of Substitute Offers***. These affect the profit of an industry by placing a ceiling on what it can charge through offering an alternative price/feature option.

2 Constructing the Tool

The concept can simply be used as a checklist to prompt planners to cover relevant issues during market analysis and strategy development. However, it is most powerful when good analysis is put behind the thinking so that judgements can be made with the benefit of real data. Industry reports and original research can be summarised into the model and used as criteria by which to develop competitive responses or critical success factors.

3 Use of the Tool

The tool can be used to guide debate and is also effective as a communications device. Its clarity summarises graphically and quickly the competitive landscape and can be used as part of the rationale for competitive programmes. It is best used, however, as a background planning tool in the market planning process.

4 Use of the Tool with Scenarios

This structure of a market lends itself well to work with scenarios. Having completed a process to identify the various forces and structures, different scenarios of how it might develop can be created. For example, a future development of the market might be for customers to develop more power, causing suppliers to compete for share. Different scenarios of how this competition might evolve can be modelled and used to anticipate marketing requirements.

RESEARCH

Application: Client, Competitor or Market Insight

1 The Tool

Field research is familiar to many business leaders and managers. They may have seen results of research presented at internal meetings or read research reports while training. Unfortunately, familiarity can breed contempt, making the processes, the techniques and the outcomes seem deceptively simple. As a result, there are many unconvincing or poor research reports resulting from poor specification or poor use of the research industry.

Yet, undertaken properly, field research yields insights into customer needs, competitor performance and market trends (Figure A2.21). It can reveal the different elements of an offer that buyers value and how they combine with different price points to form packages that they will buy. Moreover, it can reveal how these vary between different groups, creating opportunities through variation of an offer in different market segments. It can also save money by stopping new product ideas or marketing programmes which the market will reject. Yet to do all this it has to be properly specified and managed. It needs a brief and a managerial process if it is going to produce results. This needs to ensure that the sample frame, the approach, the technique and the questionnaires are appropriate.

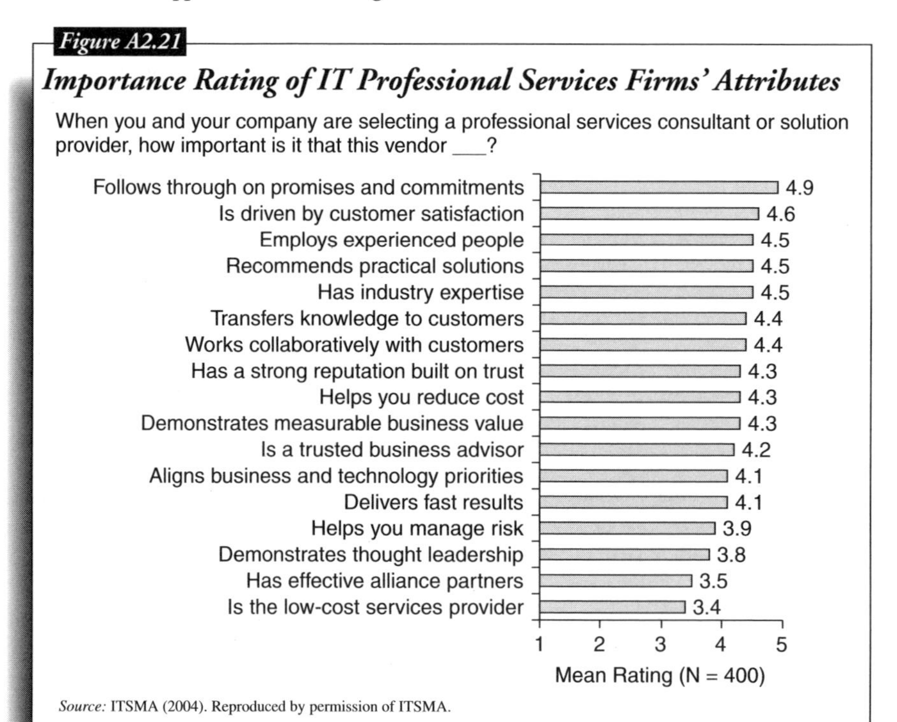

2 *Constructing Research Projects*

There are two main types of research. The first is the qualitative or "in depth" approach. This involves spending time with a relatively small number of buyers and seeking deep answers to questions. It gives colour to views and can reveal underlying feelings and motivations that can be enormously valuable. Quantitative research, on the other hand, involves a wider number of contacts, normally to investigate trends. Both have their strengths and their weaknesses.

Methods used to collect data vary enormously. They range from face-to-face interviews and observed discussion groups to telephone, postal or internet surveys. There are, however, several different research techniques.

- ***Conjoint Research.*** This uses questions (either in face to face meetings with clients or via mail or telephone) designed to trade off different pairs of values or ideas. Interviewees are forced to choose. It mimics the thought processes of clients when considering purchase and yields the type of detailed output illustrated in the diagram above. It can provide powerful insight into new offers and adjustments needed to service.

- ***Observational Research.*** As the name suggests this involves a researcher observing behaviour of clients. It can give real insight into behaviours which reflect customer views.

- ***Explorative Research.*** This is normally used in developing a new proposition or identifying a new customer segment, this technique follows issues until a trend suggests that they are likely to be substantive. The work can be iterative, checking back and adjusting the idea as interviewees respond.

- ***Concept Testing.*** This involves testing ideas for new propositions or approaches with customers before launch. They are shown an idea or marketing programme and asked to comment on it in a structured way.

3 Use of the Tool

Field research ought to carry an arrogance warning. Managers and leaders in all sectors of industry can be very dismissive of it. Many have been heard to remark that there is little that field research can tell them about their buyers. Yet they are almost always wrong. In fact, some very senior business leaders have been chastened by the direct comments they have heard their buyers make when sitting behind two-way mirrors watching focus groups.

Research does, however, need to be used properly. It needs to fill a gap in knowledge. It is sensible to first conduct an exhaustive desk review to see if libraries, professional societies or academic institutions have conducted research or provided commentary on the subject in question. Many people in large companies which lack a structured research library find, after a brief search, that their own company has conducted research near to the subject in question on previous occasions.

Once this preliminary work has been completed, the gap in knowledge ought to be clearly defined in a brief to a specialist research agency. This should specify the purpose of the research, which might be to test a new service idea, to test segmentation dimensions, to understand a new concept or to identify client needs. The exercise will be confused if there are too many objectives. In particular, the information yield that is expected must be made clear to the supplier.

When results are received, careful interpretation is needed. It is important to understand not only the statistically valid representation of results but also their meaning. Human beings often do not know what they want and, sometimes, why they behave in a particular way. They will say they want cheapness yet spend outrageous sums on a product from a branded supplier.

There are numerous examples of mistakes due to poor interpretation. In the late 1980s, for example, one American telecoms supplier commissioned a leading consultancy firm to judge the ultimate size of the worldwide mobile phone market.

The consultancy, which was not a specialist research firm, interviewed people in various parts of the world and estimated that the size of the mobile phone market would "never exceed a million handsets". They did not understand people's social need to chat, move fast and get a grip of personal communications.

Research therefore needs careful commissioning, good execution and enlightened interpretation. Yet the expense and effort is more than worth while. It can lead to profitable new insights that build strong future revenue streams and it can obviate mistakes.

4 Use of the Tool with Scenarios

Scenarios are very powerful representations of research results. Rather than literal tabulation of questions and findings, the pictures created by different scenarios can help to facilitate debate and develop strategy.

SWOT ANALYSIS

Application: Strategy Development

1 The Tool

Probably the best known of the strategy tools this matrix (Figure A2.22) helps to structure discussion by summarising a firm's strategic position into: strengths, weaknesses, opportunities and threats.

Figure A2.22

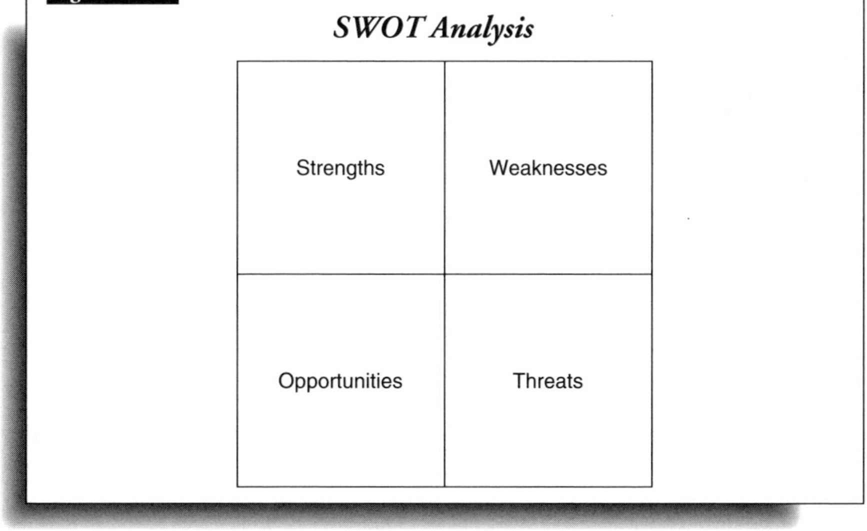

SWOT Analysis

Strengths	Weaknesses
Opportunities	Threats

2 *Constructing the Matrix*

A SWOT analysis can easily be created during discussion among a management team. Valuable insight and debate can emerge from its succinct summary of the firm.

It can, however, be constructed using detailed analysis. The market analysis techniques outlined in Chapter 2 can be summarised into it. Competitive analysis will reveal "threats", for example, and client research will give insight into "opportunities". On the other hand, an environmental analysis, which reviews "PEST" (political, economic, social, technological) factors, can contribute to both of these.

Those wishing to take a thorough, analytical approach can use the "TOWS" method. This suggests that each item in the matrix is numbered. Then each threat is compared against each weakness and each opportunity against each strength, in a systematic search for strategic options. As the strengths and weaknesses arise from debate about the firm's competencies, the strategist is, in fact, checking these against market developments through this process.

3 *Use of the Tool*

The tool is best used in the strategy development process to summarise analysis. It allows senior people to focus debate and decision-making.

4 *Use of the Tool with Scenarios*

The different combinations of strengths with opportunities and weaknesses with threats can be built into scenarios. Once agreed and prioritised, they can form the basis of a clear marketing strategy.

REFERENCES

Ansoff, I. (1957) "Strategies for diversification", *Harvard Business Review*, Sept/Oct.

BCG (1968) *Perspectives on Experience*. Boston Consulting Group.

Berry, L. and Parasuraman, A. (1991) *Marketing Services: Competing through Quality*. Free Press.

Doyle, P. (1976) "The realities of the product life cycle", *Quarterly Review of Marketing*.

Hakansson, H. and Snehota, I. (1995) *Developing Relationships in Business Networks*. International Thompson Business Press.

Hofstede, G. (1980) *Culture's Consequences: International Differences in Work Related Values*. Sage Publications.

ITSMA (2004), *State of the Profession Address*. Information Technology Services Marketing Association.

Johnson, G. and Scholes, K. (2004) *Exploring Corporate Strategy Text and Cases 7/ed*. FT Prentice Hall.

Porter. M. E, (1979) "How competitive forces shape strategy", *Harvard Business Review*, March.

Young, L. D. (1996) *Making Profit from New Service Development*. Pearson Education.

Young, L. D. (2005) *Marketing the Professional Services Firm.* John Wiley & Sons Ltd.

Zeithaml, V. Parasuraman, A. and Berry, L. L. (1990) *Delivering Quality Service*. Free Press.

Zeithaml, V. Bitner, J. and Gremler, D. D. (2000) *Services Marketing*. McGraw-Hill/Irwin.

APPENDIX THREE
A History of Scenarios

AFTER THE SECOND WORLD WAR

The Second World War mobilised large numbers of academics into government, researchers to new areas, and provided the crucible for a number of breakthroughs. Examples which are widely discussed include atomic and nuclear energy, radar, and the computer.

In *The Age of Heretics*, Art Kleiner (1996) wrote:

> *World War Two had been an extraordinary catalyst for the study of complex systems. Just as the war had mingled social scientists in unprecedented numbers, it had also assembled physicists, mathematicians, logicians and physiologists to work on problems beyond the range of any individual discipline. These were . . . students of the nature of complex systems and developers of wars to manage them more effectively by translating them into mathematical models . . .*
>
> *These operations researchers helped military leaders . . . set up complex radar mechanisms, calculate how the fewest boats could patrol the largest stretch of water . . . Then after the war they adopted similar game theory and decision analysis techniques to the business arena.*

Hermann Kahn—pioneer

After the war, the RAND Corporation was set up to research new forms of weapons technology. RAND's Hermann Kahn pioneered the technique of "future-now"

Scenarios in Marketing. Edited by G. Ringland and L. Young.

thinking, aiming through the use of detailed analysis plus imagination to be able to produce a report, written as it might be written by people living in the future.

The description "scenario" was given to these stories by the writer Leo Rosten, who suggested the name based on Hollywood terminology. Though the terminology was obsolete, he didn't think the more current term "screenplay" sounded dignified enough. Hermann Kahn adopted the term because he liked the emphasis it gave, not so much on forecasting, but on creating a story or myth.

When he founded the Hudson Institute in the mid-1960s, he specialised in stories about the future aimed at helping people to break past their mental blocks and consider "unthinkable" futures. He was well known for his idea that the best way to prevent nuclear war was to think through in detail what would happen if the war did occur, and publicise the results.

Stanford Research Institute

Meanwhile, on the West Coast, Stanford University had set up the Stanford Research Institute (SRI) in 1947, to offer long-range thinking for business incorporating operations research, economics and political strategy alongside hard science and military consulting.

SCENARIOS IN THE 1960s

Science and Prediction

In the 1960s, the world was fascinated by the apparent triumphs of science. So, for instance, twenty-seven top scientists at the leading US industrial company TRW in 1966 were asked the question: "What will the world want and need in the next twenty years?" Kahn (Kahn and Weiner, 1967) reports on the wide publicity and discussion arising from these predictions of undersea motels, factories and recreation centres powered by nuclear power, commercial passenger rockets to the moon by 1980, that by 1977 low-cost 3D colour TV would reduce business travel, and that by 1973 there would be large-scale educational teaching machine systems.

Of the 335 predictions released, however, nearly every prediction was wrong (Schnaars, 1989). The scientists ignored the economic aspects of markets: their mental model included state-driven mega-projects, which by the late 1960s had started to decline after the moon-shot had succeeded.

Societal Futures Thinking

The late 1960s saw a shift in the work done by organisations like SRI as interest increased in finding ways to look further into the future to help plan for changes in society, an interest underpinned by the upheavals resulting from the Vietnam War.

In early 1968 the SRI "futures group" began to use a variety of methods, from straight-line numeric forecasts to literature searches on utopias and dystopias from science fiction to create plausible scenarios for the USA to the year 2000. The customer was the Office of Education, which wanted to envisage the sort of society for which children were being educated, and to see if the system should change.

They poured through forecasts, coded trends into punched cards, and fed them into a mainframe to examine a range of alternative futures. The result is illustrated in Figure A3.1.

The scenarios were based round two questions:

- Would society be good at controlling its destiny? Or not?

- Would society be flexible, open and tolerant or would it be authoritarian, violent and efficient?

The alternates posed by the group do not necessarily correlate with the assumptions we might make today—considering the number of regimes that are violent and authoritarian but notoriously not efficient. However, by considering different combinations of these factors, they created five scenarios, i.e. all the four combinations of the possible answers to the questions, plus the "official future".

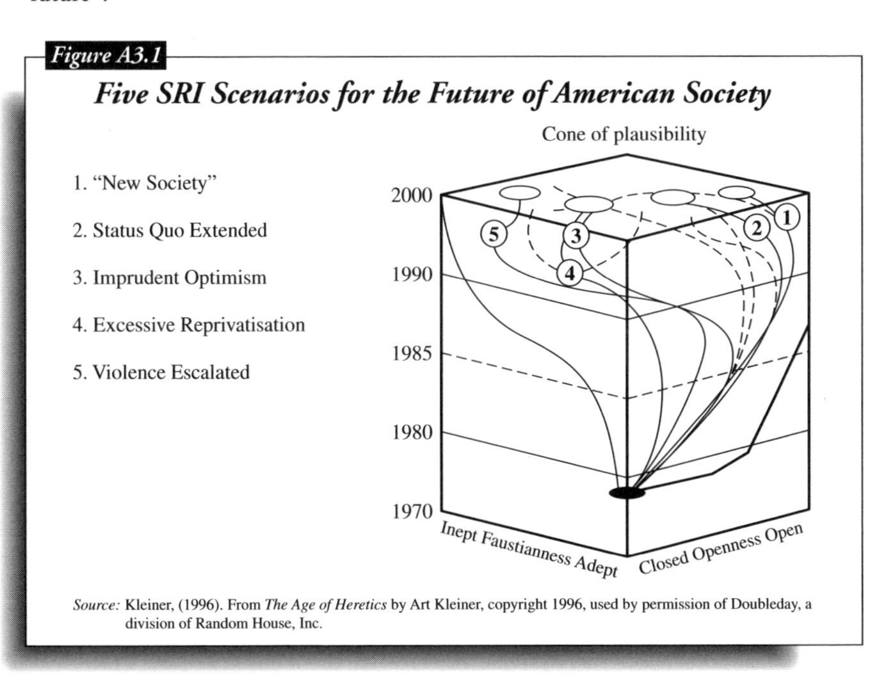

Figure A3.1

Five SRI Scenarios for the Future of American Society

Source: Kleiner, (1996). From *The Age of Heretics* by Art Kleiner, copyright 1996, used by permission of Doubleday, a division of Random House, Inc.

Four SRI Scenarios

The Official Future—Status Quo Extended was that the problems of population growth, dissent, ecological destruction, would "take care of themselves". The other scenarios were ***Imprudent Optimism*** where bureaucracy and a raging recession met head on; ***Violence Escalated***, with terrorism increasing and schools taken over by street gangs; and the ***New Society*** scenario, in which openness was combined with adeptness to create effectiveness, and which attracted wide attention. It was tied to a USA in which consumerism was no longer king, and in which government adopted an ecological ethic.

The SRI researchers believed that the ***New Society*** scenario provided a more desirable future than any of the other scenarios, but that it realistically could not happen under the existing government and corporate structures. It was inconsistent with the values of the industrial society.

How the Scenarios were Used

The message reached the sponsors, the US Office of Education, at a time when Richard Nixon's election as president represented the entrenchment of a set of values that made the offered scenario "impossible"—a good example of scenarios needing to find echo in their intended audience in order to have an effect.

The work did lead, later, to a major research programme, VALS (Values and Lifestyles), on the American consumer. This described consumers according to nine categories, and is still used extensively as a system for predicting consumer behaviour. SRI also did subsequent work for the Environmental Protection Agency (EPA), creating 10 to 12 scenarios of the future. Each scenario was built around a central concept or theme, arrived at by brainstorming. The process was free form, a lot of original thinking occurred, but the connection to decision-making was loose.

SYSTEMS THINKING

Meanwhile Professor Jay Forrester of the Massachusetts Institute of Technology had used the concepts he had developed to describe supply chains and demand (Forrester, 1961) to look at the interconnection of population, and supply and demand on the world.

The famous Club of Rome model was developed in 1970 using the same feedback loop concepts. It tracked five key variables - population, food production, industrial production, pollution, and natural resources. However, all the worlds which were simulated with the model seemed to suffer in that growth got out of control. An analysis of the results was published in *Limits to Growth* by Donella (Dana) Meadows (republished as Meadows et al., 1992). The argument over growth and the use of resources was loud and energetic and continues today. The originators of the work were clear in their aims (which were not always understood by others): they were not predicting the future; they were developing a model which would help people to understand aspects of the nature of growth and open up the public debate.

The Hudson Institute

The Hudson Institute started to seek corporate sponsors in the 1960s, which exposed companies like Shell, Corning, IBM and General Motors to this style of thinking. Ted Newland started to introduce thinking about the future into Shell.

THE 1970s: CORPORATE PLANNING AND THE IMPACT OF THE 1973 OIL SHOCK

Corporate Planning

Meanwhile, computers were being introduced to companies, although they were the province of central staffs. The computers ran the accounting systems and were beginning to be used for planning. The role model in planning during the 1970s was the US Corporation, General Electric (GE). This approach was based on top-down planning by a corporate staff, computer models, forms, charts and graphs.

GE used scenarios as part of its planning process, to think about the environmental factors affecting its businesses. The method involved using Delphi panels to establish and verify critical variables and indicators, while both trend–impact analysis and cross–impact analysis would then help to assess the implications of the interactions among critical variables and indicators. GE pioneered an approach whereby the cross–impact effects among likely developments are dealt with qualitatively, with plus or minus signs, which would then lead to the development of probable scenarios for the environment.

BOX A3.1 THE DELPHI TECHNIQUE

The Delphi technique, named after the ancient Greek oracle, was developed by the RAND Corporation in the 1950s as a method for gathering information about the future. It was based on asking experts in their various fields to estimate individually the probability that certain events will occur in the future. The goal is to get them to converge on future views by comparing the answers with those of the other experts.

Delphi became part of formal planning techniques in the 1970s (see Amara and Lipinksi, 1983).

Planning at Shell

At this time, Shell (the Royal Dutch/Shell Group) had a basic planning system that was very similar to GE's. As Pierre Wack, the *"undisputed intellectual leader in the area of scenario-based strategic thinking"* (van der Heijden, 1996) pointed out in his classic articles for the *Harvard Business Review* (Wack, 1985), for 10 years after the Second World War, planning at Shell was very physically oriented, with the main challenge being to coordinate business activities and plan the schedules for setting up new facilities.

Numbers began to play a greater role from 1955 to 1965, as planning became more financially oriented, with research and evaluation done on the economics and the perspective rate of return of projects. By 1965 a new technique called Unified Planning Machinery (UPM) was developed to enable Shell to plan for the whole chain of activity, from the oil in the ground through to its sale at petrol stations, with a horizon of six years.

However, Wack pointed out in 1967 that, because of the time scale on which oil companies worked, even six years was too short a time for planning. So a study was set up to look at Shell's position to the year 2000. An exercise was carried out from 1969 to 1970 called Horizon Year Planning, in which a dozen of the largest Shell companies around the world, as well as executives in areas such as marketing and production, were asked to look forward to 1985. This suggested that the predictable, surprise-free environment, in which oil prices were based on predictable factors of supply and demand, would not continue, and that a shift in power from the oil companies to the oil producers in the Middle East for a variety of reasons could create major increases in the oil price.

As Ted Newland said:

> *Having developed this view, the problem was to get it into Shell's corporate culture. I did not have a track record that would let us challenge the culture directly. So we produced a set of impersonal, mechanical scenarios about the future of oil prices. One of them was that prices would remain as they were. One expressed the idea—that oil prices would rise. Even this dispassionate presentation of the idea had a dramatic effect.*

Scenarios after the Oil Shock

Once the Yom Kippur War broke out in the Middle East, the oil embargo by the producing countries did indeed lead to a sharp increase in the oil price with the inevitable depressing results on the world economy, changes in supply lines, and changes in behaviour and attitudes.

Shell's ability to act quickly has been credited with moving the company into the lead in the oil industry (van der Heijden, 1996). The effect of this on corporate planning, based on sets of key numbers that had described the business over the past few years, was to look for ways of including the effects of uncertainty.

By the late 1970s scenario planning was adopted by a significant fraction of the Fortune 1000 companies, based on a variety of techniques. Many of these used multiple scenarios. Roughly three-quarters of the firms had adopted the approach after the oil embargo provided such a deep shock to previously stable views of the future (Dyson, 1990).

THE 1980S: THE WORLD ORDER BEGINS TO CHANGE

During the 1980s, however, the use of scenarios decreased from the peak of interest in the 1970s. The threat of the oil price shock had decreased, and corporate staffs were reduced in the recessions of the early 1980s. By the mid-1980s, restructuring in a range of industries had prompted an interest in strategic thinking.

Art Kleiner (1996) suggests that the large losses of corporate bell-wethers—which he ascribes to use of formulae like the BCG matrix—had a dramatic effect.

> *The stage was now set for the great managerial event of the late 1970s and early 1980s: the realisation by mainstream managers that they did not have the answers. In 1978, Chrysler lost $205 million. General Electric, Kodak, Xerox, General Foods, all saw their market share drop precipitously—if not to Japanese competition, then to smaller firms in the West.*

In this environment, the approach needed to change. For instance, Michael Porter (1985) went back to basics and proposed that companies consider the forces on their markets as a backdrop to planning. He considered scenarios to be important tools for understanding and so getting ahead of trends, and recommended the building of alternative scenarios as a form of sensitivity analysis.

Development of Scenario Methodologies

This was the environment in which a number of consulting organisations were developing their scenario methodologies. For example, Huss and Honton, (1987) identified three categories in use in the 1980s:

- Intuitive Logics, first described by Pierre Wack in the *Harvard Business Review* and used by SRI International and Shell. It is widely used by, for instance, Global Business Network, SRIC-BI and SAMI Consulting.

- Trend–impact analysis, used by the Futures Group, as described by Boroush and Thomas (1995).

- Cross–impact analysis, used by Battelle with BASICS (Battelle Scenario Inputs to Corporate Strategies), and by Michel Godet and the French school (Godet, 1993).

Shell in the 1980s

During the 1980s, Shell maintained its reputation for using scenario thinking and two examples of successful anticipation are cited:

- Oil would become a commodity with prices set by the market, not by either the companies or producers. Prices would thus behave like those of commodities such as nickel, copper and wheat. Once oil began indeed to act like other commodities, Shell had designed an oil-trading system, so was once again in pole position compared to its rivals.

- Oil and gas prices could drop. With oil, OPEC's unified façade could crumble, worsened by a slowing demand for oil because of better energy conservation and efficiency. Even more strikingly, the continuation of the Soviet system was not assured, which could have implications for the natural gas market. Shell avoided investing in new oil fields or following the acquisition trail being trodden by its major competitors, who were engaged in an acquisition spree, buying other oil companies at premium prices. Once the dust had settled following the price drop, Shell was able to pick up additional assets at bargain prices.

As Peter Schwartz (1991) relates:

> *In 1983, we presented the Royal Dutch/Shell managing directors with two scenarios; one called* ***Incrementalism****, and the other called the* ***Greening of Russia****. By that time, we knew enough about the Soviet government to say that if a virtually unknown man named Gorbachev came to power, you'd see massive economic and political restructuring; an opening to the West; arms control; declining tensions in the West; and major shifts in international relationships. It was not that Gorbachev, as an individual, would cause the changes. Rather, his arrival in power would be a symptom of the same underlying causes.*

THE 1990S: SCENARIOS WIDEN THEIR APPLICATION

Scenarios and Strategy

The resurgence of interest in scenarios in the mid-1990s was part of a new emphasis on sources of value and growth in corporations, after the downsizing and retrenchment of the 1980s. So, for instance,

- Pralahad and Hamel (1994) put the emphasis on the strategic context for the corporation.

- Henry Mintzberg (1994) foresaw the need for strategy in light of the turbulence to come.

THE NEW MILLENNIUM

New Uses

Since then, other changes have also affected the rise in the use of scenarios in organisations.

- Many senior managers now have MBAs and "know about" scenarios—however, maybe with a jaundiced view (O'Brien, 2004) through hurried exposure.

- The public sector in Europe has proactively developed the use of scenarios in policy discussion (e.g. European Commission, 2005).

- The non-governmental organisation (NGO) sector has realised the effectiveness of scenarios for harnessing the energies of members and the public.

These factors have meant that new uses of scenarios have become prominent:

- Scenario creation as a management development tool. This uses workshops—typically two days—to develop young high flyers, to create a common language in a management team (for instance after a merger), or to brainstorm ideas as a framework for research.

- Using scenarios already developed, perhaps with some implications for the organisation drawn out, as a basis for decisions on research and development, country risk, mergers and acquisitions, corporate social responsibility, portfolio management or the location and capacity of manufacturing plants.

- Using scenarios already developed to "wind tunnel" test a business plan or strategy, by asking the question: "What if this scenario happens?"

- Using scenarios already developed as a basis for action planning. An example was the use of existing Foresight 2020 scenarios (Berkhout and Hertin, 2002) to provide a framework for action planning for the Arts Marketing Association.

- As part of the communication during change management in an organisation or public consultation in local or national government.

REFERENCES

Amara, R. and Lipinski, A. J. (1983) *Business Planning for an Uncertain Future: Scenarios and Strategies*. Pergamon.

Berkhout, F. and Hertin, J. (2002) "Foresight Futures scenarios—developing and applying a participative strategic planning tool", *Greener Management Journal*, **37**, 37–52.

Boroush, M.A. and Thomas, C.W. (1992) "Alternative scenarios for the defence industry after 1995", *Planning Review*, May/June.

Dyson, R. G. (ed.), (1990) *Strategic Planning: "Models and Techniques"*. John Wiley & Sons, Ltd.

European Commission (2005) *Converging Technologies: Shaping the Future of European Societies*. Luxemburg.

Forrester, J. (1961) *Industrial Dynamics*, MIT Press (republished by Productivity Press of Oregon).

Godet, M. (1993) *From Anticipation to Action*, (2nd edition). UNESCO, Paris.

Huss, W. R. and Honton, E. J. (1987) "Scenario planning, what style should you use?" *Long Range Planning*, **20**, April.

Kahn, H. and Weiner, A. J. (1967) *The Year 2000: A Framework for Speculation on the Next Thirty Years.* Macmillan Publishing.

Kleiner, A. (1996) *The Age of Heretics.* Doubleday.

Meadows, D. H. Meadows, D. L. and Randers, J. (1992) *Beyond the Limits.* An updated version of *Limits to Growth*, published by Chelsea Green Publishing Company.

Mintzberg, H. (1994) "The fall and rise of strategic planning", *Harvard Business Review*, January.

O'Brien, F. A. (2004) "Scenario planning: Lessons for practice from teaching and learning", *European Journal of Operational Research*, **152**, 709–722.

Pralahad, C. K. and Hamel, G. (1994) *Competing for the Future*. Harvard Business School Press.

Schnaars, S. P. (1989) *Megamistakes*. Macmillan Inc.

Schwartz, P. (1991) *The Art of the Long View*. Doubleday.

Schwartz, P. (2003) *Inevitable Surprises*. The Free Press.

van der Heijden, K. (1996) *Scenarios, The Art of Strategic Conversation.* John Wiley & Sons, Ltd.

Wack, P. (1985) "Scenarios, uncharted waters ahead", *Harvard Business Review*, September.

Index

Index compiled by Terry Halliday